MTEL English as a 54 Second Language (ESL)

Teacher Certification Exam

Sharon A Wynne, M.S.

XAMonline, INC.
Boston

XAMonline, Inc.
21 Orient Avenue
Melrose, MA 02176
Toll Free 1-800-509-4128
Email: info@xamonline.com
Web: www.xamonline.com
Fax: 1-617-583-5552

Library of Congress Cataloging-in-Publication Data
Wynne, Sharon A.
MTEL English as a Second Language (ESL) 54 Teacher Certification / Sharon A Wynne.
    ISBN: 978-1-60787-466-9, 2nd edition

1. English as a Second Language (ESL)   2. Study Guides.   3. MTEL
4. Teachers' Certification & Licensure.   5. Careers

Disclaimer:
The opinions expressed in this publication are the sole works of XAMonline and were created independently from the National Education Association (NES), Educational Testing Service (ETS), or any State Department of Education, National Evaluation Systems or other testing affiliates. Between the time of publication and printing, state specific standards as well as testing formats and website information may change that are not included in part or in whole within this product. XAMonline develops sample test questions, and they reflect similar content as on real tests; however, they are not former tests. XAMonline assembles content that aligns with state standards but makes no claims nor guarantees teacher candidates a passing score. Numerical scores are determined by testing companies such as NES or ETS and then are compared with individual state standards. A passing score varies from state to state.

Printed in the United States of America   œ-1
MTEL English as a Second Language (ESL) 54
ISBN: 978-1-60787-466-9

TABLE OF CONTENTS

Section 1 About XAMonline

XAMonline – A Specialty Teacher Certification Company

Created in 1996, XAMonline was the first company to publish study guides for state-specific teacher certification examinations. Founder Sharon Wynne found it frustrating that materials were not available for teacher certification preparation and decided to create the first single, state-specific guide. XAMonline has grown into a company of over 1800 contributors and writers and offers over 300 titles for the entire PRAXIS series and every state examination. No matter what state you plan on teaching in, XAMonline has a unique teacher certification study guide just for you.

XAMonline – Value and Innovation

We are committed to providing value and innovation. Our print-on-demand technology allows us to be the first in the market to reflect changes in test standards and user feedback as they occur. Our guides are written by experienced teachers who are experts in their fields. And, our content reflects the highest standards of quality. Comprehensive practice tests with varied levels of rigor means that your study experience will closely match the actual in-test experience.

To date, XAMonline has helped nearly 600,000 teachers pass their certification or licensing exams. Our commitment to preparation exceeds simply providing the proper material for study - it extends to helping teachers **gain mastery** of the subject matter, giving them the **tools** to become the most effective classroom leaders possible, and ushering today's students toward a **successful future**.

Section 2 About this Study Guide

Purpose of this Guide

Is there a little voice inside of you saying, "Am I ready?" Our goal is to replace that little voice and remove all doubt with a new voice that says, "I AM READY. **Bring it on!**" by offering the highest quality of teacher certification study guides.

Organization of Content

You will see that while every test may start with overlapping general topics, each are very unique in the skills they wish to test. Only XAMonline presents custom content that analyzes deeper than a title, a subarea, or an objective. Only XAMonline presents content and sample test assessments along with **focus statements**, the deepest-level rationale and interpretation of the skills that are unique to the exam.

Title and field number of test

→Each exam has its own name and number. XAMonline's guides are written to give you the content you need to know for the specific exam you are taking. You can be confident when you buy our guide that it contains the information you need to study for the specific test you are taking.

Subareas
→These are the major content categories found on the exam. XAMonline's guides are written to cover all of the subareas found in the test frameworks developed for the exam.

Objectives
→These are standards that are unique to the exam and represent the main subcategories of the subareas/content categories. XAMonline's guides are written to address every specific objective required to pass the exam.

Focus statements
→These are examples and interpretations of the objectives. You find them in parenthesis directly following the objective. They provide detailed examples of the range, type, and level of content that appear on the test questions. **Only XAMonline's guides drill down to this level.**

How do We Compare with Our Competitors?
XAMonline – drills down to the focus statement level
CliffsNotes and REA – organized at the objective level
Kaplan – provides only links to content
MoMedia – content not specific to the test

Each subarea is divided into manageable sections that cover the specific skill areas. Explanations are easy-to-understand and thorough. You'll find that every test answer contains a rejoinder so if you need a refresher or further review after taking the test, you'll know exactly to which section you must return.

How to Use this Book
Our informal polls show that most people begin studying up to 8 weeks prior to the test date, so start early. Then ask yourself some questions: How much do you really know? Are you coming to the test straight from your teacher-education program or are you having to review subjects you haven't considered in 10 years? Either way, take a **diagnostic or assessment test** first. Also, spend time on sample tests so that you become accustomed to the way the actual test will appear.

This guide comes with an online diagnostic test of 30 questions found online at www.XAMonline.com. It is a little boot camp to get you up for the task and reveal things about your compendium of knowledge in general. Although this guide is structured to follow the order of the test, you are not required to study in that order. By finding a time-management and study plan that fits your life you will be more effective. The results of your diagnostic or self-assessment test can be a guide for how to manage your time and point you towards an area that needs more attention.

Week	Activity
8 weeks prior to test	Take a diagnostic test found at www.XAMonline.com
6-3 weeks prior to test	For each of these 4 weeks, choose a content area to study. You don't have to go in the order of the book. It may be that you start with the content that needs the most review. Alternately, you may want to ease yourself into plan by starting with the most familiar material.
2 weeks prior to test	Take the sample test, score it, and create a review plan for the final week before the test.
1 week prior to test	Following your plan (which will likely be aligned with the areas that need the most review) go back and study the sections that align with the questions you may have gotten wrong. Then go back and study the sections related to the questions you answered correctly. If need be, create flashcards and drill yourself on any area that you makes you anxious.

Section 3 About the MTEL English as a Second Language (ESL) 54

What is the MTEL English as a Second Language (ESL) 54?
The MTEL English as a Second Language (ESL) 54 exam is meant to assess mastery of the basic pedagogical knowledge and skills required to teach ELL students in Massachusetts public schools. It is administered by Pearson Education on behalf of the Massachusetts Department of Education.

Often **your own state's requirements** determine whether or not you should take any particular test. The most reliable source of information regarding this is your state's Department of Education. This resource should have a complete list of testing centers and dates. Test dates vary by subject area and not all test dates necessarily include your particular test, so be sure to check carefully.

If you are in a teacher-education program, check with the Education Department or the Certification Officer for specific information for testing and testing timelines. The Certification Office should have most of the information you need.

If you choose an alternative route to certification you can either rely on our website at www.XAMonline.com or on the resources provided by an alternative certification program. Many states now have specific agencies devoted to alternative certification and there are some national organizations as well, for example:
National Association for Alternative Certification
http://www.alt-teachercert.org/index.asp

Interpreting Test Results

Contrary to what you may have heard, the results of the MTEL English as a Second Language (ESL) 54 are not based on time. More accurately, you will be scored on the raw number of points you earn in relation to the raw number of points available. Each question is worth one raw point. It is likely to your benefit to complete as many questions in the time allotted, but it will not necessarily work to your advantage if you hurry through the test.

Follow the guidelines provided by Pearson for interpreting your score. The web site offers a sample test score sheet and clearly explains how/whether the scores are scaled and what to expect if you have an essay portion on your test.

What's on the Test?

The Massachusetts Test for Educator Licensure (MTEL) - English as a Second Language exam consists of one hundred multiple choice questions and two open-ended responses. The MTEL is a four hour, computer-based exam designed to measure your knowledge of subject matter, teaching practices, and issues essential to teaching English Language Learners (ELL). The test is aligned with the state curricular frameworks as well as the state's educational regulations.

The test is comprised of three areas. See the table below for descriptions of their content, number of questions, and weight in determining the final test score. A passing score on the MTEL is 240.

Sub-area	Number of test questions	Approximate test weighting
I: Foundations of second-language instruction	43-45	35%
II: Second-language and content learning	55-57	45%
III: Integration of knowledge and understanding	2 open response items	20%

In the open response items of sub-area III, you will be asked to prepare a detailed analysis that integrates your understanding of the foundations of second-language instruction and the relationship between second-language learning and content learning. This section focuses on the application of knowledge and will be assessed based on:

- How well your response addresses the task;
- How well you apply knowledge in completing the task;
- The evidence you use to support your argument; and
- Your understanding of the subject matter.

Details of the content covered in sub-areas I and II are contained within this testing guide.

Question Types

You're probably thinking "enough already, I want to study!" Indulge us a little longer while we explain that there is more than one type of multiple-choice question. You can thank us later after you realize how well prepared you are for your exam. There are two main types of multiple choice questions; single item and items with stimulus.

Single item questions may look like this:

1. **Which of the Following**. One way to test your answer choice for this type of question is to replace the phrase "which of the following" with your selection. Use this example: Which of the following words is one of the twelve most frequently used in children's reading texts:

   a. There
   b. This
   c. The
   d. An

   Don't look! Test your answer. _____ is one of the twelve most frequently used in children's reading texts. Did you guess C? Then you guessed correctly.

Items with stimulus questions may look like this:

2. **Complete the Statement**. The Dolch Basic Sight Words consist of a relatively short list of words that children should be able to:

   a. Sound out
   b. Know the meaning of
   c. Recognize on sight
   d. Use in a sentence

   The correct answer is C. To check your answer, test out the statement by adding the choices to the end of it.

Stimulus questions may include reading excerpts, infographics, or classroom situations as the stimulus.

Another example:

In the following graph (not statistically accurate) in how many years did more men take the MTEL exam than women?

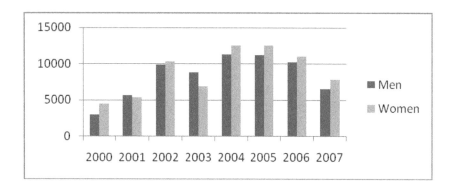

    a. None
    b. One
    c. Two
    d. Three

It may help you to simply circle the two years that answer the question. Make sure you've read the question thoroughly and once you've made your determination, double check your work. The correct answer is C.

Make sure that you read all questions carefully to determine whether it asks for a very specific answer or a broad interpretation of the visual.

Watch out for negative questions. This type of question contains words such as "not," "least," and "except." Each correct answer will be the statement that does not fit the situation described in the question. Such as: Multicultural education is not

    a. An idea or concept
    b. A "tack-on" to the school curriculum
    c. An educational reform movement
    d. A process

Think to yourself that the statement could be anything but the correct answer. This question form is more open to interpretation than other types, so read carefully and don't forget that you're answering a negative statement.

Section 4 Helpful Hints

Study Tips

You are what you eat. Good eating habits while studying, and on the day of the test, are very important. Eating well and staying hydrated help you learn and retain information. In addition, certain foods contain compounds that help increase neurotransmitter levels, supporting memory and recall of information. Eating the following foods will support your hungry brain as you study and learn:

- Milk
- Nuts and seeds
- Rice
- Eggs
- Turkey
- Fish
- Vegetables
- Whole Grains

The better you eat, the better you'll feel as you study, and most importantly, on the day of the exam!

1. **See the forest for the trees**. In other words, get the concept before you look at the details. One way to do this is to take notes as you read, paraphrasing or summarizing in your own words. Putting the concept in terms that are comfortable and familiar may increase retention.

2. **Question authority**. Ask why, why, why. Pull apart written material paragraph by paragraph and don't forget the captions under the illustrations. For example, if a heading reads *Stream Erosion* put it in the form of a question (why do streams erode? Or what is stream erosion?) Then find the answer within the material. If you train your mind to think in this manner you will learn more and prepare yourself for answering test questions.

3. **Play mind games**. Using your brain for reading or puzzles keeps it flexible. Even with a limited amount of time your brain can take in data and store it for later use. In ten minutes, you can: read a few paragraphs, quiz yourself with flash cards, or review notes. Even if you don't fully understand something on the first pass, your mind stores it for recall, which is why frequent reading or review increases chances of retention and comprehension.

4. **The pen is mightier than the sword**. Learn to take great notes. A by-product of our modern culture is that we have grown accustomed to getting our information in short doses. We've subconsciously trained ourselves to assimilate information into neat little packages. Messy notes fragment the flow of information. Your notes can be much clearer with proper formatting. *The Cornell Method* is one

such format. This method was popularized in *How to Study in College,* Ninth Edition, by Walter Pauk. You can benefit from the method without purchasing an additional book by simply looking the method up online. Below is a sample of how *The Cornell Method* can be adapted for use with this guide.

← 2 ½" →	← ——————— 6" ——————— →
Cue Column	Note Taking Column 1. Record: During your reading, use the note-taking column to record important points. 2. Questions: As soon as you finish a section, formulate questions based on the notes in the right-hand column. Writing questions helps to clarify meanings, reveal relationships, establish community, and strengthen memory. Also, the writing of questions sets the state for exam study later. 3. Recite: Cover the note-taking column with a sheet of paper. Then, looking at the questions or cue-words in the question and cue column only, say aloud, in your own words, the answers to the questions, facts, or ideas indicated by the cue words. 4. Reflect: Reflect on the material by asking yourself questions. 5. Review: Spend at least ten minutes every week reviewing all your previous notes. Doing so helps you retain ideas and topics for the exam.
↑ 2" ↓	Summary After reading, use this space to summarize the notes from each page.

*Adapted from *How to Study in College,* Ninth Edition, by Walter Pauk, ©2008 Wadsworth

5. **Apply what you are learning to the classroom**. It is not enough to memorize the theories, instructional strategies, standards, and assessment types in this book. To do well on the exam, you will need to understand the material well enough to apply them to specific school, classroom, and student scenarios. Many of the questions on the MTEL provide you with a school, classroom, or student scenario and ask you to identify the relevant theory, strategy, or assessment practice from a list of possible options. When you study, make sure you spend time applying what you are learning.

6. **Place yourself in exile and set the mood**. Set aside a specific place and time to study that best suits your personal needs. If you're a night person, burn the midnight oil. If you're a morning person set yourself up with some coffee and get to it. Make your study time and place as free from distraction as possible and

surround yourself with what you need, be it silence or music. Studies have shown that music can aid in concentration, absorption, and retrieval of information. Research indicates that classical music is most effective.

7. **Get pointed in the right direction**. Use arrows to point to important passages or pieces of information. It's easier to read than a page full of yellow highlights. Highlighting can be used sparingly, but add an arrow to the margin to call attention to it.

8. **Check your budget**. You should review all the content material before your test, but allocate the most amount of time to the areas that need the most refreshing. It sounds obvious, but it's easy to forget. You can use the study rubric above to balance your study budget.

Current Teaching Trends

Digital pedagogy and the use of 21st century teaching methods have shifted the landscape of teaching to create a bigger focus on student engagement. Student-centered classrooms now utilize technology to create efficiencies and increase digital literacy. Classrooms that once relied on memorization and the regurgitation of facts now push students to *create* and *analyze* material. The Bloom's Taxonomy chart below gives a great visual of the higher order thinking skills that current teachers are implementing in their learning objectives. There are also examples of the verbs that you might use when creating learning objectives at the assignment, course, or program level.

21st Century Bloom's Taxonomy

Lower- order			Higher- order		
Remember	Understand	Apply	Analyze	Evaluate	Create
• Define • Describe • Recall	• Classify • Explain • Summarize	• Determine • Organize • Use	• Deduct • Estimate • Outline	• Argue • Justify • Support	• Construct • Adapt • Modify

Most importantly, you'll notice that each of these verbs will allow teachers to align a specific assessment to assess the mastery of the skill that's being taught. Instead of saying "Students will learn about parts of speech," teachers will insert a measurable verb into the learning objective. The 21st century model uses S.M.A.R.T. (Specific, Measurable, Attainable, Realistic, Time-bound) assessment methods to ensure teachers can track progress and zero in on areas that students need to revisit before they have fully grasped the concept.

When reading the first objective below, you might ask yourself the following questions:

Students will:

1. Learn about parts of speech

How will they learn? How will you assess their learning? What does "learn" mean to different teachers? What does "learn" look like to different learning styles?

In this second example, the 21st century model shows specific ways students will use parts of speech.

Students will be able to:

1. Define parts of speech (lower)
2. Classify parts of speech (lower)
3. Construct a visual representation of each part of speech (higher)

Technology in the 21st Century Classroom

Student-centered classrooms now also rely heavily on technology for content delivery (PowerPoint, LMS) assessment (online quizzes) and collaborative learning (GoogleDrive). Particular to ESL classrooms, teachers can now record themselves speaking using lecture capture software. Students can then watch the video multiple times to ensure they've understood concepts. They have the ability to pause/rewind/replay any sections they are confused about, and they can focus on taking better notes while having the ability to watch the video a second or third time.

Online assessments also give students and teachers a better idea for comprehension level. These quick, often self-grading assessments give teachers more time to spend with students instead of grading. They eliminate human error and give teachers data needed to zero in on concepts that need to be revisited. For example, if 12 of 15 students got number 5 wrong, the teacher will know to discuss this concept in class. Online assessments may include listening, speaking, reading, and/or writing practice. This reinforces the content that was taught in the classroom and gives opportunity for practice at students' leisure. In addition, adaptable learning will help teachers by tracking user data to demonstrate learning gains. This can be completed in pre-posttest form, with conditionals within an assessment, or through small, formative assessments.

SMART Technologies, Inc. is a very popular company that creates software and hardware for educational environments. You may have heard of a "SmartBoard" before. These are promethean boards (interactive whiteboards) and are most commonly gained using grant money. They can be used as a projector for PowerPoints, their speakers can be used for audio practice, and their video options can allow you to "bring" a guest speaker into your classroom using videoconferencing, such as Skype. They record notes made on the whiteboard and record audio from lectures, which can then be saved and sent to students that were absent, or used to review for tests on varying concepts.

Google has created ample opportunity for secondary teachers in creating efficiencies for document sharing, assessment tools, and collaborative learning environments. Their drive feature can allow for easy transfer of assignment instructions, essays, and group projects. Slides can be used to create and post PowerPoints for students to have ongoing access. Forms is a great way to create quizzes, and the data can be sorted and manipulated in a number of ways. They can also be used for self-assessment, peer evaluation, and for pre-post analyses.

As technology continues to evolve, it's critical for teachers to continue to implement tools that make their classrooms more effective and efficient while also preparing students to successfully function in a technology-driven society. Through simple lessons and technology demonstrations, students will have a great start at applying technology skills in the outside world. The classroom is a great starting place for ESL students to learn how to use technology and how to practice their own reading, writing, listening, and speaking.

Testing Tips

1. **Get smart, play dumb**. Sometimes a question is just a question. No one is out to trick you, so don't assume that the test writer is looking for something other than what was asked. Stick to the question as written and don't overanalyze.

2. **Do a double take**. Read test questions and answer choices at least twice because it's easy to miss something, to transpose a word or some letters. If you have no idea what the correct answer is, skip it and come back later if there's time. If you're still clueless, it's okay to guess. Remember, you're scored on the number of questions you answer correctly and you're not penalized for wrong answers. The worst-case scenario is that you miss a point from a good guess.

3. **Turn it on its ear**. The syntax of a question can often provide a clue, so make things interesting and turn the question into a statement to see if it changes the meaning or relates better (or worse) to the answer choices.

4. **Get out your magnifying glass**. Look for hidden clues in the questions because it's difficult to write a multiple-choice question without giving away part of the answer in the options presented. In most questions, you can readily eliminate one or two potential answers, increasing your chances of answering correctly to 50/50, which will help out if you've skipped a question and gone back to it (see tip #2).

5. **Call it intuition**. Often your first instinct is correct. If you've been studying the content you've likely absorbed something and have subconsciously retained the knowledge. On questions you're not sure about, trust your instincts. A first impression is usually correct.

6. **Become a clock-watcher**. You have four hours to answer the questions. Don't get bogged down laboring over a question you're not sure about when there are ten others you could answer more readily. The MTEL test allows you to skip a question and flag it for review so that you can go back to it. If you finish early, you can go back and check all of your answers carefully.

Do the Drill

No matter how prepared you feel it's sometimes a good idea to apply Murphy's Law. Be sure not to trip on these basic rules of conduct and etiquette:

1. **Remember, there is no food or drink of any kind allowed in the exam room**, including gum. You will put all food, drink and any other personal items in a locker before you enter the exam room.

2. **You're not too sexy for your test**. Wear comfortable clothes. You'll be distracted if your belt is too tight, or if you're too cold or too hot.

3. **Lie to yourself**. Even if you think you're a prompt person, pretend you're not and leave plenty of time to get to the testing center. Map it out ahead of time and do a dry run if you can. There's no need to add road rage to your list of anxieties.

4. **No ID, no test**. Bring one piece of current, government-issued, photo identification printed in English with your signature, in the name in which you registered. (E.g., driver's license, passport, state ID, etc.) Check the test site before you go to make sure that your ID is acceptable.

5. **You can't take it with you**. Leave any study aids, dictionaries, notebooks, computers, and the like at home.

6. **Prepare for the desert**. Any time spent on a bathroom break cannot be made up later, so use your judgment on the amount you eat or drink.

7. **Quiet, please! Keeping your own time is a good idea, but not with a timepiece that has a loud ticker. If you use a watch, take it off and place it nearby, but not in a place where it distracts you. Cell phones are not allowed in the test area.**

To the best of our ability, we have compiled the content you need to know in this book and in the accompanying online resources. The rest is up to you. You can use the study and testing tips or you can follow your own methods. Either way, you can be confident that there aren't any missing pieces of information and there shouldn't be any surprises in the content on the test.

If you have questions about test fees, registration, electronic testing, or other content verification issues please visit www.mtel.nesinc.com.

Good luck!
Sharon Wynne
Founder, XAMonline

DOMAIN I   **FOUNDATIONS OF SECOND LANGUAGE ACQUISITION**

COMPETENCY 1.0   **LINGUISTIC AND SOCIOLINGUISTIC CONCEPTS RELATED TO INSTRUCTION FOR ENGLISH LEARNERS**

Skill 1.1   **Understands the influence of first language on second language learning (e.g., phonology, morphology, syntax, semantics, discourse)**

Skills 1.2 through 1.6 outline the major aspects of phonology and phonetics, morphology and morphemes, semantics, syntax, pragmatics, and discourse.

Skill 7.7 outlines the ways in which the similarities and differences between first and second languages can influence second language learning.

Skill 1.2   **Demonstrates knowledge of phonetics and phonemics (e.g., distinguishing among classes of sound)**

The definition of **phonology** is "the way in which speech sounds form patterns" (Diaz-Rico, Weed, 1995). Phonology is a subset of the linguistics field, which studies the organization and systems of sound within a language.

When babies babble, or make what we call baby sounds, they are actually experimenting with all of the sounds represented in languages. As they learn a language, they become more proficient in the sounds of that language and forget how to make sounds that they don't need or use.

Phonemes, pitch, and **stress** are all components of phonology. Because each affects the meaning being communicated, they are variables that ELLs must recognize and learn.

Phonology analyzes the sound structure of the given language by:

- determining which phonetic sounds have the most significance
- explaining how these sounds influence a native speaker of the language

For example, the Russian alphabet has a consonant, which, when pronounced, sounds like the soft 'g' sound from the word "rouge" in French. English speakers typically have difficulty pronouncing this sound pattern since it is only occasionally encountered (Díaz-Rico & Weed, 1995).

Mastering a sound that does not occur in the learner's first language requires ongoing repetition, both of hearing the sound and attempting to say it. The older the learner, the more difficult this becomes, especially if the learner has only spoken one language before reaching puberty. Correct pronunciation may require years of practice because the learner may not hear the sound correctly at first. Expecting an ELL to master a foreign pronunciation quickly leads to frustration for the teacher and the learner. With enough focused repetition, and listening and speaking practice, the learner may eventually hear the difference and then become able to imitate it.

A phoneme is the smallest unit of sound that affects meaning. In English, there are approximately 44 speech sounds yet only 26 letters, so the sounds, when combined, become words. For this reason, English is not considered a phonetic language with one-to-one correspondence between letters and sounds. The vowel 'a', for example, can be pronounced in different ways (as in 'make' or 'tag').

As an example of phonemes, consider the two words, "pin" and "bin." The only difference is the first consonant of the words, the "p" in "pin" and "b" in "bin." This makes the sounds "p" and "b" phonemes in English, because the difference in sound creates a difference in meaning.

Focusing on phonemes to provide pronunciation practice allows students to have fun while they learn to recognize and say sounds. Pairs or groups of words that have a set pattern make learning easier. For example, students can practice saying words that rhyme but begin with a different phoneme, such as tan, man, fan, and ran. Other groups of words might start with the same phoneme followed by various vowel sounds, such as ten, ton, tan, and tin. This kind of alliteration can be used to compose tongue twisters that students find challenging and fun. Vowels and consonants should be introduced in a deliberate order to allow combinations that form real words.

Pitch in communication plays a role in determining the context or meaning of a series of words. A string of words can communicate more than one meaning. For instance, the phrase "I can't go" acts as a statement, if the pitch or intonation falls. However, the same phrase becomes the question "I can't go?" if the pitch or intonation rises for the word "go."

Stress can occur at a word or sentence level. At the word level, different stresses on the syllable can actually modify the word's meaning. Consider the word "conflict." To pronounce it as a noun, one would stress the first syllable, as in "CONflict." However, to use it as a verb, the second syllable would be stressed, as in "conFLICT."

Different dialects sometimes pronounce the same word differently, even though both pronunciations have the same meaning. For example, in some parts of the United States the word "insurance" is pronounced by stressing the second syllable, while in other parts of the country the first syllable is stressed.

At the "sentence" level, stress can also be used to vary the meaning. For example, consider the following questions and how the meaning changes according to the stressed words:

He did that? (Emphasis is on the person.)
He **did** that? (Emphasis is on the action.)

He did **that**? (Emphasis is on object of the action.)

This type of meaning differentiation is difficult for most ELL students to grasp and requires innovative teaching, such as acting out the three different meanings. Since pitch and stress can change the meaning of a sentence completely, students must learn to recognize these differences in order to develop proficiency in English language speaking and listening skills.

Phonographemics refers to the study of letters and letter combinations. Unlike Spanish and French and many other languages, in English one symbol can represent many phonemes, and there are multiple pronunciations of vowels and consonants. Phonetic rules are crucial to learning to read and write. However, because of the numerous exceptions, the rules themselves do little to assist listening and speaking skills, which makes English a difficult language to master.

When teaching English to speakers of other languages, the wide variation of phonemes represented by a single symbol must be taught and *drilled*. If it is difficult for native speakers to learn the English spelling system, it is a great leap for the foreign-language learner. Graphemes, the written letter or group of letters that represents a single sound, should be introduced long after spoken English. Students must first be able to speak and hear the language before they can be taught to spell it.

Phonographemic differences between English words are a common source of confusion and thus need to be taught explicitly with numerous learning activities to enable learners to understand the various distinctions. Some areas of focus for the ESOL classroom include:

- **Homonyms:** A general term that describes words that have two or more meanings
- **Homographs:** Two or more words that have the same spelling or pronunciation but different meanings, e.g., stalk (part of a plant) / stalk (follow)
- **Homophones:** Two or more words that have the same pronunciation but different meanings and spellings, e.g., wood/would, cite/sight
- **Heteronyms:** Two or more words that have the same spelling, but have a different pronunciation and meaning, e.g., Polish/polish

Some useful activities for instruction would be to identify misspelled words, to recognize multiple meanings of words in sentences, to spell words correctly within a given context, and to match words with their meanings.

Sound-symbol correspondence is more difficult in English than some other languages because each letter can make a variety of sounds. Recognition of repeating patterns helps students develop decoding skills. Consonant blends such as /ch/, /ph/, and /sh/ are readily recognizable and make the same sound with quite a bit of consistency. Earliest beginners can scan for those language patterns and recognize the sounds they make.

Skill 1.3   Applies use of morphology and lexicon to analyze a word's structure, function, and meaning

Morphology refers to the process of how the words of a language are formed to create meaningful messages. ESOL teachers need to be aware of the principles of morphology in English so they can provide meaningful activities that will help in the process of language learning.

Morphemic analysis requires breaking a word down into its component parts to determine its meaning. It shows the relationship between the root or base word and the prefix and/or suffix to determine the word's meaning.

A **morpheme** is the smallest unit of a language system that has meaning. These units are more commonly known as: the roots, the prefix, and the suffix. They cannot be broken down into any smaller units.

- **The root word or base word** is the key to understanding a word, because this is where the actual meaning is determined.
- **A prefix** is a syllable or syllables which appear in front of the root or base word and can alter its meaning.
- **A suffix** is a letter or letters which are added to the end of the word and can alter the original tense or meaning of the root or base word.

The following is an example of how morphemic analysis can be applied to a word:

- Choose a root or base word, such as "kind."
- Create as many new words as possible, by changing the prefix and suffix.
- New words would include "unkind", "kindness", and "kindly."

Learning common roots, prefixes, and suffixes greatly helps ELLs to decode unfamiliar words. This can make a big difference in how well a student understands written language. Students who can decode unfamiliar words become less frustrated when reading in English, and are likely to enjoy reading more. They have greater comprehension and their language skills improve more quickly. Having the tools to decode unfamiliar words enables ELL students to perform better on standardized tests because they are more likely to understand the question and answer choices.

Guessing at the meaning of words (using knowledge of morphemes) should be encouraged. Too often, students become dependent on translation dictionaries, which causes the students not to develop morphemic analysis skills. Practice should include identifying roots, prefixes, and suffixes, as well as using morphemic knowledge to form new words.

ESOL learners need to understand the structure of words in English, and how words may be created and altered. Some underlying principles of the morphology of English are:

1. Morphemes may be free and able to stand by themselves (e.g., chair, bag), or they may be bound or derivational, needing to be used with other morphemes to create meaning (e.g., read-able, en-able).
2. Knowledge of the meanings of derivational morphemes such as prefixes and suffixes enables students to decode word meanings and create words in the language through word analysis (e.g., un-happy means not happy).
3. Some morphemes in English provide grammatical rather than semantic information to words and sentences (e.g., of, the, and).
4. Words can be combined in English to create new compound words (e.g., key + chain = keychain).

ESOL teachers also need to be aware that principles of morphology from the native language may be transferred to either promote or interfere with the second-language learning process.

Recognition of cognates and false cognates is very helpful in decoding and can be directly taught. Many words are identical in English and Spanish, with the only difference being pronunciation. Fortunately for students, as they develop skills in content areas such as math and science, the incidence of these cognates increases. Some examples of English-Spanish cognates are:

- *hotel*
- *radio*
- *religion*
- *eclipse*
- *editor*

Many words are the same in English and Spanish, with the addition of a changed vowel at the end of the word. Here are some examples:

- *cost: costo*
- *cause: causa*
- *minute: minute*
- *medicine: medicina*
- *list: lista*
- *map: mapa*

Here are some of the common false cognates between English and Spanish:

- *libreria*—It's not a *library*, but a *bookstore*
- *embarazada*—It doesn't mean *embarrassed*, but *pregnant*
- *asistir*—It doesn't mean *to help*, but *to attend* or *be present*

Prefixes and suffixes can be directly taught to give the student scaffolding in decoding new words. For instance, *-ful* and *-less* can be taught and then combined with known words to make new ones.

- *Help + ful = helpful*
- *Help + less = helpless*
- *Care + ful = careful*
- *Care + less = careless*

Skill 1.4 Applies knowledge of syntactic features (e.g., a verb phrase) in oral language and written text

Syntax involves the order in which words are arranged to create meaning. Different languages use different patterns for sentence structure. Syntax also refers to the rules for creating correct sentence patterns. English, like many other languages, is a subject-verb-object language, i.e., in most sentences the subject precedes the verb, and the object follows the verb. ELLs whose native language follows a subject-verb-object pattern will find it easier to master English syntax.

THE ENGLISH SYNTACTIC SYSTEM

English classifies eight parts of speech, each with a specific role in sentences. Understanding the parts of speech can be quite difficult for ELLs because the same word can have a different role in different sentences, and a different meaning entirely. Identifying the subject and predicate of the sentence helps to distinguish what role a particular word plays in a sentence. Since English is a subject-verb-object (S-V-O) language, the placement of a word in a sentence relative to the subject or verb indicates what part of speech it is.

- That TV *show* was boring.
- I will *show* you my new dress.
- The band plays *show* tunes at half time.

In these examples, the word *show* is first a noun, then a verb, and finally an adjective.

The Eight Parts of Speech	
Noun	A person, place, thing or idea. Common nouns are non-specific, while proper nouns name a specific person, place, thing, or idea, and are capitalized. Nouns may be **countable** or **uncountable**. Countable nouns describe countable objects, e.g., an apple, twelve chairs, six geese, a cup of coffee. Uncountable nouns describe things that cannot be counted, e.g., liberty, coffee, or politics. *Many* and *few* are used when referring to countable nouns, and *much* and *little* when referring to uncountable nouns.

Verb	An action or state of being.

Pronoun	A word that takes the place of a noun. A pronoun refers to the word it replaces—its **antecedent**.
	There are three types of pronouns:
	• *Personal pronouns* can be
	  ○ first, second, or third person (I, you, he, she, it)
	  ○ singular or plural (I/we, you/you, he, she, it/they)
	  ○ subjective or objective (I/me, you/you, he/him, she/her, it/it, we/us, they/them)
	• *Possessive pronouns* show ownership (my, mine, your, yours, his, her, hers, its, our, ours, your, yours, their, and theirs).
	• *Indefinite pronouns* refer to persons, places, things or ideas in general, such as any, each, both, most, something.

Adjective	A word that modifies a noun or pronoun. Adjectives answer the questions, *What kind? How many?* and *Which?*
Adverb	A word that modifies a verb, an adjective, or another adverb. Adverbs answer the questions, *How? When? Where? How often?* and *To what extent?*
Preposition	A word that, in a phrase with a noun or pronoun, shows the relationship between a noun or pronoun and another word in a sentence. Prepositions describe or show location, direction, or time. Prepositional phrases can have as few as two words, but can include any number of adjectives.
Interjection	A word that shows surprise or strong feeling. An interjection can stand alone (*Help!*) or be used within a sentence (*Oh no, I forgot my wallet!*)
Conjunction	Conjunctions may be either coordinating or subordinating. **Coordinating conjunctions** (*and, but, or, nor*) connect words or phrases that have the same grammatical function in a sentence. The coordinating conjunction pair *either/or* is used for affirmative statements; the pair *neither/nor* is used for negative statements. *Parallel structure* is desired when using coordinating conjunctions, e.g., *to ride, to sing, and to dance.* (Similar structures for clauses are indicated.) The coordinating conjunctions (*so, for, yet*) may also be used to connect two independent clauses. **Subordinating conjunctions** are words used to introduce adverbial clauses. Some* of the subordinating conjunctions used for _____ are: • **time**: *after, before, when, while, as, as soon as, since, until* • **cause and effect**: *because, now that, since* • **contrast**: *although, even though, though*

	• **condition**: *if, only if, unless, whether or not, in that case, e.g.,* "When we were in Brazil, we went to Rio de Janeiro and Sao Paulo." "We went to Rio de Janeiro and Sao Paulo when we were in Brazil." (*There are many, many more subordinating conjunctions.)

SENTENCES

A sentence is a group of words that has a subject and predicate, and expresses a complete idea. A subject tells us what or whom the sentence is about and the predicate makes a statement about what the subject is or does.

Example sentence: <u>The snow</u> *falls quietly*	
Subject	The subject, or the topic of a sentence, consists of a noun or a pronoun and all the words that modify it. "The snow" is the subject in the above example. The simple subject is the main part of the subject. *Snow* is the simple subject.
Predicate	The predicate makes a statement or a comment about the subject and it consists of a verb and all the words that modify it; *falls quietly* is the predicate in the above example. The simple predicate is the main part of the predicate and is always the verb; *falls* is the simple predicate.
Compound subject	A subject that consists of two or more nouns or pronouns, e.g., <u>Books and magazines</u> *filled the room.*
Compound predicate	A predicate that contains more than one verb pertaining to the subject, e.g., <u>The boys</u> *walked and talked.*

Sentence Types
Subjects and predicates can be modified and combined in different ways to make simple, compound, or complex sentences.

Sentence Types	
Simple	A simple sentence, or independent clause, is a complete thought consisting of a subject and a predicate: <u>The bus</u> *was late.*
Compound	A compound sentence consists of two independent clauses joined together by a coordinator (*and, or, nor, but, for, yet, so*): <u>Tom</u> *walked to the bus station,* **and** <u>he</u> *took the bus.*
Complex	A complex sentence is a sentence consisting of a dependent clause (a group of words with a subject and predicate that are not a complete thought) and an independent clause joined together using a subordinator (*although, after, when, because, since, while*): After <u>I</u> *write the report,* <u>I</u> *will submit it to my teacher.*

Sentence Purposes

Sentences serve different purposes. They can make a statement (declarative); ask a question (interrogative); give a command (imperative); or express a sense of urgency (exclamatory). Understanding the different purposes for sentences can help ELLs understand the relationship between what they write and the ideas they want to express.

Sentence Purpose	
Declarative	A declarative sentence makes a statement: "Anna will feed the dog."
Interrogative	An interrogative sentence asks a question: "Anna, have you fed the dog?"
Imperative	An imperative sentence gives a command: "Anna, please feed the dog."
Exclamatory	An exclamatory sentence expresses a sense of urgency: "Anna, go feed the dog right now!"

Constructing sentences involves combining words in grammatically correct ways to communicate the desired thought. Avoiding fragments and run-ons requires continual sentence analysis. The test of a complete sentence is: Does it contain a subject and predicate and express a complete idea?

 ELLs often over-generalize that sentence fragments are short and complete sentences are long. When they truly understand what constitutes a sentence, they will realize that length has nothing to do with whether a sentence is complete or not.

For example:

- "He ran." is a complete sentence.
- "After the very funny story began" is a fragment.

To make these distinctions, learners must know the parts of speech and understand the difference between independent clauses and dependent clauses. Practice identifying independent clauses, dependent clauses, and phrases will help ELLs to write complete sentences.

Clauses and Phrases	
Independent clause	Independent clauses can stand alone or can be joined to other clauses.
Dependent clause	Dependent clauses contain at least one subject and one verb, but they cannot stand alone as a complete sentence. They are structurally dependent on the main clause.

Phrase	A phrase is a group of words that does not have a subject and a predicate and cannot stand alone. The most common types of phrases are: Prepositional: "in the room" Participial: "walking down the street" Infinitive: "to run"

Sentence Transformations

Sentences are transformed to add, delete, or permute informational content. There are many kinds of grammar. Chomsky proposed transformational grammar beginning in the 1950s. The term is still used to explain the relationships between the spoken word and its underlying meaning by distinguishing between sounds, words (and word parts), groups of words, and phrases. According to generative grammarians, sentences have a surface structure and an underlying structure. The rules that interpret the underlying structures and modify them to create the same surface structure are called **transformations**.

There are numerous possible transformations in the English language. Some of the most common ones used in ESOL teaching are listed below.

Sentence Transformations: ways in which the sentence adds, deletes, or permutes components	
Yes/no questions	**Sentences may be transformed into yes/no questions.** **auxiliary verb + subject + main verb + rest of sentence:** He lives in Chicago. Does he live in Chicago? Yes, he does. No, he doesn't.
Information questions	**Sentences may be transformed into information questions.** **question word + auxiliary verb + subject + main verb + rest of sentence:** Susan lives near Orlando. Where does Susan live? Near Orlando/She lives near Orlando. Will Julius be living alone in the house? How will Julius be living in the house? Alone./Julius will be living alone in the house.

Active voice to passive voice or vice versa	**Sentences may be changed from one voice to another voice.** I saw John. John was seen by me. John was being helped by me. I was helping John.
Indirect objects	**The word "to" (phrase marker) may be deleted.** I gave a cookie to him. I gave him a cookie. I mailed the article to the newspaper. I mailed the newspaper the article.
Imperatives	**The imperative or commands have no expressed subject.** You, sit. You, jump. Sit! Jump!
Negatives	**Linguists distinguish between two types of negation. Affirmative sentences may be transformed into negative sentences where the whole sentence is negative.** Marion is happy. Marion is not happy. **Parts of sentences may be negative.** Juliana is happy. Juliana is unhappy.

Verb Tense

The basic English verb tenses are itemized below. Tense refers to any conjugated form expressing time, aspect, or mood. The charts omit the negative and interrogative forms.

Verb Tenses	Simple	Progressive	Perfect	Perfect progressive
Present	I write	I am writing	I have written	I have been writing
Past	I wrote	I was writing	I had written	I had been writing
Future	I will write	I will be writing	I will have written	I will have been writing

This table, of course, omits several additional forms that are part of the basic system:

- The intensive present: *I do write*
- The intensive past: *I did write*
- The habitual past: *I used to write*
- The "shall future": *I shall write*

- The "going-to future": *I am going to write*
- The "future in the past": *I was going to write*
- The conditional: *I would write*
- The perfect conditional: *I would have written*
- The subjunctive: *if I be writing, if I were writing*.

Skill 1.5   Applies knowledge of semantics in determining meaning in connected discourse

Semantics encompasses the meaning of individual words, as well as combinations of words. Native speakers use their language to function in their daily lives at all levels. Through experience, they know the effects of intonation, connotation, and synonyms. This is often untrue of non-native speakers. In an ESOL class, we are trying to teach as quickly as possible what the native speaker already knows. The objectives of beginning ESOL lesson plans should deliberately build a foundation that will enable students to meet more advanced objectives.

Teaching within a specific context helps students to understand the meaning of words and sentences. When students can remember the context in which they learned words and recall how the words were used, they retain that knowledge and can compare it with different applications of the same words as they are introduced.

Using words in a variety of contexts helps students reach deeper understanding of the words. They can then guess at new meanings that are introduced in different contexts. For example, the word "conduct" can be taught in the context of conducting a meeting or an investigation. Later the word "conductor" can be used in various contexts that demonstrate some similarity but have distinctly different uses of the word, such as a conductor of electricity, the conductor of a train, the conductor of an orchestra, and so forth.

Second language learners must learn to translate words and sentences that they already understand in their primary language into the language they wish to acquire. This can be a daunting task because of the many ways meaning is created in English. Voice inflection, variations of meaning, variations of usage, and emphasis are some of the factors that affect meaning. The lexicon of language includes the stored meaning and contextual meaning from word association, as well as knowledge of pronunciation, grammar, and morphemes.

Skill 1.6   Demonstrates knowledge of discourse features in oral and written text

The term discourse refers to linguistic units composed of several sentences and is derived from the concept of "discursive formation" or communication that involves specialized knowledge of various kinds. Conversations, arguments, or speeches are types of discourses. Discourse shapes the way language is transmitted, as well as how we organize our thoughts.

The structure of discourse varies among languages and traditions. For example, Japanese writing does not present the main idea at the beginning of an essay; rather, writing builds up to the main idea, which is presented or implied at the end of the essay. This is completely different than English writing, which typically presents the main idea or thesis at the beginning of an essay and repeats it at the end.

In addition to language and structure, topic or focus affects discourse. The discourse in various disciplines approaches topics differently, such as feminist studies, cultural studies, and literary theory. Discourse plays a role in all spoken and written language, and affects our thinking.

Written discourse ranges from the most basic grouping of sentences to the most complicated essays and stories. Regardless of the level, English writing demands certain structure patterns. A typical paragraph begins with a topic sentence which states directly or indirectly the focus of the paragraph, adds supporting ideas and details, and ends with a concluding sentence that relates to the focus and either states the final thought on that topic or provides a transition to the next paragraph. As with spoken discourse, organization, tone, and word choice are critical to transferring thoughts successfully and maintaining interest.

Vocal discourse varies significantly depending on context. People speak in different styles depending on who they are talking to and what the occasion demands. A candidate who is running for president and speaking to a group will use more formal speech than when having a casual conversation. The message conveyed may also vary, depending on whether the group is one of supporters or people who hold different political views. In either case, the candidate must make choices about how to organize what he or she says to ensure comprehension and to hold the audience's interest.

ELLs might initially practice set conversations to learn the patterns of English discourse. Practicing in pairs using a question and answer format gives both participants an opportunity to learn the structures of discourse as well as information about the other person or the other person's culture. Such practice also gives students practice with other language skills and can increase vocabulary. The teacher may provide a set of questions, and learners can alternate asking and answering. Short skits that repeat a limited number of words also provide helpful practice. Allowing students time to converse informally is also useful, perhaps including suggested topics to continue to reinforce speech patterns.

Polite discourse includes what is called "empty language" or perfunctory speech, that has little meaning but is important in social exchanges. Frequently, English speakers start a conversation by asking, "How are you?" even though they have no real interest in the other person's health. An appropriate response would be, "Fine," even if the person may not feel well. The exchange is simply a polite means of starting a conversation. Likewise, at the end of a discourse empty language is frequently employed: "It was good to see you." "Good to see you, too." This type of discourse is part of the Basic Interpersonal Communication Skills (**BICS**) that learners must acquire to function in social situations. It is generally less demanding than Cognitive Academic Language Proficiency (**CALP**), and allows learners to participate in informal conversations.

Written discourse ranges from the most basic grouping of sentences to the most complicated essays and stories. Regardless of the level, English writing demands certain structure patterns. A typical paragraph begins with a topic sentence, which states directly or indirectly the focus of the paragraph; adds supporting ideas and details; and ends with a concluding sentence that relates to the focus and either states the final thought on that topic or provides a transition to the next paragraph when there is more than one. As with spoken discourse, organization, tone, and word choice are critical to transferring thoughts successfully and maintaining interest.

As skills increase, paragraphs are combined into stories or essays. Each type of writing has specific components and structures. Story writing requires setting, plot, and character. Initially, following a chronological order is probably easiest for ELLs, but as learners become more skillful, other types of order should be practiced, such as adding descriptions in spatial order or using flashbacks in a story.

Teachers frequently rely on the standard three- or five-paragraph essay to teach essay writing because it provides a comprehensible structure for organizing and expanding ideas within a single focus. It mirrors the paragraph structure organizationally in that the first introductory paragraph provides the main idea or focus of the essay, each body paragraph adds and develops a supporting idea and details, and the concluding paragraph provides a summary or other type of conclusion that relates to the main idea or focus stated in the first paragraph. For English Language Learners, the structure of the 3-5 paragraph essay teaches the basic organizational concept of English essay writing. By offering strictly defined limits, the teacher reduces the number of variables to learn about essay writing.

Starting with a blank page can be overwhelming for ELLs. Working within this structure enables learners to focus on developing each paragraph. As learners become more able to control their writing and sustain a focus, variations can be introduced and topics expanded.

Academic discourse refers to formal academic learning. This includes all of the four language skills: listening, reading, speaking, and writing. Academic learning is important for students to succeed in school. Cummins differentiated between two types of language proficiency: basic interpersonal communication skills (BICS) and cognitive academic language proficiency (CALP). According to research, an average student can acquire BICS within two to five years of language learning whereas CALP can take from four to seven years. A lot of factors are involved in the acquisition of CALP, such as age, language proficiency level, literacy in the first language, etc.

Academic discourse includes not only the knowledge of content-area vocabulary, but also the knowledge of various skills and strategies that are essential to successfully complete academic tasks in a mainstream classroom. It includes skills such as inferring, classifying, analyzing, synthesizing, and evaluating. Textbooks used in classrooms require abstract thinking relating to information that is context reduced. As students reach higher grades, they are required to think critically and apply this knowledge to solve problems.

Additionally, the language of academic discourse is complex for English language learners. With respect to reading and writing, complex grammatical structures are frequently found in academic discourse, which makes it challenging for the learners. Also, passive voice is normally used to present science and other subject-area textbooks. Similarly, the use of reference, pronouns, modals, etc. is a common feature of academic discourse that might cause problems for ESL learners. All of the language features of academic discourse help to convey the intended meaning of the author; therefore, it is necessary to teach these language features to students in order for them to become skilled readers and writers.

Furthermore, genre is an important aspect of academic discourse. Each genre employs a style of writing that is unique to itself. The organization of a text structure differs according to the purpose of the author. For example, mystery versus romance. Likewise, in academic reading, students come across multiple texts that vary in organization and style according to the purpose of the author, and the audience in question. Students need to understand the different features of multiple texts to become efficient readers. With respect to writing, students need to determine the purpose of their writing - for example, argumentative writing versus story writing.

In short, explicit instruction of these language skills—grammar, vocabulary, and genre—should be provided to students to help them learn academic discourse so they can succeed in a school setting.

Oral discourse analysis is often referred to as conversational analysis. In oral discourse, the emphasis is on the behavior of the participants and social constraints such as politeness and face-saving phenomena. Oral discourse analysis is concerned with who initiates the conversation, turn-taking, how not to interrupt, and who speaks next.

Written discourse is generally analyzed for how the text hangs together. **Cohesion** is the "surface" characteristics of the semantic relationships between the elements of the text. **Coherence** is the deeper meaning of the logical elements of the text. Other elements of written discourse include theme, anaphora, topic progression, and grammatical choices at the clausal level.

Skill 1.7   Understands the role of pragmatics in determining meaning in connected discourse

Pragmatics is the study of how the context impacts the interpretation of language. Situations dictate language choice, body language, the degree of intimacy, and how meaning is interpreted. For example, when customers walk into a bar and sit down on

stools, they expect a bartender will ask them several questions: "What would you like to drink?" and "Would you like to start a tab?" This sequence of events and cues is a typical pattern of interaction in a bar. Pragmatic knowledge provides the customer with a set of expectations for the flow of events. Pragmatic knowledge sets customer expectations. Typically, people in a bar expect a certain level of social exchange that allows congeniality without intrusiveness. They expect to receive a certain level of service, and to use a certain manners. These types of exchanges are expected in bars, but would be completely inappropriate in a more formal setting - for example, when conversing with the president of a corporation.

Gestures, the appropriate distance between speakers, seating arrangements, nodding and shaking of the head, signs, and touch are all examples of nonverbal pragmatic conventions. These elements vary in different cultures and may be taught as such.

In the ESL classroom, pragmatics can be illustrated and practiced by repeating the same situation in different contexts. For example, students can write or act out how they would explain why they failed a test to three different people: their best friend, their teacher, and their parent. With a little imagination, different scenarios can be chosen that pique student interest and make learning fun. For example, explain an embarrassing event in different contexts, such as in front of a boy/girl you want to impress, a close friend, and an authority figure. For students with very low language skills, pantomime can encourage participation, teach the concept, and create an opportunity for using language to describe what has happened.

For students from other cultures, pragmatics involving nonverbal cues and body language can be confusing. It is the teacher's responsibility to be sensitive to these different behaviors and acknowledge them when they become obvious in the classroom, and to guide students to adopt behaviors appropriate to their audience, purpose, and setting.

Students may be unaware that others feel uncomfortable because they are standing too close or not making eye contact. These situations are very common examples of cultural differences in nonverbal communication. In some cultures, it is considered impolite to look a teacher in the eye—exactly the opposite behavior expected of North Americans! The problem could be addressed directly by discussing appropriate behaviors in different cultures, perhaps by focusing on behavior appropriate to the teacher as a model.

Other examples of nonverbal communication are gestures, tone, volume, stress, and intonation. Appropriate use varies in different social settings. All students (and not just ELLs) need to learn the appropriate voice volume for different settings such as the library, hall, gymnasium, supermarket, and movie theater. An appropriate correction for young children would be to ask all the class members to use their "inside" voices and not their "outside" (playground) voices when speaking in the classroom.

Skill 1.8   Incorporates knowledge of the differences between social and academic language into instruction (e.g., vocabulary, grammatical constructions).

See also 1.6.

Academic discourse refers to formal academic learning. This includes all four core skills: listening, reading, speaking, and writing. Academic learning is important in order for students to succeed in school. As noted previously (1.6), Cummins differentiated between two types of language proficiency: basic interpersonal communication skills (BICS) and cognitive academic language proficiency (CALP). A lot of factors are involved in the acquisition of CALP, such as age, language proficiency level, literacy in the first language, etc.

Academic discourse not only includes the knowledge of content-area vocabulary, but also the knowledge of various skills and strategies that are essential to successfully complete academic tasks in a mainstream classroom. It includes skills such as inferring, classifying, analyzing, synthesizing, and evaluating. Textbooks used in a classroom require abstract thinking where the information is context-reduced. As students reach higher grades, they are required to think critically and apply new knowledge to solve problems.

Skill 1.9   Understands important sociolinguistic concepts (e.g., factors affecting language variation, register, etc.)

Sociolinguistics is the study of how social conditions influence the use of language. Social factors such as ethnicity, religion, gender, status, age, and education all play a role in how individuals use language. Dialects differ depending on these and other factors. Sociolinguistics tries to understand the relationship between language and social elements. Different dialects, or how language is spoken, are frequently referred to today as varieties of a language. Varieties of a language may be considered separate languages if there is a strong literary, religious, or other tradition.

MAJOR THEORISTS

Fishman
Studied how language evolved and changed over time. His work with Gaelic, Welsh, and Yiddish helped identify the forces in society that may help languages survive. Fishman differed from Ferguson's (1959) original concept of diglossia - a situation in which two varieties of the same language are used under different conditions (usually related to status or situations of formality/informality) within the same community. Diglossia previously applied to languages in which there are very distinct formal and colloquial versions. Fishman, however, believed there could be more than two unrelated languages within a diglossic community. Thus, diglossia ranges from the use of separate dialects to the use of separate languages.

Hymes

Hymes' early work focused on the relationship between language and its social context. His notion of communicative competence was devised (using the SPEAKING acronym below) to study how people talked. Hymes believed that native speakers' competence to speak their language is not sufficient to explain their ability to use grammatically correct forms. He felt that the native speaker also knows when and where to use them, leading to communicative competence.

Hymes' model of discourse analysis explaining the relationship between society, culture, and language may be remembered using this acronym:

SPEAKING:

S- setting and scene
P- participants (speaker and audience)
E- ends, purpose, goals
A- act sequence (form and order of event)
K- key (cues that establish the tone, manner or spirit)
I - instrumentalities (forms and styles of speech)
N - norms (social rules)
G- genre (kind of speech act or event)

Historical variation may occur in the sound system, the grammar, or the lexicon. It may be a gradual change in the pronunciation of a word, or it may be abrupt, as in the case of pidginization of the language when contact with a new culture occurs. It is beyond anyone's control, but language is constantly changing. In the words of H. L. Mencken, "A living language is like a man suffering incessantly from small hemorrhages, and what it needs above all else is constant transactions of new blood from other tongues. The day the gates go up, that day it begins to die." France is a prime example of a country that has tried to keep its language "pure." Despite tremendous efforts, the French language has evolved. It has acquired new terms for twentieth- and twenty-first-century technology and experiences. It has been modified by immigrants who have moved to France. Living languages are simply not static.

Social language is different from academic language. The languages are used in different contexts and for different purposes. Their vocabularies are distinct. Structures and grammar may also be distinct. Social language is generally used with peers, in relaxed and informal contexts. Academic language is often used to convey scholarly concepts with concern for accuracy, objectivity, and dispassionate comment.

The United States has experienced disparate social influences, which accounts for the substantial differences between American and other varieties of English, even British English from which American English originated. Ralph Waldo Emerson said, "The English language is the sea which receives tributaries from every region under heaven." Most obvious of these tributaries has been the continuous flow of immigrants who have brought their customs and languages to the United States. Each culture contributes new words, and new immigrants continue to change the language today.

Language is influenced by the geography of the land in which it is spoken. Imagine the different words needed to describe the geographical features of the snowy, icy northern countries and the words needed to describe the lands of the harsh, barren deserts. Nomadic peoples in these areas use different vocabularies with words not easily translated because the people living in other regions have no concepts upon which to base the words.

Contemporary culture changes language significantly. Advertisers have such great success that brand names come to represent entire categories of products, such as Kleenex for tissue, Xerox for photocopy, Hoover for vacuum cleaner, and Coke for cola. People pick up and use phrases from popular TV shows: like, cool, man; and D'oh! Other cultural trends, such as music, sports, and fads add new words to the language.

Political rhetoric also influences language. We hear sports metaphors (a success referred to as a homerun); war metaphors (victories or defeats); and business metaphors (ending up in the red or the black). Politicians like to "send a message" to enemies, political rivals, or the American people. Candidates like to be "the candidate of change" or "the education candidate."

Technology and science may have changed language more than any other factor in the past century. An estimated five hundred thousand technical and scientific terms have been added to English. Many of these words affect our daily lives. Fifty years ago, people didn't routinely use computers, cell phones, the Internet, or satellite dishes. They hadn't had an MRI or wondered if genetically modified organisms (GMOs) were safe to eat.

Text messaging has created a kind of shorthand variation of English: CUL8R means "see you later"; BRB means "be right back"; and TTYL means "talk to you later." ESL teachers might be surprised at how adroit their students are with technological language. Students who make English-speaking friends and want to adapt to U.S. culture will quickly learn this new language.

Work-related language (jargon) is often different from the language of laypeople. To the professionals using it, jargon may be a kind of shorthand. Consider the multitude of terms used to refer to those learning English as an additional language - e.g., ESL students, EFL students, ELL, and LEP - to name a few. Teachers may be referred to as TESOL, ESL, or EFL teachers. Laypeople would be hard-pressed to understand the distinctions made by professionals using these terms.

The merging of languages into English has contributed to the inconsistencies and exceptions to rules that make the language so difficult to learn. It has also increased the number of words one must learn to communicate in English. We can be certain that English will continue to change and language will continue to be vital in new forms.

"Register" refers to choice of language for a specific discourse. Register varies with many factors including context, age, gender, culture, level of education, social class, and vocation. British linguist Michael Halliday first defined the broadened term of register as three factors leading to variations in the formality between the participants:

- **Field of discourse:** A reference to the subject matter being discussed
- **Mode of discourse:** Speaking or writing, and the choice of format
- **Manner of discourse:** A reference to the social relations between the participants

American English usage is influenced by the social and regional situation of its users. Linguists have found that speakers adapt their pronunciation, vocabulary, grammar and sentence structure depending on the social situation. For example, the decision to use "ing" or "in'" at the end of a present participle depends on the formality of the situation. Speakers talking with their friends will often drop the "g" and use "–in'" to signal that the situation is more informal and relaxed. These variations are also related to factors such as age, gender, education, socioeconomic status, and personality.

We call this type of shift a "change in register," how language is used in a particular setting or for a specific purpose. People change their speech register depending on such sociolinguistic variables as:

- Formality of situation
- Attitude towards topic
- Attitude towards listeners
- Relation of speaker to others

Changing speech registers may be completely subconscious for native speakers. For example, if a university professor takes his/her car in for servicing, the manner and speech s/he uses to communicate with the mechanic differs significantly from the manner and speech s/he uses to deliver a lecture. Likewise, when the mechanic explains the mechanical diagnosis, s/he most likely chooses a simplified vocabulary rather than using completely technical language, or jargon, that the professor wouldn't understand. Using the jargon of a profession or field with which the listener is unfamiliar will likely make communication difficult or awkward.

 ESOL teachers should be aware of these sociolinguistic functions of language and compare different social functions of language with their students. Knowing and being able to use appropriate registers allows learners to function more effectively in social and academic situations. Learners must acquire the social, as well as linguistic, aspects of American English. Sociolinguistic functions of a language are best acquired by using the language in authentic situations.

Sociolinguistic diversity, which is language variations based on regional and social differences, affects teachers' language attitudes and practices. Teachers must respect the validity of any group's or individual's language patterns, while at the same time teaching traditional English. Vernacular versions of English have well-established patterns and rules to support them. Making learners aware of language variations leads to increased interest in language learning and better ability to switch among one or more registers or dialects and Standard English.

COMPETENCY 2.0   PROCESSES AND STAGES OF LANGUAGE
ACQUISITION AND FACTORS AFFECTING SECOND-
LANGUAGE DEVELOPMENT

Skill 2.1   Demonstrates knowledge of major theories of first-language
acquisition and second language acquisition and learning (e.g.,
Vygotsky, Chomsky, Pinker, Krashen, Cummins)

Contemporary theories of language acquisition are the results of years of research on
many different language learners in many different cultures. These theories have led to
a solid basis upon which to base teaching practices and can guide teachers in their
interactions with learners of all types. Below are brief summaries of some of the most
important theories about the language acquisition process.

CHOMSKY: THE UNIVERSAL HYPOTHESIS

Chomsky's Universal Hypothesis theory asserts that humans are born with a special
biological brain mechanism, called a Language Acquisition Device (LAD). His theory
proposes that the ability to learn language is innate, that nature is more important than
nurture, and that experience using language is only necessary to activate the LAD.
Chomsky based his assumptions on his work in linguistics. His work shows that
children's language development is much more complex than what is proposed by
behaviorist theory, which asserts that children learn language merely by being rewarded
for imitating. However, one criticism of Chomsky's theory is that he underestimates the
influence that cognition and language have on each other's development.

PIAGET: COGNITIVE CONSTRUCTIVISM

Piaget's central interest is children's cognitive development. Piaget argues that learning
is a process of active discovery and knowledge is something that is actively
constructed; that the best learning takes place when students are provided with
opportunities to play, to practice, to scaffold, and to cognitively process what they are
learning. For Piaget, skill and drill techniques are not effective methods for real learning
and knowledge acquisition.

VYGOTSKY: SOCIAL CONSTRUCTIVISM AND LANGUAGE

Unlike Chomsky and Piaget, Vygotsky's central focus is the relationship between the
development of thought and language. He was interested in the ways that different
languages affect a person's thinking. He suggests that what Piaget saw as the young
child's egocentric speech was actually private speech; the child's way of using words to
think about something, which progressed from social speech to thinking in words.
Vygotsky views language first as social communication, which gradually promotes both
language itself and cognition.

PINKER: LANGUAGE INSTINCT

Pinker argues that humans are born with an innate capacity for language. He states that
language is an instinct, as children are able to learn language because the "basic
organization of grammar is wired into their brains" through biological evolution. Pinker

claims language was created through evolution to solve communication problems among social hunter-gathers. He believes language is universal and that specific structures in the brain are activated during the critical period of childhood. When this period is over, Pinker argues, these structures are disassembled, allowing the brain to use this energy for other purposes. Pinker disagrees with theorists who assert that language and thought are the same. He says that they are separate both in the genes and in the mind from other instincts that comprise the human mind.

KRASHEN: THE MONITOR MODEL

Krashen's Monitor Model consists of 5 main hypotheses.

- **The Acquisition/Learning Hypothesis:** Distinguishes between "acquisition", a subconscious event resulting from natural communication where emphasis is on communication and "learning" which occurs as the result of conscious study of formal properties of language.
- **The Natural Order Hypothesis:** Claims learners follow an invariable path when learning a language, and that grammatical structures are acquired in a predictable order.
- **The Monitor Hypothesis:** States a learner uses an internal monitor to edit "learned" language production. The three conditions for successful 'monitor' use are: sufficient time, a focus on form and not on meaning, and the user must know the grammar rule (or have had instruction in the language form).
- **The Input Hypothesis:** Is based on Krashen's belief that "acquisition" takes place when the learner is exposed to comprehensible input a little beyond the learner's current level of competence, or at "i + 1".
- **The Affective Filter Hypothesis:** Controls the amount of input a learner comes in contact with and how much of that input becomes intake. The Affective Filter is low in learners with high motivation and self-confidence, but high in learners with low motivation and self-confidence. The Affective Filter does not affect the route of language development.

CUMMINS: BICS AND CALPS

Cummins distinguishes between Basic Interpersonal Communication Skills (BICS) and Cognitive Academic Language Proficiency (CALPS). BICS are the "surface" skills that language students acquire quickly. CALPS are skills needed to perform in an academic setting. Cummins states that children can acquire BICS in approximately 2 years of immersion in the target language, CALPS need between 5-7 years to develop.

Language proficiency requires both BICS and CALP. While they have clear distinctions, they also have underlying similarities that contribute to overall language learning. In addition, students should also recognize Common Underlying Proficiency (**CUP**). These are skills, ideas, and concepts that learners can transfer from their first language to their English learning. Similarities and differences between languages can both help learners comprehend and learn aspects of English.

RECENT THEORIZING: INTENTIONALITY

Some contemporary researchers and theorists criticize earlier theories and suggest that children, their behaviors, and their attempts to understand and communicate are misunderstood when the causes of language development are thought to be "outside" the child or mechanistically "in the child's brain." They recognize that children are active learners who co-construct their worlds. Children's language development is part of their holistic development, emerging from cognitive, emotional, and social interactions. These theorists believe that language development depends on the child's social and cultural environment, the people in it, and their interactions. The way children represent these factors in their minds is fundamental to language development. They believe that a child's agenda and the interactions generated by the child promote language learning. The adult's role, actions, and speech are still considered important, but adults need to be able to "mind read" and adjust their side of the co-construction to relate to an individual child's understanding and interpretation.

These types of theories about language development help us see that enjoying "proto-conversations" with babies (treating them as people who understand, share, and have intentions in sensitive interchanges), and truly listening to young children are the best ways to promote their language development. Between two and three years of age, most children will be able to use language to influence the people closest to them.

Brain research has shown that the single most important factor affecting language acquisition is the onset of puberty. Before puberty, a person uses one area of the brain for language learning; after puberty, a different area of the brain is used. A person who learns a second language before reaching puberty will always process language learning as if prepubescent. A   person who begins to learn a second language after the onset of puberty will likely find language learning more difficult and depend more on repetition.

Many researchers have focused on analyzing aspects of the language to be acquired. Factors they consider include:

- **Error analysis:** Recognizing patterns of errors
- **Interlanguage:** Analyzing which aspects of the target language are universal
- **Developmental patterns:** The order in which features of a language are acquired and the sequence in which a specific feature is acquired

Skill 2.2   Applies knowledge of the characteristics of various stages of first- and second language acquisition

Language acquisition is a gradual, hierarchical, and cumulative process. This means that learners must go through and master each stage in sequence, much as Piaget theorized for learning in general. In terms of syntax, this means learners must acquire specific grammatical structures, first recognizing the difference between subject and predicate; putting subject before predicate; and then learning more complex variations, such as questions, negatives, and relative clauses.

While learners must pass through each stage and accumulate the language skills learned progressively at each stage, learners use different approaches to mastering these skills. Some use more cognitive processing procedures; more of their learning takes place through thought processes. Others tend to use psycholinguistic procedures, processing information through speaking. Regardless of how learners process information, they must all proceed through the same stages, from the least to the most complicated.

Experts disagree on the exact definition of the phases, but a set of six general stages would include:

Stage of Development	Examples
1. Single words	I; throw; ball
2. SVO structure	I throw the ball.
3. Wh-fronting	Where you are?
Do fronting	Do you like me?
Adverb fronting	Today I go to school.
Negative + verb	She is not nice.
4. Y/N inversion	Do you know him? Yes, I know him.
Copula (linking v) inversion	Is he at school?
Particle shift	Take your hat off.
5. Do 2nd	Why did she leave?
Aux 2nd	Where has he gone?
Neg do 2nd	She does not live here.
6. Cancel inversion	I asked what she was doing.

Each progressive step requires the learner to use knowledge from the previous step, as well as new knowledge of the language. As ELLs progress to more advanced stages of syntax, they may react differently, depending on their ability to acquire the new knowledge that is required for mastery

Skill 2.3 Understands cognitive processes involved in internalizing language rules and learning vocabulary in a second language (e.g., memorization, categorization, metacognition)

COGNITIVE STRATEGIES
Cognitive strategies are vital to second-language acquisition; their most salient feature is the manipulation of the second language. The most basic strategies are: practicing, receiving and sending messages, analyzing and reasoning, and creating structure for input and output, which can be remembered by the acronym PRAC.

- **Practicing:** Practice constant repetition, make attempts to imitate a native speaker's accent, concentrate on sounds, and practice in a realistic setting to help promote the learner's grasp of the language.

- **Receiving and sending messages:** These strategies help the learner quickly locate salient points and then interpret the meaning: skim through information to determine "need to know" vs. "nice to know," use available resources (print and non-print) to interpret messages.
- **Analyzing and reasoning:** Use general rules to understand the meaning and then work into specifics, and break down unfamiliar expressions into parts.
- **Creating structure for input and output:** Choose a format for taking meaningful notes; practice summarizing long passages; use highlighters to focus on main ideas or important specific details.

METACOGNITIVE STRATEGIES

The ESOL teacher is responsible for helping students become aware of their own individual learning strategies and constantly improve and add to those strategies. Each student should have his/her own toolbox of skills for planning, managing, and evaluating the language-learning process.

Some salient points for ELLs to keep in mind:

- **Center your learning:** Review a key concept or principle and link it to existing knowledge, make a firm decision to pay attention to the general concept, ignore input that is distracting, and learn skills in the proper order.
- **Arrange and plan your learning:** Take the time to understand how a language is learned; create optimal learning conditions, i.e., regulate noise, lighting, and temperature; obtain the appropriate books, etc.; and set reasonable long- and short-term goals.
- **Evaluate your learning:** Keep track of errors that prevent further progress and keep track of progress, e.g., reading faster now than the previous month.

SOCIOAFFECTIVE STRATEGIES

Socioaffective strategies are broken down into affective and social strategies.

Affective strategies are those that help the learner control the emotions and attitudes that may hinder progress in learning the second language and at the same time help him/her learn to interact in a social environment. There are three sets of affective strategies learners can use to reduce the impact of negative attitudes or emotions—lowering your anxiety, encouraging yourself, and taking your emotional temperature—which are easy to remember with the acronym LET.

- **Lowering Anxiety:** These strategies encourage the learner to maintain emotional equilibrium with physical activities, meditation and/or deep breathing, listening to calming music, reading a funny book or watching a comedy.

- **Self-Encouragement:** These strategies help support and motivate the learner to stay positive through self-affirmations, taking risks, and giving themselves rewards.

Krashen: affective Filter.

- **Taking your Emotional Temperature:** These strategies help learners control their emotions by understanding what they are feeling emotionally as well as why they are feeling that way. These strategies include listening to your body's signals; creating a checklist to keep track of feelings and motivations during the second-language-acquisition process; keeping a diary to record progress and feelings; and sharing feelings with classmates or friends.

Social strategies affect how the learner interacts in a social setting, including the classroom setting. The following are three useful strategies to help learners interact socially: asking questions, cooperating with others, and empathizing with others, which can be remembered with the acronym ACE.

- **Ask questions:** Ask for clarification or help. Request that the speaker slow down, repeat, or paraphrase, and ask to be corrected when you are speaking.

- **Cooperate with others:** Interact with more than one person: Work cooperatively with a partner or small group and work with a native speaker of the language.

- **Empathize with others:** Learn how to relate to others, remembering that people usually have more things in common than things that set them apart. Empathize with another student by learning about his/her culture and being aware and sensitive to his/her thoughts and feelings. Understanding and empathizing will help the other student but it will also help you.

PRIOR KNOWLEDGE
Schemata, or the prior knowledge students have when beginning a new foreign language, is a valuable asset to be exploited in their language learning. The schema theory (Carrell and Eisterhold, 1983) explains how the brain processes knowledge and how this facilitates comprehension and learning. A schema is the framework around information that is stored in the brain. As new information is received, schemata are activated to store the new information. By connecting what is known with what is being learned, understanding is achieved and learning can take place. If students lack sufficient prior knowledge, they cannot be expected to understand a new lesson.

Children may or may not have prior educational experiences upon which to build their new language skills. However, even children who have little or no formal education may have been taught the alphabet or simple mathematics by their parents. Children from oral cultures may have quite sophisticated language structures already in place upon which to base new language learning.

COGNITIVE/LEARNING STYLES
A student's learning style includes cognitive, affective, and psychological behaviors that indicate his/her characteristic and consistent way of perceiving, interacting with, and responding to the learning environment (Willing, 1988).

Willing, an Australian researcher, identified four main learning styles used by ESL learners:

- **Concrete learning style:** People-oriented, emotional, and spontaneous
- **Analytic learning style:** Object-oriented, with the capacity for making connections and inferences
- **Communicative learning style:** Autonomous, prefers social learning, likes making decisions
- **Authority-oriented learning style:** Defers to the teacher, does not enjoy learning by discovery, intolerant of facts that do not fit (ambiguity)

Reid (1987) identified four perceptual learning tendencies:

- **Visual learning:** Learning mainly from seeing words in books, on the board, etc.
- **Auditory learning:** Learning by hearing words spoken and from oral explanations, from listening to tapes or lectures
- **Kinesthetic learning:** Learning by experience, by being involved physically in classroom experiences
- **Tactile learning:** Hands-on learning, working on models, lab experiments, etc.

Skill 2.4   Demonstrates knowledge of the levels of English language proficiency described in the WIDA English Language Development (ELD) Standards

WIDA describes six levels of language proficiency that outline the linguistic development of a student learning English as a new/additional language. They are:

- Entering
- Beginning
- Developing
- Expanding
- Bridging
- Reaching

This continuum of language development provides detailed descriptions of what students can do at each level and at each grade level within the different domains of language - speaking, listening, reading and writing. Keep in mind that students may be at higher proficiency levels in one domain than in another. For example, a student may demonstrate faster progress in speaking than in reading comprehension. The six language proficiency levels outline the progression of language development in the acquisition of English as an additional language, from 1, Entering the process, to 6, Reaching the end of the continuum.

Examples of skill progression on the WIDA continuum

From Entering	To Reaching
Concrete concepts in English	Understanding of abstract concepts
Comfort using informal language	Facility in using a formal register
Single word responses	Extended conversation or writing
Non-standard language use	Standard use of English
Basic, general vocabulary	Domain specific vocabulary

Students at the Reaching level of English proficiency will be able to function like their native English speaking peers. Though this does not necessarily mean that they won't have gaps in language (unfamiliar vocabulary, occasional errors in syntax, etc.) students at the reaching level demonstrate a high level of proficiency in English and can function independent of instructional support or scaffolding for language learners.

WIDA has also created detailed examples of continua describing expected performance by students within specific content area. For example, an elementary school age student asked to investigate and collect information about weather and its impact might demonstrate the following skills at each respective level in reading and writing.

- Entering - Name weather conditions using prompts like charts
- Beginning - Restate weather conditions and their effects
- Developing - Describe the effects of weather conditions
- Expanding - Discuss weather conditions and their effects
- Bridging - Explain in detail weather conditions and their effects

The language proficiency levels delineate expected performance and describe what ELLs can do within each language domain of the standards for designated grade level clusters. These are extremely useful tools for the ESOL teacher, but they are too detailed to include all of them here. Teachers are encouraged to refer to the WIDA website to find detailed descriptions that can helpful in assessing student progress, communicating with parents, working with content-area or classroom teachers, and/or designing instruction.

Skill 2.5   Understands connections and interactions between English language proficiency and cognitive and academic levels

It is important for ESOL teachers to understand that English language proficiency is both independent from and interrelated to students' cognitive and academic levels. Some English language learners are intellectually gifted, some have learning disabilities, and some may have both. Just like native English speaking students, ELLs may have multiple exceptionalities.

Students may arrive at a new school with special education needs undiagnosed or with families not sharing previous academic or cognitive data with the school. ESOL teachers, together with parents and other school staff, should endeavor to assess and support ELLs who they think may need additional learning supports.

The sooner ELLs with exceptionalities are identified the better, but teachers and school staff must be careful not to misdiagnose students who are struggling with English as students who are learning disabled. (See 2.7 and 9.7).

ESOL teachers should communicate with other colleagues and school staff about students' progress in different classrooms and school settings. This will help provide ELLs of all cognitive and academic levels with the best opportunities for English language proficiency and content/subject area knowledge and skill achievement.

Skill 2.6   Understands the role of the first language in second-language development (e.g., language transfer, interlanguage development)

EDUCATIONAL EXPERIENCE

ELLs come to the United States for many different reasons: joining family, job transfers, the search for a better life, fleeing war zones and oppressive governments, or to escape economic difficulties. In many cases, ELLs have entered the school system in their native land and done very well. In other cases, they have had little or no educational experience. In either case, it is imperative that, before or upon enrollment, assessment of the student take place—if possible, in their first language. By building on their previous knowledge of literacy, language, and experience, English language instruction will be more successful (Au, 1993, 2002; Ovando et al., 2006).

Shumm (2006) emphasizes that not only are reading-level characteristics important, but also the differences between the first and second language, as these may influence the assumed level of the student. Some of the questions she proposes for eliciting these similarities and differences are useful for further evaluation of reading-level characteristics:

- Is the L1 writing system logographic, as is Arabic; syllabic, as is Cherokee; or alphabetic, as are English and Greek?
- How does the L1 syntax compare with L2 syntax?
- Are the spelling patterns phonetic with consistent grapheme-phoneme relationships (e.g., Spanish or French), or are there multiple vowel sounds (e.g., English)?
- Do students read from left to right and top to bottom in their L1?
- Are there true cognates (Spanish: *instrucción*, and English: *instruction*) and false cognates (Spanish: *librería* [bookstore], and English: *library*) that will help or confuse the ELL?

- Are the discourse patterns and writing styles of L1 and L2 similar or different?
- Does the L1 writing style emphasize description and detail? Or does it emphasize direct, clear language with supporting arguments?

POSITIVE AND NEGATIVE LANGUAGE TRANSFER

L1 (or first language) transfer refers to the effect the native tongue has on the language being acquired. It can be positive or negative. **Negative transfer** is illustrated in many of the errors ELLs make when using the new language.

Positive transfer occurs when similar structures in the L1 facilitate the learning of the new language. An example of this would be when cognates are able to transfer to the target language.

INTERLANGUAGE DEVELOPMENT

Interlanguage is a strategy used by a second language learner to compensate for his/her lack of proficiency while learning a second language. It cannot be classified as first language (L1), nor can it be classified as a second language (L2), rather it could almost be considered a third language (L3), complete with its own grammar and lexicon. Interlanguage is developed by the learner, in relation to the learner's experiences (both positive and negative) with the second language. Larry Selinker introduced the theory of interlanguage in 1972 and asserted that L2 learners create certain learning strategies, to "compensate" in this in-between period, while the learner acquires the language.

Interlanguage Learning Strategies	
Overgeneralization	Overgeneralization occurs when the learner attempts to apply a rule "across-the-board," without regard to irregular exceptions. For example, a learner is over-generalizing when he/she attempts to apply an "ed" to create a past tense for an irregular verb, such as "buyed" or "swimmed."
Simplification	Simplification refers to the L2 learner using resources that require limited vocabulary to aid comprehension and allow the learner to listen, read, and speak in the target language at a very elementary level.
L1 interference or language transfer	L1 Interference or language transfer occurs when a learner's primary language influences his/her progress in the secondary language, L2. Interference most commonly affects pronunciation, grammar structures, vocabulary and semantics

Selinker theorizes that a psychological structure is "awakened" when a learner begins the process of second language acquisition. He attached great significance to the notion that the learner and the native speaker would not create similar sounds if they attempted to communicate the same thought, idea, or meaning.

Fossilization is a term applied by Selinker to the process in which an L1 leaner reaches a plateau and accepts that less-than fluent level, which prevents the learner from achieving L2 fluency. Fossilization occurs when non-L1 forms become fixed in the interlanguage of the L2 learner. L2 learners are highly susceptible to this phenomenon during the early stages.

Skill 2.7 Demonstrates knowledge and understanding of typical and atypical development in home and new languages.

Each child is different, and teachers should be responsive to and aware of the factors that can influence an English language learner's progress in acquiring language. Previous school experience, social/emotional factors, age, and environment are just a few examples of possible influences on a student's progress in English.

It is, however, important to be aware of typical language development, particularly in students' first/home language. If there are concerns that a child may have a learning disability that affects new language acquisition, it is valuable to investigate his/her first language history of language development. Since it may not be easy to find tools to evaluate students in their first language, a language history can be an essential tool in determining whether there may be a potential learning hurdle.

Some major milestones in typical first language development include:

- 12-18 months - vocabulary of 5-20 words (mostly nouns); repeats phrases; follows simple commands
- 18-24 months - can name many objects from day-to-day surroundings; vocabulary of 150-300 words; starting to use pronouns; combining words
- 2-3 years - three word sentences are common; can relate experiences; uses pronouns like 'I' and 'you' correctly; understands simple questions about environment and activities (though may not always respond)
- 3-4 years - starting to know colors; understands contrast (e.g., small and smaller); can identify common objects in picture books; speaks often, even while carrying out activities; knows prepositions
- 4-5 years - uses possessives; mispronounces words often; vocabulary of around 900 words; expresses ideas and feelings verbally; usually follows requests and can accept explanations; can use the third person
- 5-6 years - speech is generally easy to understand and very social; can tell a story
- 6-7 years - simple reading; responds to and can produce opposites (tall/short); simple writing
- 7-8 years - can refer to books for information; reads aloud; can explain how to do something; descriptive language in retelling something; simple and compound sentences

In a new language, common stages include:

- Pre-production - often described as the silent period; very limited comprehension of simple phrases and terms; little or no production

- Early production - increasing though still limited comprehension; very simple responses of a few words; many errors
- Emergent - increasing comprehension; forms simple sentences; does not correct errors; may seem to reach a plateau in which progress stalls
- Intermediate fluency - comprehension is fairly strong; sentences become more complex; errors in speech usually when trying to use complex sentence structure; starts to correct errors when they are pointed out or corrected
- Stabilization - fluency of speech; no comprehension difficulty; self-corrects errors in speech; fossilization can occur in which errors in the new language can become fixed

Though some students may progress in some skills more quickly than others (i.e. for some, listening comprehension may develop more quickly than speech), knowledge of these common stages is helpful in planning and defining expectations. For example, it would not make sense to expect an ELL student in the pre-production phase to do a presentation as an assessment of content-learning.

COMPETENCY 3.0   ESL INSTRUCTIONAL APPROACHES AND BEST
                  PRACTICES THAT PROMOTE ENGLISH LANGUAGE
                  DEVELOPMENT

Skill 3.1   Demonstrates knowledge of various English language learning program models

The Bilingual Education Act, Title VII of the Elementary and Secondary Education Act of 1965 created an energetic debate on bilingual education programs. Second language acquisition consists of three distinct programs: immersion (also called submersion), English as a Second Language (ESL), and bilingual education. Immersion programs have tried, with varying degrees of success, to engage our linguistically diverse population in mainstream U.S. education programs. In this program model, students are expected to "sink or swim". They are given no native language linguistic support and are expected to perform at a level equivalent to native speakers. The main goal of immersion programs is that students acquire English as soon as possible through continuous and constant submersion within the language (Brisk; Baker & Jones, 1998).

Two-Way Bilingual Education
The Two-Way Bilingual Education Model is based on strong content and academic achievement in both a heritage language and a new language. For example, Spanish and English speakers in the same class could spend part of each day learning in Spanish and part in English – building literacy and content-area skills in both. Teachers use hands-on activities, thematic units, peer interaction, multiple clues, and whole language approaches to teach ELLs and English native speakers content in a language that is not their heritage language (while also building literacy in their first language). The goals of such programs are to provide students with ample exposure to both languages and allow them to progress academically in both languages while appreciating another culture (CAL, 1999). While the goals are the same, the methods used to achieve these goals may vary by:

- **Content:** Social studies and math are taught in one language, while math, arts, and music are taught in English.
- **Time:** Instruction is given in each language on alternate days
- **Person:** One teacher uses one language and one teacher uses English
- **Language development methods:** Start at 90% instruction in native language (so 90-10, 80-20, 70-30, 60-40, 50-50...) Used in the Amigos Program in Cambridge, Massachusetts (reported on by Cabazon, Lambert & Hall, 1992).
  - ○ Students were basically satisfied with the program.
  - ○ Students did not believe that their academic progress had been hampered.
  - ○ Investigators believe that student perceptions of a program are essential to the evaluation of a program's effectiveness.

Lambert (1990) also distinguished between Second Language Learning and Foreign Language Learning, citing differences in:

- Training, goals, orientations, and their practice are directed at different users.
- There is a more serious demand than by those being educated for higher levels of competence in foreign language and second languages than usually occurs in school-based programs.
- Time constraints limit the amount of time spent on English language development if it interferes with math, sciences, humanities, and social science.

Ramirez: Proponent of Late Exit

The U. S. Department of Education (1991) reported the results of a national longitudinal study, informally known as the Ramirez Report after its primary investigator. Data was collected from over 2,300 Spanish-speaking students in 554 classrooms (K-6) in New York, New Jersey, Florida, Texas and California (Samway & McKeon, 1999 in Cruz). The study compared Structured English Immersion programs to two types of bilingual programs. Investigators observed the classrooms over a period of four years to verify the presence of hypothesized differences in the programs. The only hypothesized difference found to occur in actual practice was the percentage of instructional time teachers taught in English compared to Spanish (Baker, 1998)

The study concluded that students in immersion and early-exit transitional programs progressed at the same rate as students from the general population. While the students in the immersion and early-exit programs did not fall behind other students, neither were they able to bridge the gap between the two groups. Students who spent longer in programs that supported their home language development were more successful in closing those gaps. Cummins & Genzuk (1991) stated that the study provides support for the belief that primary language skill development facilitates the acquisition of English language skills.

Gersten: Early Exit Programs

In 2000, Gersten, Russell, Baker, and Scott published research gathered over a four-year period using the qualitative multivocal method of Ogawa & Malen (1991). They conducted five work groups consisting of researchers, teachers, administrators, psychologists, and staff developers. Their twin goals were to understand what these professionals viewed as recurrent problems in instruction and what terms practitioners used to describe current practices (2000). Their findings indicate that:

- Language growth and academic growth are difficult to distinguish between and should be more closely studied.
- English- language development in bilingual education and bilingual special education is a major problem, especially for special education students because they cannot keep up.
- A good English-language program should include three components:
  - Development of both fluency and proficiency in English social and academic communication.
  - More high quality study of the formal, grammatical aspects of the English language.
  - Emphasis on learning academic content.

- A drastic increase in the quality and quantity of instructional intervention studies of English language learners, including studies with ELL students with disabilities.
- New research in the field needs to be well-designed and valid.
- The professionals' work resulted in a set of principles and practices that will be useful in defining best practices.

In other work, Gersten and Baker (2001) have called for teachers to reduce their English language demands when students are challenged cognitively, and reduce cognitive content when students are learning English.

Rossell & Baker

Rossell and Baker released a study in 1996 in which they evaluated the effectiveness of bilingual education programs. They selected only 72 (of 300) programs to be methodologically acceptable and concluded that little evidence exists that bilingual education works.

Many theorists, including Cummins and Krashen, have challenged their findings. Cummins noted that when Rossell and Baker compared transitional bilingual education (TBE) with structured immersion in reading performance, no differences were found in 17% of programs while in 83% of programs structured immersion in English was superior (Cummins, 1998). Cummins pointed out, however, that their evidence was not based on transitional bilingual programs but rather on long-term bilingual programs that seek full bilingualism (such as those used in Canada to promote French/English bilingualism).

Krashen questioned the rigor of many studies included in their evaluation, claiming they included as methodologically acceptable all the studies unfavorable to bilingual education, and many studies were unpublished in professional literature (Krashen in Crawford, 1998). In addition, Rossell and Baker used a narrative technique (vs. meta-analysis of numerous variables) counting votes for or against bilingual education (Dunkel in Crawford, 1998).

Skill 3.2   Applies knowledge of language acquisition theories to instruction to promote language and content learning.

Sheltered instruction (SI) allows teachers to select and adapt content area materials in a way that addresses students' cognitive and linguistic needs. In sheltered classes, a core teacher instructs the students throughout the day. Teachers make grade-level content comprehensible by activating and building background knowledge. Teachers speak in clear, direct, simple English and use scaffolding techniques such as visuals, gestures, manipulatives, paraphrasing, etc. (i.e. anything that conveys the meaning to the EL). The classes have clear grade level content and language objectives.

Below are some examples of language learning theories and instructional strategies that support language and content-area learning.

THEORY: IN ORDER FOR THE L2 LEARNER TO BEGIN PRODUCTION IN THE TARGET LANGUAGE (TL), THE FOLLOWING PRINCIPLES MUST BE OBSERVED AND IMPLEMENTED

- During the silent period (when learners listen, instead of speaking), the instructors must use comprehensible input, corresponding to the learners' level of understanding in the TL.
- Attempts to speak and produce language on the part of the L2 learner will gradually occur.
- The class curriculum must be aligned with specific speech production skills, i.e., instead of a linear-grammatical approach, instruction should be topically-centered, such as nonsequential lessons on weather, things found in a house, how to tell time, etc.

Strategy: The Natural Approach

T. Terrell and S. Krashen are the researchers behind the most comprehensive CBA/CBL approach: the "Natural Approach." The underlying assumption is that any learner of any age has the ability to receive comprehensible speech input and determine its pattern, without someone else having to spell it out for them. According to Terrell & Krashen, the approach involves large amounts of comprehensible input, whether it is situational, from visual aids/cues, or grammatical. This input is respectful of "the initial preproduction period, expecting speech to emerge not from artificial practice, but from motivated language use, progressing from early single-word responses up to more and more coherent discourse" (Celce-Murcia, 1991). Terrell also maintains that being grammatically correct is not as important as the learner enjoying the learning process. Critics of Terrell maintain that by not correcting the learner's errors early on, fluency is achieved at the expense of accuracy.

THEORY: LEARNERS NEED NOT ONLY INPUT, BUT OUTPUT: IN ORDER TO LEARN A LANGUAGE, THEY MUST USE IT. CLT EMPHASIZES THE LEARNER AS AN INDIVIDUAL, THE VIEW OF LANGUAGE WHICH INCLUDES COMMUNICATIVE AND SOCIAL FACTORS IN ADDITION TO THE LINGUISTIC ONE

Strategy: Communicative Language Teaching (CLT) Emphasis is on:

There are many models of CLT which include most, if not all, of the following elements in varying degrees:

- Appropriacy, not correctness
- Use, not usage
- Value (contextual, pragmatic meaning), not signification (meaning)
- Utterance, not sentence
- Illocutionary act (defined in terms of function), not proposition (specific request or statement, does not have to be interpreted to have significance)
- Coherence (describes how a text hangs together, makes sense as ideas are clearly and logically stated), as opposed to coherence (formal features of a text which unite text at a linguistic level, e.g. pronouns, linking words, etc.)

- Communicative abilities (e.g. speaking, listening), not linguistic skills (e.g. speaking and hearing)
- Lexis should be the basis of CLT, not grammar
- Task-based learning
- Self-directed learning, not teacher-centered classroom
- Learning to learn, i.e. teacher trains students in learning techniques
- Learner generated syllabus, i.e. learning communicative and linguistic skills needed to conduct real-world tasks

Learner autonomy is another feature of CLT. This feature encourages the ELL to gradually outgrow the need for a teacher by becoming more self-aware, self-reliant, and better able to learn directly from the experience (Trim, 1981).

THEORY: IF THE INSTRUCTIONAL ENVIRONMENT FOR L2 LEARNERS IS CHARACTERIZED BY HIGH EXPECTATIONS FOR SPEAKING CORRECTLY, TOTAL MEMORIZATION OF GRAMMATICAL RULES AND VOCABULARY, AS WELL AS CONSTANT ERROR CORRECTION, THE L2 LEARNER WILL QUICKLY LOSE MOTIVATION TO CONTINUE THE LEARNING PROCESS

Strategy: Total Physical Response (TPR)
A "command-driven" instructional technique developed by the psychologist James Asher. TPR is a useful tool in the early developmental stage of second language acquisition, as well as for LEP students without any previous exposure to English. The main tenet of TPR is that input is very comprehensible, in the form of commands and gestures and is also fun for the L2 learner. Asher supports this theory with the idea that the process mirrors the process that young children use when acquiring their primary language (i.e., children gradually develop both their awareness and attempts to communicate, until listening comprehension skills have reached a comfortable level). At this point, the child will begin to speak. Through TPR, instructors interact with students by way of commands/gestures, and the students respond with a physical response. TPR emphasizes listening rather than speaking; students are encouraged to speak only when they feel ready.

See 9.3 and 9.4 for additional information on sheltered models and content learning

Skill 3.3 **Uses research-based instructional practices that are developmentally appropriate to promote English language acquisition and proficiency (including developing and integrating language skills, vocabulary, and the ability to recognize and utilize varied levels of linguistic complexity).**

Vocabulary

Research has shown that the same 1000 words (approximately) make up 84 percent of the words used in conversation and 74 percent of the words in academic texts (*The Nation*, 2001). The second most frequently used 1000 words increases the percentages to 90 percent of the words used in conversation and 78 percent used in academic texts. The ELL needs to understand 95 percent to achieve comprehension of higher level academic texts. ELLs need to acquire the 2000 most used words and work on academic content words at the same time. In order to help students acquire the vocabulary they need for school, consider the following.

- Vocabulary development for young children is increased using the same methods used with native speaker beginning readers: ample exposure to print, word walls, realia, signs or objects around the room, and so on.
- Older children may take advantage of all these methods in addition to studying true and false cognates, creating personal dictionaries, journal writing between themselves and their teacher, and using learning strategies to augment their vocabulary.
- Other strategies, from Peregoy and Boyle (2008) are:
  - Activate the prior knowledge of the ELL.
  - Repeat the new word in meaningful contexts.
  - Explore the word in depth through demonstrations, direct experience, concrete examples, and applications to real life.
  - Have students explain concepts and ideas in writing and speaking using the new words.
  - Provide explicit strategy instruction so that students can independently understand and use the new words.

In addition, ESOL teachers build academic language proficiency with their ELLs by introducing academic language that consists of more than just content area vocabulary. English language learners benefit from consistent reinforcement of academic vocabulary so that they don't just memorize the words for an assessment and then forget them. Assessment is a key part of this process and teachers should work hard to ensure that they are assessing ELLs' academic vocabulary knowledge in a meaningful way.

→ reinforce!!!
– Daily Practice.

Skill 3.4   Plans and implements ESL instruction aligned with language and content curriculum standards (e.g., the WIDA ELD Standards; Massachusetts curriculum frameworks)

See 5.3, 7.3, and 8.4 for descriptions of ELD standards on reading, writing, speaking and listening as well as the WIDA website (https://www.wida.us/standards/eld.aspx). For complete details on the state curriculum frameworks, please see https://www.wida.us/standards/eld.aspx.

In addition to their work with ELL students to develop language proficiency in all domains of language (speaking, listening, reading and writing), ESOL teachers play a crucial role in supporting students in building content area knowledge. Through scaffolding, sheltered instruction, and working directly with content-area teachers to design instruction, ESOL teachers help to ensure that English language learners maximize learning of content in subjects such as math and science.

Students with limited English proficiency often have greater difficulty acquiring skills and knowledge in classes like biology if they do not have language support to understand procedures and domain-specific terminology. ESOL teachers working with students in such classes must have knowledge of the academic and procedural knowledge (e.g., for laboratory experiments) necessary for students to learn content and language necessary for success in these classes. A key element of this type of work is often planning with content-area teachers to determine essential language for demonstrating learning.

Skill 3.5   Understands and responds to the needs of special populations of English language learners (e.g., newcomers, ELLs with limited or interrupted formal education, etc.).

All students face the challenges of learning new content in different subjects, but for ELL students, this challenge can be compounded by the additional need to learn new vocabulary and new language structures. Teaching specific learning skills and strategies can support ELL students in learning the language structures necessary to both understand and express learning in different disciplines while also helping them to master and integrate new content-area knowledge. For students with limited or interrupted formal school experiences, these can be essential tools.

Strategies to consider include:

- Note-taking - Students need to learn to synthesize large chunks of information presented orally or in writing in order to remember and apply essential ideas. Note-taking strategies vary tremendously, and different students will respond better to different methods.
- Research - All students will need to do research in different subject areas. This is a challenging process that includes searching for information, selecting what is relevant, synthesizing it into usable 'chunks', and integrating it into writing or

*Super essential.

projects. Students need methods for finding, saving, and annotating. Some students will find this easiest with traditional paper/pen and a notebook while others will benefit from digital tools (like Evernote or Diigo) that allow them to save sources and then annotate them. Research is a cross-disciplinary skill that should be used in multiple classes, but the ESOL teacher will play a special role in supporting ELL students.

- Study skills - Students may need practice in how to review for a test or prepare for an assessment. Teachers can assist students in creating flashcards (digital or paper) or learning ways of review (quizzing oneself/a partner, reviewing notes, etc.).
- Test-taking - Particularly in an era of high stakes testing, students may need guidance on how to pace themselves during assessments, when to skip items for later review, how to create an outline, or simply following procedural directions.
- Building vocabulary - For ELL students, content area vocabulary can pose a challenge. Students may need support in learning how to categorize words, how to use new terms in context, or even the importance of looking up unfamiliar words to determine meaning.
- Comprehension - Inference is an important part of reading comprehension. For students learning English, extra time is often needed to develop skills for recognizing implied meaning.

Skill 3.6   Understands and responds to the needs of English language learners with disabilities.

Students with disabilities are guaranteed an education under Public Law 94-142 of 1975. A key feature of the law is the requirement of an individualized education program (IEP) for any student receiving special funds for special education.

Learning disabilities refer to either physical, emotional, cognitive, or social components that severely limit what is considered "normal" functioning behavior. Children who fall into this category can be one or more of the following: emotionally challenged; hearing, vision, or speech impaired; intellectually challenged, and so on. One similarity between second language development and learning disabilities is comprehensive diagnostic testing before placement.

A language disorder or learning disability is characterized by the learner experiencing difficulties in communication and speech motor skills, and typically the learner will be noticeably behind his/her classmates in language acquisition or speech skills. The following summaries outline both the similarities and differences between second language development and language disorders. Remember that an English language learner who has proficiency in his/her native language but struggles in the English language environment is not considered to have a language disorder.

Some language disorders cause the learner to:

- mispronounce phonemes (the smallest unit of a word)

- have issues with properly identifying a word in context (either verbally or nonverbally)
- have difficulty associating words and their appropriate meanings
- confuse proper grammatical structures
- have difficulty understanding advanced vocabulary
- struggle to follow directions

All of these characteristics of language disorders are problems experienced by the English language learner during the process of second language acquisition – the only exception being the problem with following directions. [This difficulty falls under language disorders if the learner understands directions but is not cognitively able to follow them.] During the early stages of second language acquisition, learners experience all the characteristics that are similar to language disorders. However, this is due primarily to unfamiliarity with the structure of the second language, not to dysfunctions of communication or speech motor skills.

Differences: The differences between language disorders and second language learning are more apparent than their similarities. First, learners experiencing problems with speech motor skills face the following challenges:

- inability to produce certain sounds such as "r" or "l"
- voice quality issues (such as pitch or volume)
- "dysfluency" or stuttering
- difficulty creating speech that is understandable to others

Topics to investigate in determining whether an ELL student has a learning disability include:

- History of language delay in his/her native language;
- Difficulty in developing literacy skill in his/her native language;
- A family history of reading difficulties;
- Specific language weakness in his/her first language; and
- Relatively little progress relative to ELL peers after participating in reading interventions designed for ELL students.

In addition, schools must develop identification and exit criteria for ELL students with disabilities receiving services or participating in learning support programs.

Teachers should know, understand and follow Massachusetts regulations as they work with English language learners with disabilities. State learning standards and regulations for accessibility and accommodations can be found on this website (http://www.doe.mass.edu/mcas/accessibility/)

Skill 3.7 Applies effective instructional approaches for promoting the content area learning of English language learners at different ages, especially those who have experienced gaps and interruptions in their education

English language learners who have had their education interrupted face the dual challenge of learning grade-level content and learning the basic tenets which support it. For ELLs, the challenge is daunting as they must also learn English at the same time.

Some researchers believe there is a critical age at which the learners of a foreign language can maximize their learning. Penfield and Roberts (1959) expounded the theory of critical age in language learning based upon their studies of L1 and brain damage studies. Their studies showed that children who suffered brain damage before puberty typically recovered and developed normal language. Adults, however, rarely recover from such injuries and language remains fixed at the point of recovery reached 5 months after damage. Lenneberg (1967) supports Penfield and Roberts (1959) claim of neurological mechanisms responsible for maturational change in language learning abilities.

Chomsky's Universal Grammar (UG) suggests that language is an innate function of humans who have a language acquisition device (LAD) in their brains. The LAD allows children to construct a grammar out of raw input in their environment. Universal Grammar does not describe an optimal age for language acquisition, but the theory implies that younger children learn languages more easily as their LAD is still active. Older learners lose this ability and rarely achieve complete fluency. Therefore, research suggests that UG may govern all languages, it becomes increasingly difficult for older learners to access their LAD and explicit instruction is needed to achieve language proficiency.

Piaget considers the brain to be a computational device with language acquisition only one part of general learning. He believes that language is controlled by external influences and social interactions. The research of Newport and Supalla (1987) support Piaget's theories as their studies showed that language abilities decline with age just as other cognitive abilities do.

Both Krashen (1975) and Felix (1985) proposed theories for the close of the Critical Period of L2 at puberty based on Piaget's cognitive stage of formal operations beginning at puberty.

Cognitive processes are used by the learner to organize and direct second language acquisition. Examples of these processes are problem-solving, method of approaching the learning of new information, and choices regarding what to ignore and what to notice (Díaz-Rico, Weed, 1995). Developing these skills leads to language acquisition, but these skills also bridge languages and serve to enhance cognition in the first language.

Piaget: language is controlled by external influences and social interactions.

Research demonstrates that learning and using more than one language:

- Enhances problem solving and analytical skills
- Allows better formation of concepts
- Increases visual-social abilities
- Furthers logical reasoning
- Supports cognitive flexibility

Cognitive skills are any mental skills that are used in the process of acquiring knowledge, including reasoning, perception, and intuition. Using these skills in second-language learning applies L2 vocabulary and sentence patterns to thought processes that have already formed in the L1.

Memorization of the words and rules of a second language is insufficient to integrate the second language into the learner's thought patterns. L2 learners use cognitive processes to form rules, which allow them to understand and create novel utterances. The creation of novel utterances, whether grammatically correct or not, offers proof that the L2 learner is not simply mimicking chunks of prescribed language, but rather is using cognitive processes to acquire the second language. People use their own thinking processes, or cognition, to discover the rules of the language they are acquiring.

Planning what actions to take when confronted with an academic (or social) challenge demonstrates understanding of the problem and the ability to confront it. By engaging the cognitive skills, the student can plan where and how to search for information, how to organize it and how to present the information for review.

Organizational skills may show differences in different cultural contexts. For example, when organizing information for writing, the English speaker normally goes from a smaller unit to a larger unit. In addresses, for example:

Dr. Randal Price
Department of English as a Second Language
University of Georgia
Athens, Ga.
USA.

A Japanese speaker would begin with the larger unit and go to the smaller one. For example:

USA
Athens, Ga.
University of Georgia
Department of English as a Second Language
Dr. Randal Price

Teachers cannot assume their students know these skills. Even the most basic organizational skill concepts must be reviewed or fully taught if necessary.

COMPETENCY 4.0   FACTORS THAT INFLUENCE TEACHINGA ND
                    LEARNING OF ENGLISH LANGUAGE LEARNERS

Skill 4.1   Understands factors affecting second-language acquisition (e.g., age, motivation, learning style, environmental factors)

AGE

According to Ellis (1985), age does not affect the "route" (order) of second-language acquisition (SLA). Thus, children and adults acquire language in the same order, that is, they go through the same stages. With respect to rate of acquisition, teens appear to surpass both children and adults, especially in learning the grammatical system (Snow and Hoefnagel-Hohle, 1978). Some research shows that achievement in a foreign language is strongly related to the amount of time spent on the language, and that the earlier a second language is started, the better the pronunciation (Burstall et al., 1974). Krashen (1982) disagrees that age is the most important factor, believing instead that SLA is related to the amount of comprehensible input (i.e., the younger child will receive more comprehensible input) and that younger learners are more open emotionally to SLA.

Other theorists have formulated different hypotheses about age in SLA related to affective factors. In the critical period hypothesis, Penfield and Roberts (1959) state that the first ten years are the best age for SLA as the brain retains its plasticity. After puberty, this plasticity disappears and the flexibility required for SLA is lost. Guiora et al. (1972) believe that around the age of puberty, the ability to acquire native-like pronunciation of the foreign language is no longer present.

Cognitive explanations are also used to explain the effects of age on SLA. These theories assert that children are more prone to use their Language Acquisition Device (LAD), while adults are better able to use their inductive reasoning because of more fully developed cognitive faculties. Rosansky (1975) explains SLA in terms of Piaget's "period of concrete operations." Rosansky believes the child is more open and flexible to new language than an adult who identifies more closely with the differences in the native language and the language to be acquired. Krashen (1982) believes that adolescents and adults probably have greater access to comprehensible input than children and that this is the real causative variable, rather than age itself.

AFFECTIVE FACTORS

The term **affective domain** refers to the feelings and emotions in human behavior that affect how a second language is acquired. Self-esteem, motivation, anxiety, and attitude all contribute to the second language acquisition process. Internal and external factors influence the affective domain. ESOL teachers must be aware of each student's personality and must stay attuned to the affective factors in their students, such as:

- **Self-esteem:** Learning a second language puts learners in a vulnerable frame of mind. While some learners are less inhibited about taking risks, all learners can easily be shut down if their comfort level is surpassed. Using teaching techniques that lower stress and emphasize group participation, rather than focusing on individuals getting the right answer, reduces anxiety and encourages learners to attempt to use the new language.

- **Motivation:** Researchers Gardner and Lambert (1972) have identified two types of motivation in relation to learning a second language:
  - **Instrumental motivation:** Acquiring a second language for a specific reason, such as a job
  - **Integrative motivation:** Acquiring a second language to fulfill a wish to communicate within a different culture

Neither type stands completely alone. Instructors recognize that motivation can be viewed as either a "trait" or a "state." As a trait, motivation is more permanent and culturally acquired, whereas as a state, motivation is considered temporary because it fluctuates, depending on rewards and penalties.

- **Anxiety:** Anxiety is inherent in second-language learning. Students are required to take risks, such as speaking in front of their peers. Without a native's grasp of the language, second language learners are unable to express their individuality, which is even more threatening and uncomfortable. However, not all anxiety is debilitative. Bailey's (1983) research on "facilitative anxiety" (anxiety that compels an individual to stay on task) is a positive factor for some learners, closely related to competitiveness.

- **Attitudes:** Attitude typically evolves from internalized feelings about oneself and one's ability to learn a language. On the other hand, one's attitude about language and the speakers of that language is largely external and is influenced by the surrounding environment of classmates and family.

If non-native speakers of English experience discrimination because of their accent or cultural status, their attitude toward the value of Second Language Learning may diminish. Schools can significantly improve the attitude towards SLAs by encouraging activities between native speakers and ELLs. This can be particularly beneficial to both groups if students learning the SLA's first language work on projects together. When native speakers get a chance to appreciate the SLA's language skill in their first language, attitudes change and ELLs have an opportunity to shine.

In some cultures, children who learn a second language at the expense of their primary language might be viewed negatively by family and friends. This can cause mixed feelings about school in general and can adversely affect second language acquisition.

LEARNING STYLES
Students have different learning styles or preferences that affect the way in which they learn and express themselves. Oftentimes, there are cultural factors which affect their

learning styles (e.g. role of minors in the family structure and their society, the learning/teaching styles used in the native culture, the ability to "look the speaker in the eye", and the distance between speakers). Individual learning styles within cultures affect ELLs differently.

Researchers have devoted considerable time to analyzing learning styles. Learning styles may fit into more than one category, and students may exhibit more than one type of learning style.

RESEARCHERS	LEARNING STYLES
Hruska-Reichmann and Grasha (1982)	• Competitive vs. cooperative • Dependent vs. independent • Participant vs. avoidant
Keefe (1987)	• Physiological variables (nutrition, health, time of day preferences, sleeping and waking habits, need for mobility, and needs for and response to varying levels of light, sound, and temperature) • Affective variables (amount of structure of supervision student needs, level of anxiety or curiosity student displays, degree of persistence in face of frustration) • Incentive variables (personal interests, level of achievement motivation, enjoyment of competition vs. cooperation, risk taking vs. caution, reaction to rewards vs. punishment, social motivation coming from family, school, and ethnic background, and internal vs. external control) • Cognitive variables (field dependent vs. field independent, conceptual/analytical vs. perceptual/concrete, broad vs. focused attention, easily distracted vs. capable of controlled concentration, leveling {tendency to lump new experiences with previous ones} vs. sharpening {ability to distinguish small differences}, high cognitive complexity {accepting of diverse, perhaps conflicting input} vs. low cognitive complexity {tendency to reduce conflicting information to a minimum})
Sonbucher (1991)	• Combination of information-processing styles (preferences for reading, writing, listening, speaking, visualizing, or manipulating) and work environment preferences (such as differences in motivation, concentration, length of study sessions, involvement with others, level of organization, prime times for study, amount of noise, light, heat and need for food/drink
Tharp (1989)	• Identified two sets of contrasting learning styles: visual/verbal and holistic/analytic. Schools typically prefer students who are verbal and analytical.

Kolb (1976)	• Studied adult learners and developed a theory of experiential learning. Four-stage process: a learner's experience forms the basis for observation and reflection, which in turn permits the learner to make decisions and solve problems, creating the basis for new experiences. • Four learning types: active experimentation vs. reflective observation and abstract conceptualization vs. concrete experience
McCarthy (1983)	Four learning styles similar to Kolb's learning styles • Innovative: personally involved through social interaction • Analytic learner: thinks through ideas and concepts • Commonsense learner: hands-on experience and enjoys solving practical problems • Dynamic learner: uses intuition and trial and error, taking risks and jumping to conclusions
Myers/Briggs (See Murphy, J.M., 1998 and Keirsey, D. 1998).	Based on Jung's theory of personality Classified learners into 4 opposing dimensions which when combined make up 16 different dimensions • Introversion/extroversion • Sensing/perception • Thinking/feeling • Judging/perceiving

Adapted from Díaz-Rico, 2008.

Skill 4.2   Applies knowledge of sociocultural factors (e.g., cultural, and linguistic identity; language variation) that can affect English language learners linguistic development and motivation (e.g., patterns of communication, approaches to learning)

While there is a continuous effort to establish a "Standard English" to be taught for English Language Learners (ELLs), English learning and acquisition depends on the cultural and linguistic background of the ELL, as well as preconceived perceptions of English Language cultural influences. These factors can act as a filter, causing confusion and inhibiting learning. Since language, by definition, is an attempt to share knowledge, the cultural, ethnic, and linguistic diversity of learners influences both their own history as well as how they approach and learn a new language.

ELLs tend to adapt linguistic structures to their familiar culture, modifying specific concepts and practices. Teachers must identify these variations, call attention to them, and teach the appropriate English equivalent. Various functional adaptations of English have great significance to the cultural groups that use them. Attempting to eliminate variations is not only futile, but raises hostility and reluctance to learn English. Stable, socially shared structures emerge from the summed effects of many individual communication practices. The goal is not to eliminate linguistic diversity, but rather to enable learners to control their language use so that they can willfully use standard English *in addition to* their cultural variation.

Teachers must assess the English Language Learner to determine how cultural, ethnic, and linguistic experience can impact the student's learning. This evaluation should consider many factors, including:

- The cultural background and educational sophistication of the ELL
- The exposure of the ELL to various English language variants and cultural beliefs

No single approach, program, or set of practices fits all students' needs, backgrounds, and experiences. The ideal program for a Native American teenager attending an isolated tribal school may fail to reach a Hispanic teenager enrolled in a suburban district.

CULTURAL FACTORS

Culture encompasses the sum of human activity and symbolic structures that have significance and importance for a particular group of people. Culture is manifested in language, customs, history, arts, beliefs, institutions, and other representative characteristics, and is a means of understanding the lives and actions of people.

Customs play an important part in language learning because they directly affect interpersonal exchanges. What is polite in one culture might be offensive in another. For example, in the U.S., making direct eye contact is considered polite. Some cultures may view eye contact, especially with someone in a position of authority, as aggressive or rude. Teachers who are unaware of this cultural difference could offend an English Language Learner, or misjudge them, and unwittingly cause a barrier to learning. However, teachers who are familiar with this custom can make efforts not to offend the learner and can teach the difference between the two customs so that the ELL can make more informed decisions about behaviors.

In designing learning experiences, the ESOL teacher must be aware of the potential impact of cultural differences on the effectiveness of certain teaching methods. Group work, for example, has tremendous potential to create opportunities for communication and authentic language use both by ELLs and between ELLs and native speakers. This has clear benefits for student language acquisition.

Many cultures promote group loyalty and cooperation over competition and the idea of winning. Some students may be reluctant to participate in activities that they perceive could cause their peers to 'lose' or be embarrassed. Similarly, within groups some students may defer to others because of perceived status. Recognizing these potential effects will help ensure that teachers create the best possible learning situations for a diverse student body.

Beliefs and institutions have a strong emotional influence on ELLs and should always be respected. While customs should be adaptable (similar to switching registers when speaking) no effort should be made to change the beliefs or institutional values of an ELL. Presenting new ideas is a part of growth, learning, and understanding. Even though the beliefs and values of different cultures often have irreconcilable differences, they should be addressed respectfully. In these instances, teachers must respect alternative attitudes and adopt an "agree to disagree" attitude. Presenting new, contrasting points of view should not be avoided because new ideas can strengthen original thinking as well as change it. All presentations should be neutral, however, and no effort should be made to alter a learner's thinking. While addressing individual cultural differences, teachers should also teach tolerance of all cultures. This is especially important in a culturally diverse classroom but will serve all students well in their future interactions.

Studying the **history and various art forms** of a culture reveals much about the culture and offers opportunities to tap into the interests and talents of ELLs. Comparing the history and art of different cultures encourages critical thinking and often reveals commonalities as well as differences, leading to greater understanding among people.

Culture constitutes a rich component of language learning. It offers a means of drawing learners into the learning process and greatly expands their understanding of a new culture, as well as their own. Second language acquisition, according to the findings of Saville-Troike (1986), places the learner in the position of having to learn a second culture. The outcome of learning a second culture can have negative or positive results, not only depending on how teaching is approached, but also outside factors. How people in the new culture respond to ELLs makes them feel welcome or rejected. The attitudes and behavior of the learner's family are particularly important. If the family is supportive and embraces the second culture, then the effect is typically positive. However, if acculturation is perceived as rejecting the primary culture, then the child risks feeling alienated from both cultures.

There are many unique ways that students are affected by the cultural differences in their native culture and at home when compared with the culture being acquired through schooling and daily life in a foreign culture.

The following points, adapted from Peregoy and Boyle (2008), illustrate some of the ways that culture affects us daily and thus affect students in their participation, learning, and adjustment to a different society and its schools.

- **Family structures:** What constitutes a family? What are the rights and responsibilities of each family member? What is the hierarchy of authority?
- **Life cycles:** What are the criteria for defining stages, periods, or transitions in life? What rites of passage are there? What behaviors are considered appropriate for children of different ages? How might these conflict with behaviors taught or encouraged in school?
- **Roles and interpersonal relationships:** How do the roles of girls and women differ from those of boys and men? How do people greet each other? Do girls work and interact with boys? Is deference shown, and to whom and by whom?

- **Discipline:** What is discipline? Which behaviors are considered socially acceptable for boys versus girls at different ages? Who or what is considered responsible if a child misbehaves? The child? Parents? Older siblings? The environment? Is blame even ascribed? Who has authority over whom? How is behavior traditionally controlled? To what extent and in what domains?

- **Time and space:** How important is punctuality? How important is speed in completing a task? How much space are people accustomed to? What significance is associated with different cultural locations or directions, including north, south, east, and west?

- **Religion:** What restrictions are there on topics discussed in school? Are dietary restrictions to be observed, including fasting? What restrictions are associated with death and the dead?

- **Food:** What is eaten? In what order and how often is food eaten? Which foods are restricted? Which foods are typical? What social obligations are there regarding food giving, reciprocity, and honoring people? What restrictions or proscriptions are associated with handling, offering, or discarding food?

- **Health and hygiene:** How are illnesses treated and by whom? What is to be considered the cause? If a student were involved in an accident at school, would any of the common first aid practices be unacceptable?

- **History, traditions, and holidays:** Which events and people are sources of pride for this group? To what extent does the group in the United States identify with the history and traditions of the country of origin? What holidays and celebrations are considered appropriate for observing in school? Which ones are appropriate for private observance?

- **Age:** Can impact second language acquisition, as well, when a culture determines what a person does, as well as when they can do it. For example, as noted by Sindell (1988), middle-class European Americans tend to expect that children will play and behave appropriately for their age, rather than take on more adult responsibilities.

It is important for ESOL teachers and English Language Learners to understand the strong connection between language and culture. Language is used to explain, express and develop culture, and cultural practices are often rooted in language specific to the cultural group(s). Language and culture are intertwined. When learning English as a new language, students are also learning about a new culture. Teachers can help students by applying this understanding to instruction and by helping students become aware of the ways in which they are learning a language and learning about a culture(s).

ELLs tend to adapt linguistic structures to their familiar culture, modifying specific concepts and practices. Teachers must identify these variations, call attention to them, and teach the appropriate English equivalent. The goal is not to eliminate linguistic diversity, but rather to enable learners to control their language use so that they can willfully use standard English in addition to their cultural variation.

Various functional adaptations of English have great significance to the cultural groups that use them. Attempting to eliminate variations is not only futile, but raises hostility and reluctance to learn English. Stable, socially shared structures emerge from the summed effects of many individual communication practices. Firmly ingrained language patterns serve a purpose within the community that uses them. Unique variations can arise in a school venue. New, nonstandard English words can represent a group's identity, or function as a means to solidify social relationships. As long as students recognize that a variation should not be used as if it were Standard English, there should be no problem with its use.

Some ways to do this include: being empathetic with the attitudes English Language Learners may bring to class that differ from the L2 culture, actively teaching about cultural aspects while teaching English, maintaining a respectful classroom environment that can observe differences while encouraging all students to celebrate and value diversity.

Skill 4.3   Understands the importance of family and community in English language learners' education.

The same cultural, environmental, social and psychological factors that may affect a student's English language development are relevant in effective communication between the teacher, the student, and the student's family. For example, based on their own cultural experience, some parents may be reluctant to ask teachers questions if they perceive the teacher as an authority figure who should not be questioned. Others may not attend meetings with the teacher or school events if they find these situations to be intimidating because of their own limited English skills. In both cases, the parents' lack of communication should not be interpreted as a lack of interest in their children's educational progress.

Since effective communication between the school and the home is an important factor in students' academic success, recognition of these factors is an important part of finding ways to communicate with all stakeholders in a child's education. Anticipating questions and creating a FAQ (frequently asked questions) to share with parents may help get conversations started. Similarly, encouraging parents to send in questions before meetings (to avoid having to ask them directly) can also break the ice. Use of home language (when possible) to reach out to parents can help draw them into the school community. Encouraging groups of parents to reach out to others in their home language is another way to connect the institution and ELL students' homes.

Often in schools, parents, grandparents, and other people involved in children's lives want to take a more active role in the educational process. It is important to provide opportunities for the public to come into the school and participate in activities designed to encourage their participation in the schooling of their children. During these programs, it is important to share information about the methodologies and strategies being implemented to support students. In this way, the public can begin to understand the methodology and programs used in ESOL instruction.

Taking the time to educate parents and other family members not only helps to enhance understanding and open communication, it can also provide more support for students than the school alone would ever be able to provide.

Some strategies for educating parents and family members include:

- open house style events
- parent workshops on various topics
- newsletters or monthly emails
- individual parent meetings
- inviting parents to observe lessons
- information shared during social times where parents are invited into the school

Communicating general information about English and appropriate English language instruction is also important. It is just as important to share specific information about student progress with parents and relevant school personnel. Once the teacher has gathered sufficient information on the students, s/he must find appropriate methods to share this information with those who need the data. Again, depending on the audience, the amount and type of information shared may vary. Some ways to share information with parents/guardians include:

- individual parent meetings
- small group meetings
- regular parent updates through phone calls, email, or other messaging tools
- charts and graphs of progress sent home
- class blogs or portals on learning management systems

Communicating about assessment methods and results is important, but so is communicating about instructional practice so that stakeholders understand the goals and the strategies for meeting goals. Stakeholders can then more effectively help develop student strengths and meet student needs. When teachers communicate effectively with parents, families, colleagues, administrators, and English Language Learners themselves, all stakeholders are more likely to work together towards the common goal of helping learners achieve communicative, academic, and social/emotional success.

DOMAIN II   SECOND-LANGUAGE AND CONTENT LEARNING

COMPETENCY 5.0   LISTENING AND SPEAKING INSTRUCTION AND ASSESSMENT

Skill 5.1   Understands the importance of first language oral language skills as a basis for English aural and oral skill development

See 7.1 for the importance of first language literacy skills as a basis for English reading and writing skill development.

See 2.6 for the general role that first language skills play in English language development.

Skill 5.2   Develops strategies and activities for developing English language learners' communicative language skills (e.g., aural comprehension, listening and speaking vocabularies, knowledge of Standard English, listening and speaking for different purposes) and communicative competence in English

Language study using authentic language and realistic uses of language have become the most important aspects of language acquisition. Theorists now believe that language use is the proper goal of language studies and that it should be studied in context instead of in isolated sentences which provide examples of only a specific grammar point or structure. In the move away from de-contextualized, graded textbooks, researchers encourage the study of discourse above the sentence level.

Teachers need to provide a wide range of materials, including educational technology to create a language-rich environment, believed to be the key to comprehensible input and high motivation.

And finally, all the four language skills—listening, speaking, reading, and writing -- should be practiced at all levels. One way of achieving the practice of all four skills, while using authentic language, is to incorporate task-based activities into the instruction (1985), defining a task as "an activity or action which is carried out as a result of processing or understanding language" (Leaver and Willis, 2004).

The teacher must use a variety of methods to encourage students to use the new language rather than focusing only on comprehension. These can include activities such as the following, in which the objective is to learn the names of classroom objects:

- TPR activities, in which the student obeys a command ("Hold up a pencil") or displays a response on a slate or 3 x 5 card ("Draw a computer mouse").
- Duet reading (the students and teacher read aloud together at the same time).
- Races (each team sends up a runner who must touch whatever classroom object the teacher names before the other team's runner).

- Team drawing on the chalkboard ("Draw a classroom with a flag above the desk. Now draw a wastebasket beside the desk," etc.).
- Singing, rated as the single easiest way to remember new vocabulary.
- Cooperative learning tasks, in which each student has one piece of information and must get other information from classmates as well as share what he/she has with them.

Ellis (1994: 596-598) concluded that two-way exchanges of information show more benefits because:

- Two-way tasks require more negotiation of meaning.
- ELLs usually produce more complex and more target-like language when they have sufficient time to plan their responses.
- Closed tasks (those with one single, correct solution) may produce more negotiation work than those which have no predetermined solution because there is more chance that participants will work through challenges.

With respect to listening skills, Ur (1996) lists some of the occasions on which we listen and appropriately respond:

- Interviews
- Instructions
- Loudspeaker announcements
- Radio news
- Committee meetings
- Shopping encounters
- Theater
- Telephone
- Lessons or lectures
- Conversation and gossip
- Television
- Story-telling

Most of these situations use language that is informal and spontaneous. In the classroom, teachers are training ELLs for real-life listening situations. Bearing this in mind, the most useful types of activities are those where the listener (ELL) is asked to listen to genuinely informal talk instead of the typical written text. The speaker should be visible to the listener and there should be direct speaker-listener interaction. Finally, there should be only one exposure to the text because, as in real-life, the listener will rarely have the opportunity to have the text "replayed."

The tasks themselves should be presented in such a way that the ELL can use his or her previous knowledge to anticipate outcomes. Saying, "You are going to hear a husband and wife discussing summer vacation plans" is far more useful than merely stating, "Listen to the passage..." Also, ELLs should be given a task to complete as they

listen (e.g., listen for information about where they are planning to go, mark this on your maps). Finally, ELLs should be permitted to answer the questions as they hear the information and not wait until the end.
(Adapted from Ur, 1996)

In recent years, the teaching of speaking skills has moved away from a focus on accuracy toward a focus on fluency and communicative effectiveness. This has affected the kinds of activities used by the teachers in the classroom. These communicative activities promote students' abilities to understand and communicate real information. It also provides opportunities for them to engage in interaction that is as close as possible to real life situations.

The selection of appropriate activities depends a lot on the level of the learners. For example, the beginning level students need form-controlled practice and drills to move to more communicative activities. On the other hand, advanced learners may be asked to engage in less structured activities on their own. Following are the examples of the kinds of activities that could promote speaking skills.

Linguistically Structured Activities
Despite a recent shift towards emphasizing fluency, accuracy is still considered an important goal for language learners. Controlled activities can be provided with context, so that they have some of the elements of a communicative activity. This would help the beginning-level student focus on accurate structure within a communicative context. An example of this is the *structured interview* where students question and answer each other, exchanging real information, while at the same time repeating and producing specific structures (e.g., yes, no, or "wh" questions).

Some language games can also provide students with controlled practice. However, it is important to model the language structures for beginning students. These and other games help students focus on and repeat specific structures as well as perform natural "authentic" tasks.

Participation Activities
Participation activities involve students in participating in some communication activity in a "natural" setting. One of these activities is the guided discussion, through which the teacher introduces a problem or a controversial topic. Students in small groups discuss the problem and try to come up with appropriate solutions. In more advanced classes, students could choose their own topic and lead a discussion about it. This activity advances turn-taking elements and topic control among the students, and reinforces accuracy of grammar and pronunciation.

Another activity is *interviewing,* wherein ELLs interview a native speaker about some meaningful or memorable experience in their lives. After the interview, the students organize the information collected and present it to the whole class.

Observation Activities

These are activities in which students record both verbal and nonverbal interactions between native speakers or advanced speakers of the target language. This process helps students become aware of the language spoken in an authentic setting. It also allows students to observe how people greet each other, make requests, interrupt each other, compliment each other, disagree, or receive compliments. A follow-up activity could be a role play created by the students to show the verbal and nonverbal behaviors appropriate in a particular situation.

Discussion Activities

- **Describing pictures:** Each group has a picture that all members of the group can see. The recorder or secretary makes a check mark for each sentence (the recorder does not have to write out the sentence) the members of the group use to describe the picture. After two minutes, the check marks are added up, and the group tries to surpass their checks by describing a second picture.
- **Picture differences:** Each pair is given a set of two pictures. Without showing their picture to their partner, they must find out what differences there are between the pictures by questioning each other.
- **Solving a problem:** Students are told that they will be on an educational advisory committee that must advise the principal on a problem with students. They should discuss their recommendations and write a letter to the principal. (Teacher needs to prepare the problem and copy it for each student or group.)

Performance Activities

In performance activities, language learners prepare for the activity beforehand and deliver a message to a group. This could vary from a student's speech or explanation of an experiment to simply telling a story from their own experience. The follow-up activity could involve videotaping the students during their performances and having them evaluate themselves. This allows the students to focus on communication about their initial performance and, in the follow-up session, deal with specific language features. Additionally, role play and dramas can be used for all language learners, making varying demands on the learners according to their proficiency levels. Finally, debates can be an effective performance activity for intermediate and advanced learners.

- **Creative drama:** This activity can be used in the language classroom to encourage dialogue technique. Students either write their own play or learn one from English literature. The activity is time consuming but increases confidence and morale of the ELLs.
- **Role plays and skits:** ELLs are each given a card describing their situation and the task or problem. The participants can be given time to practice their role play or they may improvise. This activity is usually done in pairs or small groups. (Adapted from Ur, 1996)

These activities and tasks can be adjusted to the levels and needs of the ELLs.

An ESOL instructor can use a variety of instructional methods to communicate with students. Common techniques which are suitable for all levels are:

Contextual

- Gestures
- Body language
- Facial expressions
- Props
- Visual illustrations
- Manipulatives

Linguistic Modifications

- Standardized vocabulary
- Set standard for sentence length and complexity
- Reinforcement through repetition, summarization, and restatement
- Slower speaking pace

Teaching Vocabulary

- Use of *charades* when trying to communicate a word (acting out the word with physical actions or gestures)
- Introducing new vocabulary through familiar vocabulary
- Utilizing visual props, antonyms, and synonyms to communicate vocabulary

As English Language Learners progress, these techniques are adjusted according to individual or group needs and proficiency levels.

Skill 5.3 **Selects materials and implements strategies that support English language learners' achievement of listening and speaking standards (WIDA ELD, 2011 Massachusetts Curriculum Framework for English Language Arts and Literacy)**

Massachusetts state standards are aligned with the WIDA English Language Development (ELD) Standards. WIDA (originally World-class Instructional Design and Assessment, but now simply known as WIDA) seeks to develop research-based standards and assessments for ELL students of linguistically diverse backgrounds. In 2012, WIDA published their Amplification of English Language Development Standards for Kindergarten through Grade 12.

The Massachusetts Framework implemented in 2011 reflects the Common Core English Language Arts (ELA) standards for speaking and listening (as well as reading and writing). Together these ELA and ELD standards should guide ESOL teachers' selection of materials and strategies for supporting students' learning.

Neither document prescribes specific teaching methods, but these principles should guide teachers' planning and instruction.

Instruction and activities should:

- Allow for and encourage collaboration, building students' ability to express complex ideas;
- Require students to integrate information and evidence from diverse media sources (e.g. text, infographics, presentations);
- Include activities that require analysis of complex messages presented orally;
- Incorporate visual media;
- Require students to adapt their speaking methods for different audiences;
- Emphasize the authentic use of language (e.g. presentations or debates rather than memorization of language patterns);
- Integrate speaking, listening, reading and writing to promote literacy development effectively;
- Encourage students to build on and respond to the ideas of others; and
- Speaking and listening activities involving content area knowledge and skills.

Digital tools and media offer important opportunities for ELL students as well. Digital stories, presentations, video-based projects, and podcasts are a few examples of activities that would involve authentic use of language and listening skills. These activities also offer the opportunity for students to self-evaluate language development and to set specific goals for areas to improve. As a preserved record of performance, they can also become part of a student's portfolio.

Discussions (small group and whole class), debates, interviews, presentations, projects and scripted projects (plays, films, etc.) are instructional methods that incorporate the traits above. For example, a project that requires a student to interview someone, present findings with a peer, and then use information gleaned from the process in a class discussion would involve authentic, collaborative use of language, recognition of the requirement to adapt speech (formal vs. informal), integration of evidence, and the analysis of the speech of others.

ELL students benefit from programs that draw on their previous experiences and language development. Students with strong skills in their home language are likely able to transfer and build upon those skills as they learn English. Planning and instruction should try and make use of this as a tool to support students' English language development.

See 5.2

Skill 5.4   **Demonstrates knowledge of formal and informal methods of assessing oral and aural language proficiency and understanding of effective guidelines for selecting and administering oral language assessments**

Everything a teacher does to check on student learning in the classroom is a type of informal (also called formative) assessment. This includes comprehension check activities such as thumbs up/thumbs down, verbal responses (ranging from yes/no and one or two word answers to complete sentences), end-of-lesson feedback surveys, and quizzes, to name just a few. The interview technique is especially effective for obtaining feedback regarding a student's developing oral language proficiency.

Teachers can use oral interviews, or paired student-to-student interviews, to evaluate the language the students are using or their ability to provide content information when asked questions—both of which have implications for further instructional planning. This type of assessment allows instructors to evaluate the student's level of English proficiency, as well as identify potential problem areas which may require correctional strategies.

Formal Assessments

Formal assessments (also called summative assessments) are usually conducted at the end of a unit of study, to check students' global learning of the content. These include national or state assessments, as well as chapter, unit, or other classroom tests. At the national and state levels, there are formal oral assessment instruments designed to test a student's overall achievement of oral language proficiency. These include, but are not limited to, the ACTFL Oral Proficiency Interview (OPI), Test of Spoken English (TSE) and, in Massachusetts, the Department of Secondary and Elementary Education (DESE)-mandated Massachusetts English Language Assessment – Oral, or MELA-O.

ACTFL Oral Proficiency Interview (OPI)

This assessment was originally created by the American Council on the Teaching of Foreign Languages (ACTFL) in the 1950s and has been evolving ever since. It is designed to measure functional speaking ability. Learners can choose between a one-on-one computer-based interview, which lasts about 45 minutes, or a 30+ minute phone interview between a certified ACTFL tester and a student. The phone interview is a structured, interactive conversation that continuously adapts to the interests, experiences, and abilities of the person being tested. The computer interview is individualized for the test-taker. Each interview is recorded and rated by one or more certified testers. For rating purposes, there are five major levels of proficiency: Distinguished, Superior, Advanced, Intermediate, and Novice.

If a test-taker requires an official Bilingual Language Endorsement, s/he must take the 'To Superior' version of the computer based interview.

ACCESS for ELLs Tests

The Every Student Succeeds Act or ESSA (2015), replaced the No Child Left Behind Act (2001). Key provisions of the ESSA that affect English language learners include the following:

- States must have English language proficiency standards.
- States must implement annual assessments of English language proficiency for all ELLS.

In 2019, Massachusetts schools will be required to administer the computer-based (online) version of the ACCESS for ELLs assessment. Currently, schools can choose between the online or paper version of the test. The online version of the test is adaptive; teachers do not have to pre-select tiers or levels for students – the computer determines levels and upcoming questions based on previous answers.

The listening portion of the assessment is self-paced but it generally takes students approximately 40 minutes to complete. Students listen to pre-recorded passages and select from a series of multiple-choice responses. The test platform records and scores students' answers. Students must take the Listening and Reading tests before Speaking and Writing as their performance determines their placement in Speaking and Writing.

The speaking portion of the assessment is also self-paced and takes students approximately 30 minutes to complete. Students listen to pre-recorded speaking prompts on the computer and speak into headsets with microphones to record their answers. Speaking tests are scored by the test contractor.

See the WIDA ACCESS for ELLs site (https://www.wida.us/assessment/ACCESS20.aspx) for details and sample assessment questions.

Informal Assessments

Informal assessments allow teachers to track the ongoing progress of their students regularly and often. Standardized tests measure students at one point of the school year (i.e., their cumulative development by the time of administration), whereas ongoing informal assessments can provide snapshots of the continual development throughout the year. Informal assessments allow teachers to pinpoint each student's specific problem areas, plan and implement appropriate interventions, and adapt their instructional strategies. In order to continually assess a student's oral proficiency development, a teacher should use a variety of strategies and techniques. Performance-based and portfolio assessments can help a teacher document student progress in this domain.

 All assessments, even informal ones, should be implemented using a scoring rubric to measure student progress. Students should be assessed at the very beginning of the school year to establish a baseline of their working (productive) knowledge. The first step for any teacher in the selection and administration of oral performance assessment should be to use (or create) a rubric listing outcomes outlined in the state's curriculum frameworks for their content area. For an ESL teacher in Massachusetts, these are listed in the ELPBO. Performance-based assessments typically promote a broad range of responses, rather than a single correct answer. In addition to interviews (described in Skill 6.1), other activities that can be implemented with a scoring rubric to assess students' current proficiency levels and ongoing development include:

- Reading aloud (to check for oral fluency)
- Retelling stories (to check for productive vocabulary/grammar)
- Role playing
- Giving descriptions, directions or instructions orally
- Telling a story based on visual prompts (e.g., a sequence of three or more pictures)
- Brainstorming
- Playing games
- Comprehension checks
- Exit tickets (e.g., 3-2-1: list three things you learned today, list two things you would like to know more about, list 1 thing you enjoyed/did not enjoy/did not understand at all, etc.)

With beginner/intermediate level ELLs, it is best to assess no more than three items at a time. For example, for a role-playing activity, a teacher might assess ELLs' ability to respond to "wh" questions, ask for or respond to a clarification, read addresses or telephone numbers aloud.

Informal/formative assessments should be continuous and applied on a daily, weekly, monthly continuum throughout the school year.

Formal assessment of ELLs is required by federal (ESSA) and state law. In Massachusetts, this requirement is fulfilled by administering the MEPA-R/W and MELA-O. Administration periods and requirements for this formal assessment of ELLs are specified by the Massachusetts Department of Secondary and Elementary Education. In addition, unless exempted by a documented special need, all students in MCAS grades (3-12), regardless of English proficiency level, are required to participate in the MCAS.

Skill 5.5   Interprets and uses assessment results, including differentiation between normal variation in oral language performance and performance that may indicate possible disabilities

A basic premise of assessment is "test what you teach." In the high-stakes testing of today, teachers are expected to show good results with the exit tests of their students. Teachers can use regular classroom testing to determine and monitor each individual student's strengths and weaknesses. By aligning instruction of the ELLs with the curriculum, the instructor can plan reinforcement of deficit skills as needed. This system is effective in preventing later gaps when more complex skills are introduced. By integrating language skills into the content area, the instructor can make the language classroom a motivating place, with many opportunities for further learning. Instruction may be differentiated to accommodate a variety of learning styles and levels.

Gurel (2004) claims that research evidence points to disproportionate numbers of English language learners who have been identified with learning disabilities, and at the same time, under-identification of English-language learners who have disabilities but have been dismissed because they were in the process of learning a new language. It is this conundrum that confounds the teaching of English language learners with disabilities. Of vital importance is the accurate assessment of these students.

Assessment is diagnostic and ongoing, whereas evaluation is used to judge students' learning (Cobb, 2003 in Tompkins, G. E., 2009). Authentic assessment tools and tests give a more complete picture of what the student knows about the subject matter as well as the strategies and skills they use, whereas tests compare student performance against grade-level standards (Wilson, Martens, & Arya, 2005 in Tompkins, G. E., 2009). Oftentimes, tests are more a measure of English language proficiency than the construct which they were designed to test (Figueroa & Garcia, 1994 in Quiocho & Ulanoff, 2009). Test results may be influenced by ELLs from many different language backgrounds (Quiocho & Ulanoff, 2009).

Teachers can use the information gathered from their testing in different ways (Chapman, D. W. and Snyder, Jr., C. W. 2000):

- Tests can be used to reorient teaching practices in desirable ways.
- Teachers can be motivated to improve their teaching.
- Testing gives information for remedial work.

Creece (2003 in Schumm 2006) suggests that classroom progress be used instead of IQ-achievement discrepancy as the criteria for placing students in special education classes. In the case of students demonstrating possible learning difficulties, the classroom teacher will have preliminary diagnostics with which to recommend further testing.

Watson (2011) suggests that teachers look at the following skills when evaluating oral language skills:

Strengths

- Strong articulation skills
- Quite fluent orally
- Uses voice intonation and good expression
- Grade appropriate use of grammar
- Good use of words
- Expanding vocabulary

Weaknesses

- Weak articulation skills
- Difficulty with oral language; uses lots of interjections and hesitations (umm, uh, well...
- Weak verbal expression
- Grammar skills are quite weak
- Forgets a lot of words and often can't remember what he/she was going to say
- Weak vocabulary

Many of these oral skill weaknesses can be the result of learning a second language. Caution should be used when evaluating ELLs and descriptive evaluation is recommended by many researchers as being more beneficial. **Descriptive assessment** (Quiocho & Ulanoff, 2009) is a more holistic view by using data collected by a variety of methods (language samples, narrative analysis, and rating scales). Students are then analyzed using language proficiency, previous academic performance, and an emphasis on the use of multiple measures. In all cases, when classroom performance does not improve over a period of time, even with support from ELL teachers or support staff, consideration should be given to recommending the student for special education classes and /or support.

COMPETENCY 6.0 STRATEGIES FOR PROMOTING AND ASSESSING ENGLISH LANGUAGE LEARNERS' READING SKILLS AND READING COMPREHENSION

Skill 6.1 Demonstrates knowledge of research foundations and key features of significant reading theories and models

Two types of traditional approaches to reading are the **bottom-up (phonics) approach** and **the top-down (more language-based approach)**. Each approach has its proponents.

The **bottoms-up approach** is phonics instruction designed to "break the code" of reading in a systematic way. Students start by learning the sounds of letters, followed by letter-sound, and the syllables, words, sentences, etc. Reading is viewed as a linear, systematic process. Spelling and language are taught as separate subjects. This approach has its origins in ancient Greece.

The **top-down approach** advocates exposing students to a wide variety of literature and reading materials. Words are taught as individuals need and are ready for them. The progressive education movement led by John Dewey is associated with this approach. More recently, Goodman developed a whole-language approach based on his own research, and the linguistics of Chomsky (1965). Typical characteristics of the whole-language approach are:

- Each student takes an individualized route to developing proficiency in reading
- Teachers provide mini-lessons when needed and act as facilitators
- Authentic literature and writing tasks are emphasized (as opposed to basal readers and supplementary materials)

Rumelhart (1976) and Stanovich (1980) advocate a middle ground between the two above approaches. Stanovich developed an **interactive-compensatory model** which recognizes the importance of phonics as key step in the reading process. The interactive-compensatory model:

- Suggests that students should receive early intensive instruction in phonological awareness and phonics, but with an emphasis on real reading and writing
- Teachers should have accurate data about each students' strengths and weaknesses
- Instruction should be differentiated based on each student's needs
- teachers should use research when considering what to teach and how to teach it

(Adapted from Schumm & Arguelles in Schumm, 2006)

Skill 6.2   **Understands the role of oral language in early reading development and the interrelationship of listening, speaking, reading, and writing**

Some state policies or districts fail to recognize the importance of native language literacy and its importance in English language learning. (Avalos in Schumm, 2006). Cummins (1981) formulated an **interdependency hypothesis** which explains that the degree of knowledge and processes evident in the first language can determine the ease of transfer to the new language. Many other studies since Cummins' study support this claim in English language reading (Schumm, 2006). In other words, ELLs need to develop oral language in order to develop reading skills, which in turn further develop oral language skills.

Phonological awareness is a significant part of literacy development in children. Likewise, new research has shown that phonological awareness also plays an important role as children with limited English language proficiency learn to read both in their native language (L1) and in their second language (L2). Students need to understand the words in order to read texts. To read words, they need to be aware of the letters and the sounds represented by letters. This basic learning leads to the blending of sounds that helps them to pronounce words. Reading educators have found that phonological awareness is critical to the development of comprehension skills.

Furthermore, when fluency in word recognition is achieved, the child focuses more on understanding what is read. Therefore, researchers emphasize the importance of word recognition instruction to enhance fluency. It is recommended that educators who want to improve students' comprehension skills first teach them how to decode well. Explicit instruction in sounding out words is a start in developing good comprehension skills. Word recognition skills must be developed to the point of fluency if comprehension is to be increased.

Recent research has shown that phonological awareness in the native language (L1) of the English language learners predicts successful literacy acquisition of both L1 and L2. Therefore, the closer the phonologies of L1 and L2, the more likely it is that the transfer of skills will help the English language learners in their literacy development of L2. Studies suggest beginning instruction for bilingual children with the sounds and patterns that the two languages share. Teachers can then move on to the sounds and patterns that are different between the two languages. In this way, teachers can build upon the transfer of the common sounds of both languages to help their students achieve literacy skills.

Instruction could follow with discussion of the sounds that are different between the two languages, to avoid negative transfer. In short, phonological awareness of both the native language and the target language can help increase the literacy skills of an English language learner. This awareness fosters not only their word recognition skills and their fluency, but also helps students focus their cognitive capabilities on increasing their reading comprehension.

Integration of all four language skills is beneficial for all English Language Learners, regardless of their proficiency level (Genesee et. al., 2006). Integration of the skills provides a framework for learners to exercise their writing skills. The integration of the four skills provides an effective context for writing so that the use of one leads naturally to the use of another, as in real life. In this way, learners will see how writing relates to certain communicative needs just as the other skills do.

For example, students participate in classroom conversations by articulating their opinions, sharing their observations, making comparisons, etc., through speaking and writing. They need to listen to the topic, take notes, discuss with their classmates, and read about the topic, which requires the integration of all four skills.

Oral language development and language skills such as reading, writing, speaking, and listening need to be developed in conjunction with one another. They are all interrelated and integrated naturally. Practice in any one area promotes development in the other areas as well. Connections between abstract and concrete concepts are best made when all language processes are incorporated and integrated during both practice and application.

English Language Learners benefit from opportunities to use English in multiple settings. Learning is more effective when students have an opportunity to participate fully, actively discussing ideas and information. Through meaningful interaction, students can practice speaking and making themselves understood by asking and answering questions, negotiating meaning, clarifying ideas, and other techniques. Ideally, these activities would require the use of the four language skills (reading, writing, speaking, and listening) to successfully complete each task.

Opportunities for Interaction

- Effective teachers strive to provide a more balanced linguistic exchange between themselves and their students.
- Interaction accesses the thought processes of another and solidifies one's own thinking.
- Talking with others, either in pairs or in small groups, allows for oral rehearsal of learning.

It is important to encourage students to elaborate on their verbal responses and challenge them to go beyond "yes" and "no" answers:

- "Tell me more about that."
- "What do you mean by. . .?"
- "What else. . .?"
- "How do you know?"

It is also important to allow wait time for students to formulate answers. If necessary, the teacher can also call on another student to extend his or her classmate's response.

All students, including English Language Learners, benefit from instruction that frequently includes a variety of grouping configurations. It is recommended that at least two different grouping structures be used during a lesson:

- **Flexible small groups**
  - To promote multiple perspectives
  - To encourage collaboration

- **Partnering**
  - To provide practice opportunities
  - To scaffold instruction
  - To give assistance before independent practice

Additionally, teachers should provide activities that allow interaction with varied student groupings.

- Homogenous grouping by language proficiency or language background allows for targeted instruction and skills practice.
- Heterogeneous grouping can challenge students to a higher level and provide good student models.
- Movement from whole class, to partners, to small group increases student involvement.

Cooperative Learning Ideas

- **Information gap activities:** Each student in a group has only one or two pieces of the information needed to solve the puzzle or problem. Students must work together, sharing information, while practicing their language and using critical thinking skills.
- **Jigsaw:** Jigsaw a reading task by chunking text into manageable parts (1–2 pages); students pool their information.
- **Roundtable:** Use with open-ended questions, grammar practice. Small groups of students sit at tables, with one sheet of paper and a pencil. A question, concept, or problem is given to each group by the teacher; students pass paper around table, each writing his or her own response. Teacher circulates room.
- **3-Step Interview:** Students are paired. Each student listens to the other as they respond to a topic question. At the end of three minutes, each pair joins another pair of students and shares what their partners said. This activity provides students with a good way to practice language.
- **Writing Headlines:** This activity provides a way to practice summarizing an activity, story, or project. Teacher provides models of newspaper or magazine headlines. Students work in pairs writing a headline for an activity. Pairs share their headlines with the rest of the class and the class votes on the most effective headlines.

Wait Time

Wait time varies by culture. Research has shown that the average amount of wait time in American classrooms is not sufficient. Teachers should

- Allow students to express their thoughts fully without interruption.
- Allow students to discuss their answer with a partner before sharing with the whole group.

Fluency

Fluency is developed over time through extensive practice both in speaking and in reading. Ample opportunities should be given to ELLs to develop their speaking and listening abilities to help them achieve more oral fluency. Role plays, skits, poems, singing, and telephone dialogs are good ways to increase oral fluency. Fluency in reading interacts with oral fluency. Wide exposure to print and reading will increase both reading fluency and oral fluency. The two are intertwined.

Fluent readers can grasp chunks of language, read for meaning (and not word by word), and decode automatically. They are confident readers who are able to self-monitor, and maintain comprehension. Specific instruction devoted to these areas should improve fluency rates in slower readers.

Literacy is a complex set of skills that comprise the interrelated processes of reading and writing. Reading requires decoding, accurate and fluent word recognition, and comprehension at the word, phrase, sentence, and text levels. Writing requires automatic letter formation and/or keyboarding, accurate and fluent spelling, sentence construction, and the ability to compose a variety of different text structures with coherence and cohesion.

Literacy involves the integration of speaking, listening, and critical thinking. Young children use their oral language skills to learn to read, while older children use their reading ability to further their language learning. The instructional components necessary for reading and writing include: phonemic awareness, phonics, vocabulary building, fluency development, comprehension, text structure, and writing process strategies, as well as prerequisite writing skills, such as handwriting, spelling, and grammar.

A survey of research points to the following indicators of effective instructional literacy practices:

- Motivating students according to their unique needs and interests
- Providing direct explicit instruction of reading and writing skills and strategies based on ongoing student assessment
- Modeling the effective thinking skills that good readers and writers employ
- Devoting fifty percent of the students' instructional time every day to reading and writing in the classroom

- Activating students' prior knowledge to help them make connections between what they know and what they would like to learn (e.g., KWL)
- Providing opportunities for students to make text and writing connections to their lives, forms of media, and the world
- Offering both guided and independent reading experiences
- Differentiating instruction with a plentiful supply of multi-level books to accommodate interests and ability levels
- Motivating readers by offering a choice of books to read that are at their independent reading level, and that they can read with accuracy, fluency, and comprehension
- Promoting conversation through purposeful and guided discussion about a book, piece of writing, or topic
- Guiding discussions through open-ended questioning
- Creating a more personable learning environment
- Designing projects that excite and engage students as opposed to engaging in short disconnected tasks (integration of subjects)
- Assessing student work based on common rubrics

Skill 6.3   Demonstrates knowledge of the alphabetic principle, and research-based strategies for promoting students' phonemic awareness and other critical phonological skills (e.g., phonics skills)

The International Reading Association (1997) issued a position statement on the place of phonics in reading instruction. This position paper asserts that phonics has an important place in beginning reading instruction, primary teachers value and teach phonics, and effective phonics is integrated into the total language arts program. To help children learn phonics, teaching analytical phonics in context seems to work better than teaching synthetic phonics in isolation, e.g. on worksheets.

Some of the techniques for beginning reading development, skills and strategies are glossed below:

- Teaching children to understand sentences, texts, and other materials is better than trying to teach the word skills in isolation.
- Children can learn the alphabet principles by alphabetizing lists of spelling words or groups of objects.
- Simple techniques such as holding up the left hand and recognizing the letter 'L' can help children remember which side of the text to begin reading first.
- Learning to decode words is best achieved by practicing while reading.
- Sight words can be memorized.
- Three major types of context clues are: syntactic (word order, word endings, function of words in a sentence), semantic (meaning clues), and phonemes and graphemes (/ph/ may sound like /f/ as in photograph, /ch/ sometimes sounds like a /k/ as in chemistry).

- Reading fluency may be improved by observing the following strategies (et al): reread for clarity and to improve understanding, ask for help when confused, realize that "There is no such thing as a stupid question". Venn diagrams, webs, and other graphics may be helpful in organizing texts for easier understanding.
- Vocabulary cards or dictionaries may help ELLs to recall words they don't know. Word walls and instruction on idioms, antonyms, synonyms, and homonyms are useful.
- Learning the structure of sentence patterns, question forms, and their punctuation can help the ELL to determine meaning.

Teaching decoding skills is one of the effective methods of reading instruction. The emphasis is on teaching the phoneme-grapheme correspondences. In order to develop effective reading skills, students should aim for *automaticity* i.e., the brain process of decoding letter sounds becomes automatic. Automaticity leads to fluent reading whereby the brain may process many letters, sounds, and words at the same time, which is positively related to students' achievement in reading. Once decoding skills are mastered, more attention can be given to mastering the overall meaning of a phrase or sentence (comprehension). However, students still need explicit instruction in developing strategies to improve their comprehension skills.

Phonics and other linguistic approaches to teaching reading are important in terms of word identification skills. Accurate and rapid word recognition leads to fluency in reading, which is considered one of the five critical components of the reading process (National Reading Panel). When the reader's decoding skills become automatic, she or he can focus on constructing meaning. For readers who have not yet reached automaticity of decoding skills, reading is a slow, laborious struggle. Fluent readers are more likely to engage in extensive reading than struggling readers.

The view that if readers read more, they will achieve fluency is not applicable for ESL learners. Expert teacher guidance is necessary for learners to reach fluency. Several studies have focused on the type of instruction that would increase fluency in readers.

These instructional practices include:

- Modeled reading
- Repeated reading of familiar text
- Wide independent reading
- Coached reading of appropriately selected materials
- Chunking of text
- Word reading practice

Although fluency is an important part of reading, it is not sufficient to ensure high levels of reading achievement and comprehension. Fluency is based on a foundation of oral language skills, phonemic awareness, familiarity with letter forms, and efficient decoding skills. In short, a combination of instruction in decoding and reading comprehension is required for students to achieve high levels of reading skill.

Activities should be organized to encourage English language learners to use all four language skills needed to engage in real-life communicative situations. To do this, students should speak not only with the teacher, but also with other students. The student will also listen and try to comprehend what other speakers are saying. The listener can then react by writing down for a reader his version of the information he has just heard. This sequence of activities helps ELLs brainstorm ideas in the target language before they put them on paper, thereby providing little opportunity for the student to translate his or her idea from his or her native language into English. In this scenario, prewriting techniques give the students opportunity to use all four skills to help them explore and initiate their ideas on a given topic, or to develop a topic for a writing activity based on communication activities in the classroom.

Brainstorming
Brainstorming allows students working together in the classroom in small groups to say as much as they can about a topic. This helps them generate ideas to use for their individual brainstorming on paper. This activity involves the use of both speaking and listening skills to produce effective writing.

Guided Discussion
Another way to get students to talk about a topic or to focus on specific aspects of a topic is to provide guidelines for group or whole class discussion. This technique offers the advantage of helping the students beforehand with the vocabulary and sentence forms that they might need in their discussion. This again makes use of all four skills to guide students in their writing process.

Some of the other activities that encourage students to use the four linguistic skills are:

- Interviews
- Skits
- Dictation
- Note taking
- Story telling

Second-language teaching (SLT) recognizes the importance of giving ELLs integrative tasks which help them achieve their language goals by including any or all of the following language skills: listening, speaking, reading, writing, and viewing. Tasks are loosely defined as any activities which emphasize meaning over form. Which tasks are chosen depends on the teacher who makes decisions about appropriate tasks for his or her classroom.

Candlin (1987, in Batstone 1994: 17) suggests that beneficial tasks are those that

- Encourage learners to attend to meaning
- Give learners flexibility in problem solving
- Involve learners whose personality and attitude is primary
- Are challenging, but not too demanding

- Raise ELLs' awareness of the process of language use, encouraging them to reflect on their own language use

Tasks can be divided into two different types. **Learning tasks** are those that focus on formal features of language and have specific learning outcomes.

Communicative tasks are typically focused on meaning and are frequently open-ended. Often, they are used in group work and may have a written component which summarizes the work.

Tasks may be divided into three main groups:

- **Information-gap tasks:** Involve the transfer of given information from one person to another, from one form to another, or from one place to another. The activity often involves selection of relevant information, as well, and learners may have to meet criteria of completeness and correctness in making the transfer.
- **Reasoning-gap tasks:** Involve deriving some new information from given information through processes of inference, deduction, practical reasoning, or a perception of relationships or patterns.
- **Opinion-gap tasks:** Involve identifying and articulating a personal preference, feeling, or attitude in response to a given situation.

(Adapted from Prabhu, 1987: 46-47.)

Authenticity is an important component of tasks in the classroom. Many instructors and researchers believe that learning tasks should be authentic or use "real" spoken English. According to Nunan (1989), the distinction between real world tasks and pedagogic tasks may be blurred in reality. He believes that pedagogic activities, while they may seem artificial, may in fact practice enabling skills such as fluency, discourse, and interactional skills, mastery of phonological elements, and mastery of grammar. He suggests that there may be no hard and fast distinction between real-world and pedagogic tasks.

Skill 6.4   Demonstrates knowledge of research-based strategies to help students develop their academic language levels (vocabulary, sentence, discourse)

Develop English Language Learners' academic language by frontloading vocabulary. When students are given explanations and new vocabulary they need in upcoming reading (or content classes), they are better able to handle the academic demands placed upon them. By using examples of the word in its context, asking students to decide if the word is used correctly, and asking them to draw pictures of the word, students are actively engaged in the learning process.

Provide ELLs with opportunities to learn and use forms of English language necessary to express content-subject specific academic language functions (e.g., analyzing, comparing, persuading, citing evidence, making hypotheses). ELLs need opportunities to debate, write written reports, make hypotheses, etc., but in most cases, these structures must be taught. Citing evidence and making hypotheses are academic skills used throughout an academic's life, and need to be taught beginning with simplified reports or research papers.

Teachers need to provide models of the language activity/structure they are teaching and demonstrate it to the students. The teacher can list the specific vocabulary and rhetorical structures used on the board for illustration. These forms could be copied and distributed to the class.

Provide authentic opportunities for ELLs to use the English language for content-related communicative purposes with both native and non-native speakers of English. ELLs need the opportunity to practice English regardless of their level. By grouping ELL students with native speakers and other nonnative speakers of English they are practicing language and the social elements of communication. Many ELLs have content knowledge but may have difficulty expressing it, whereas many native speakers may not have the content knowledge necessary to complete a task. Both students benefit when working in small groups on assigned tasks.

See Skills 9.1 and 9.3 for more strategies to support academic language development
See Skills 6.5 and 7.2 for more strategies to support vocabulary, sentence and discourse level

Skill 6.5   Demonstrates knowledge of research-based strategies and resources to support English Language Learners' reading comprehension skills

During efficient reading, incoming textual data is processed (bottom-up), which activates appropriate higher level schemata (top-down) against which the reader tries to give the text a coherent interpretation. The reader makes predictions on the basis of these top-down processes and then searches the text for confirmation or rejection of these partially satisfied higher-order schemata.

Reading comprehension is a highly complex process and successful readers use reading strategies in each of the three distinct phases of reading—prereading, reading, and postreading—to successfully understand a text (Peregoy and Boyle, 2008).

The purposes of the "prereading phase" are for teachers to build background knowledge through anticipation guides or field trips, motivate the reader with structured overviews or films, and establish the purpose using experiments or pictures.

The purposes of the "reading phase" are to read, based upon the established purpose, using learning logs or annotating texts to record information, improve comprehension by Directed Reading-Thinking Activities and asking questions, and utilizing background knowledge by studying headings and subheadings and answering questions.

The purposes of the "postreading phase" are to help the student with organizing and remembering information through activities such as art work, maps, or summaries and to use the information in reporting, making a film, or publishing.

Some of the techniques students need to be able to master in reading comprehension include:

- Skimming to extract main idea
- Scanning for specific information
- Predicting based upon prior knowledge
- Restating the information to indicate comprehension of the text
- Recognizing inferred information
- Sounding out unfamiliar words, guessing at their meaning based upon previous understanding of the text
- Summarizing the text.

Teachers can guide students through these steps by using scaffolding techniques and giving support as needed.

Children's and juvenile's literature includes parables, fables, fairy tales, folktales, myths, legends, novels, romances, poetry, drama, and novels. ELLs need to be taught the intricacies of plot, point of view, setting, characterization, and other literary terms just as their native speaking classmates do. Many of these terms are universal, but the instructor should be aware that the literature of other cultures may vary considerably from its English counterpart. Drawing on background knowledge of ELLs is valuable, but literary genre and terms will undoubtedly have to be taught. Encouraging and promoting wide reading of the different genre both inside and outside the classroom is one way to introduce these elements to the students.

Reading classes should include instruction of the grammatical elements which typically occur over large stretches of text. Authentic texts contain more complex grammatical constructions, like anaphoric references and cohesive devices, which result in second-language readers having difficulty synthesizing information across sentences and paragraphs. Additionally, vocabulary building is an important aspect of reading instruction in order to avoid breakdown in the process of reading. The teacher can help students read a passage by preparing them with a brief list of some of the most important terms, together with their meanings in the context before they read. However, only those words should be pre-taught which are important in order to read the text accurately and critically.

The cultural dimension to reading involves one's purposes for reading and the attitude one holds towards the book and its content. Therefore, the teacher needs to utilize techniques and instructional practices which take attitudes based on cultural background of learners into account. One effective technique is to give students ample opportunities to work in pairs and small groups in which they share with each other the process of reading and literacy in their own cultures.

Pressley (2008) discusses the mental processes of good readers and states that teachers need to understand what good reading entails. According to him, good readers rely on both decoding strategies and comprehension strategies to achieve their reading goals.

Teachers should take the following strategies into account to design effective reading instruction programs.

1. *Phonemic awareness*: Phonemes are the smallest units of sound that combine to form syllables and words. For example, the word shut has three phonemes (sh-u-t) while skip has four phonemes (s-k-i-p). Therefore, phonemic awareness enables the learner to identify and manipulate these phonemes. Some English phonemes may be absent in students' native language and are more difficult to acquire. In this case, it is necessary to teach phonemic awareness with the vocabulary word, its meaning, and its pronunciation. Additionally, teachers could learn about the phonemes that exist or do not exist in their students' first language in order to provide them with effective instruction. Meaningful activities that focus on unique sounds and letters, such as language games and word wall, are useful as are songs and poems that help teach phonemes with rhythm and repetition.

2. *Phonics*: This is the understanding of the relationship between the phonemes and graphemes (the letters and spellings that represent sound in the written language). It helps readers read familiar words and decode unfamiliar ones. Instructional activities that develop students' phonemic awareness help them understand the systematic and predictable relationship between written letters and spoken sounds. Teachers can effectively teach phonics if they have knowledge about their students' native language. For example, in Spanish the letters b, c, d, f, l, m, n, p, q, s, and t represent sounds that are similar enough to English that students may learn them with relative ease. However, the vowels look similar in English and Spanish but are named differently and have different sounds. Therefore, they may be more difficult for Spanish speakers to master when reading English (Peregoy and Boyle, 2000).

3. *Reading fluency*: Reading fluency is crucial for reading comprehension. A fluent reader not only reads words quickly and accurately but also comprehends them at the same time. Students can be taught fluency by reading passages aloud with explicit instruction from the teacher. The other way is for students to read silently on their own with less teacher guidance. However, accent should not be confused with lack of fluency, as students can learn to read fluently in English even with a native language accent.

4. *Vocabulary development*: Vocabulary development is crucial for reading comprehension. It is difficult for a reader to understand the content unless they know the meaning of most of the words in the text. Vocabulary development is particularly important for beginner ELL students both to support comprehension

and to avoid frustration. Avoiding frustration will promote a more positive attitude towards reading. When a student sounds out a word, it helps to make sense of the word if they already know its meaning and are able to understand the sentence. Therefore, vocabulary needs to be taught explicitly as a part of the daily curriculum to help ELLs comprehend academic texts.

5. *Reading comprehension strategies*: Comprehension is an active process that requires a repertoire of strategies. These strategies help students engage with the text and monitor their comprehension. Brown (2008) notes that secondary students need a wide variety of strategies in order to tackle the complex reading required of them to succeed in and out of school. Students need to be taught explicitly how, why, and when to use these strategies. Pearson and Gallagher's Gradual Release of Responsibility Model (1983) for adolescence provides guidance with teaching strategies. Teachers explicitly describe the strategies they use while reading and demonstrate them to the students during read-aloud. Students model these strategies and later adapt them to suit their individual needs. This shifts the focus of responsibility from the teacher to the learner to help them adapt and internalize the strategies.

6. *Scaffolds before, during, and after reading*: "Scaffold" is the term used for teacher support for a learner through dialog, questioning, conversation, and modeling. A number of such reading strategies such as questioning, discussion, and writing are recommended for struggling readers. Roehler and Cantlon (1997) identified five types of scaffolding: (a) offering explanations, (b) inviting student participation, (c) verifying and clarifying student understandings, (d) modeling of desired behaviors, and (e) inviting students to contribute clues for reasoning through an issue or problem. Additionally, these reading strategies/ scaffolding activities should also be used in the content-area classroom for them to be effective.

7. *Knowledge about the learner*: Diagnostic assessment is necessary to determine the strengths and weaknesses of the students to provide effective instruction. Knowledge regarding the history of students' reading difficulties would help the teacher focus more on these problematic areas. Similarly, knowledge regarding the cultural and linguistic background of the students assists the teacher in selecting reading material for the class in accordance with their interests, cultural sensitivity, and acknowledgement of their cultural beliefs and values.

COMPETENCY 7.0   UNDERSTAND READING INSTRUCTION AND ASSESSMENT FOR ENGLISH LANGUAGE LEARNERS

Skill 7.1   Understands the relationship and transfer of existing first-language reading skills to the second language and demonstrates knowledge of key factors that affect second-language reading development

Literacy development is affected not only by the individual students' educational background but also by the educational background of their families. With respect to individual ESOL students, it is paramount to note that some adolescent ELLs need to learn to read for the first time, while others are building second or third language literacy with already developed first language literacy (Peregoy & Boyle, 2000). Therefore, those students who lack literacy skills in their first language have inadequate skills to succeed in school and need basic as well as advanced literacy development.

Literacy requires a number of cognitive and metacognitive skills that students can transfer from their first language to their second or third language. In addition, students literate in their first language have more funds of knowledge or prior knowledge to comprehend the content of the text. The educational background of English language learners can give them the advantage of transferring their first language literacy skills to their second language and using their prior literacy knowledge to understand information in the new language. With respect to writing, research has shown that students who lacked first language literacy strategies displayed a similar lack of strategies for writing in their second language. Mohan and Lo (1985) suggest that students who have not developed good strategies in their first language would not have developed strategies to transfer to their second language. Similarly, transfer of knowledge from L1 literacy helps students brainstorm information to help them write about the topic at hand.

Furthermore, family literacy of the English language learners also has an impact on their literacy development. The educational level of the parents has a great influence on literacy development. Similarly, the learner's family's attitude towards education and the value they give to success in school can have an impact on language development. Parents with positive attitudes towards education are more involved in school activities and keep track of their child's progress. They attend parent-teacher conferences and are a part of the learning process.

In addition, parents who read books to children from an early age and have books, newspapers, magazines and other reading materials available at home facilitate their children's literacy development. These families spend time reading together and encourage critical thinking and high-order skills in their children. These positive attributes help students develop skills that are critical for success in school.

Teachers need to be perceptive and draw upon the child's home language and literacy experiences so that the child is better served when beginning literacy instruction.

Encouraging home involvement in the literacy process is critical. Family members are modeling reading and writing every time they read the newspaper or magazine, make a shopping list, note an appointment on a calendar, discuss their work schedule, or question the newest charges on the phone bill. Many children come from societies where oral storytelling traditions provide excellent foundations for literacy development.

If feasible, students should first learn to read in their native language and later in the second language. When instruction is begun in English, many ESOL practitioners believe that the same methods used to teach the native speaker will be beneficial to the ELL because similar literacy patterns will probably emerge. Older learners may be able to progress more rapidly in reading and writing because they use their worldly experiences to help them with comprehension and communication.

National reading authorities recommend phonemic awareness, phonics, reading fluency, and comprehension as keys to success in achieving literacy. All these elements should be considered in meaningful contexts rather than in isolation. Instruction in specific strategies (e.g., summarizing, retelling, and answering questions) will help the ELLs to become independent readers and writers.

Peregoy & Boyle (2008) state that literacy scaffolding helps ELLs with reading and writing at a level that would otherwise be impossible for them. Scaffolding allows ELLs to work at their level in both reading and writing, and at the same time, challenges them to reach their next level of development. To help students achieve their next level, several criteria are suggested:

- Use of functional, meaningful communication found in whole texts
- Use of language and discourse patterns that repeat themselves and are predictable
- A model (from teacher or peers) for understanding and producing written language patterns
- Support of students at a level Krashen refers to as $i + 1$ (or language that is just beyond students' current level causing them to 'reach' and grow).
- Discarding supports when the student no longer needs them.

Keeping in mind the scaffolding theory, teachers may use the first language in instruction—when they know it. This is not always possible. In many states, there are hundreds of language communities represented in the statewide school system. A danger of this method is that some students become dependent on instruction in their first language and are reluctant to utilize their knowledge of the second language. However, for most children, instruction in their first language has numerous advantages. First, language instruction lowers the affective filter by reducing tension, anxiety, and even fear, thus permitting faster learning; it can clarify misunderstandings in the second language content; and it can be used to explain how the two languages differ or are the same with respect to different types of reading texts or writing tasks.

Skill 7.2   Demonstrates knowledge of sheltered strategies and various reading intervention approaches for addressing the specific reading needs of English language learners

When planning pre-reading and intermediate reading intervention, the teacher may use the following intervention strategies:

WORD ANALYSIS
(e.g., concepts about print; phonemic and morphemic awareness; vocabulary and concept development; decoding; word recognition, including structural analysis, recognition of cognates, and other word identification strategies)

Sound-symbol correspondence is more difficult in English than some languages because each letter can make a variety of sounds. Recognition of repeating patterns helps students develop decoding skills. Consonant blends such as /ch/, /ph/ and /sh/ are readily recognizable and make the same sound with consistency. Earliest beginners can scan for those language patterns and recognize the sounds they make.

Recognition of **cognates** and false cognates is very helpful in decoding and can be directly taught. Many words are identical in both languages, with the only difference being pronunciation. Fortunately for students, as they develop skills in content areas such as math and science, the incidence of these cognates increases. Some examples of English-Spanish cognates are:

- Hotel
- Radio
- Religion
- Eclipse
- Editor

Many words are the same in English and Spanish, with the addition of a changed **vowel at the end of the word**. Here are some examples:

- Cost: costo
- Cause: causa
- Minute: minuto
- Medicine: medicina
- List: lista
- Map: mapa

Here are some of the common **false cognates** between English and Spanish:

- Libreria – It's not a library, but a bookstore.
- Embarazada – It doesn't mean embarrassed, but pregnant.
- Asistir – It doesn't mean to assist, but to attend or be present.

FLUENCY

(e.g., reading aloud with appropriate pacing, intonation, and expression; applying word recognition skills)

The teacher may utilize a variety of strategies to increase fluency, such as the following:

- Duet reading, where the student reads aloud simultaneously with the teacher helps the student develop proper intonation and pacing.
- Listen/repeat exercises, including short dialogues between teacher and student or student and student.
- Choral reading, where the entire class reads aloud together, starting and stopping and emphasizing at the same points
- Singing, or language that is sung, is difficult to forget. Simple common expressions set to familiar tunes such as "Happy birthday," or "Are You Sleeping?" can be quickly invented and help develop fluency.

SYSTEMATIC VOCABULARY DEVELOPMENT

(e.g., applying word recognition skills, using content-related vocabulary, recognizing multiple-meaning words, applying knowledge of text connectors, recognizing common abbreviations, and using a dictionary, using morphemes and context to understand unknown words)

The teacher understands that second language acquisition is a jigsaw process, in which a student acquires comprehension of a word, a phrase, or a concept in ways that may seem random and unmanageable. The imposition of systematic vocabulary development, whether content-related or grouping by phonics or grammatical structures, relieves anxiety and lowers the affective filter.

- Armed with recognizable text connectors (and, but, because, until, unless, etc.), a student has a method to help break down text into manageable segments.
- Use of the dictionary, with its many abbreviations (*v.t., n.,* pronunciation symbols, etc.) empowers the student to research new words with confidence.
- Recognizing common morphemes such as the prefix *un-* can help decode un-familiar and un-known words (without becoming un-happy).

READING COMPREHENSION

(e.g., features, structures, and rhetorical devices of different types of texts; comprehension and analysis of grade-level-appropriate texts; identifying fact and opinion; identifying cause and effect; using a text to draw conclusions and make inferences; describing relationships between a text and one's own experience; evaluating an author's credibility)

The teacher can use a variety of scaffolding techniques to help students recognize features of different types of texts. For instance:

- Students can be taught key words to help differentiate fact from opinion (I believe; it seems to me...);
- Students can draw arrows between listed events from the text to determine what was a cause and what was an effect;
- Students can be directly taught to make inferences (The old woman was crying. What does that tell us?);
- Students can make text-to-self connections (Have you ever_____?); and
- Students can evaluate credibility (Is the wolf a reliable narrator? Why or why not?).

LITERARY RESPONSE AND ANALYSIS
(e.g., narrative analysis of grade-level-appropriate texts, structural features of literature, literary criticism)

There are many levels of literary response and analysis the teacher can provide for even beginning ELs to use. Students can develop their own rating systems for books and movies, breaking down the text into elements that they wish to evaluate: setting, plot, characters, etc. and then applying a five-star or ten-star system to arrive at an overall evaluation.

- Students can illustrate a story to demonstrate interpretive or reflective response to it.
- Students can compare book and movie versions of the same story. Students can develop their own versions of the same story with graphic art or poetry.
- Students can use graphics to retell a story. Graphics force the student to decide which story elements are important enough to include in the blank cartoon panels provided.

Some key elements of sheltered instruction are the following:

ACCESS ENGLISH LEARNERS' PRIOR KNOWLEDGE
(e.g., concepts, vocabulary related to a lesson, including using an additive cultural approach)

 Schemata need to be activated to draw upon the previous knowledge and learning of the ELL, especially when the ELL may not have had experiences like those of the mainstream culture. The use of graphics to encourage pre-reading thought about a topic (e.g., brainstorming, web maps, and organizational charts) activates this knowledge and shows how information is organized in the students' minds. Shumm (2006) states that research has shown:

- More prior knowledge permits a reader to understand and remember more of new materials (Brown, Bransford, Ferrara, & Campione, 1983).
- Prior knowledge must be activated to improve comprehension (Bransford & Johnson, 1972).

- Failure to activate prior knowledge is one cause of poor readers (Paris & Lindauer, 1976).
- Good readers accept new information if they are convinced by an author's arguments. Likewise, they may reject ideas when they conflict with a reader's prior knowledge (Pressley, 2000).

CONTEXTUALIZE A LESSON'S KEY CONCEPTS AND LANGUAGE
(e.g., using materials, resources, and activities to support contextualization)

Teachers need to analyze the lesson's key concepts and then contextualize them in a way so that all students understand what the lesson is about. In a lesson on butterflies, for example, the teacher can bring in butterflies (or simply a caterpillar that is ready to change into a chrysalis) at different stages of development. Different resources such as realia, posters, books, and films can be used as resource materials for initiating instruction and activating background knowledge. All these resources, as well as classroom observations, can then be used in different learning experiments, projects, and writing activities.

MODIFY AND AUGMENT STATE-ADOPTED CONTENT-AREA TEXTBOOK(S) TO ADDRESS ENGLISH LEARNERS' LANGUAGE NEEDS, INCLUDING THE INCORPORATION OF PRIMARY-LANGUAGE RESOURCES
Scaffolding ELL's language needs starts with a careful analysis of the state-standards for the grade level. Differentiated instruction is permitted when the ELL does not have grade-level proficiency in the language. Planning of instruction should answer the questions of: **What** content will be taught, **Who** the student is (language and cultural background of the student), **How** (strategies and materials), and **How well** (performance goals and assessment methods). When available, resource materials in a student's first language are an acceptable scaffolding technique.

DEMONSTRATE OR MODEL LEARNING TASKS
Instructors can bring in papers, projects, mind maps, and posters from previous classes to demonstrate what is expected in a finished project. Modeling a learning task is simply illustrating whatever point or skill is expected from the learners. In Total Physical Response, a teacher would ask students to stand up (teacher stands) or sit down (teacher sits). As instructions become more complicated, the teacher illustrates (or has a student do so) the expected action.

USE QUESTIONS TO PROMOTE CRITICAL-THINKING SKILLS
(e.g., analytical and interpretive questions)

Questions are one of the most frequently used instructional and scaffolding strategies. Teachers should avoid rhetorical questions as many students find them silly or purposeless. Questions which call upon students to analyze (e.g. What are the essential elements of…?, How would you classify …?, What evidence do you find …?) or interpret a topic (e.g. How would you prioritize the facts …?, Would it be better if…?,

Based upon what you know, how would you explain...?) are questions which call upon higher level think skills and contribute to learning.

PROVIDE ENGLISH LEARNERS WITH EXPLICIT INSTRUCTION IN METACOGNITIVE AND COGNITIVE STRATEGIES
(e.g., debriefing, using text features, using self-evaluation and reflection)

Metacognitive Strategies
The ESOL teacher is responsible for helping students become aware of their own individual learning strategies. Successful students often constantly improve those strategies and add to them. Each student should have his/her own "tool-box" of skills for planning, managing, and evaluating the language-learning process.

- **Centering your learning:** Review a key concept or principle and link it to already existing knowledge, make a firm decision to pay attention to the general concept, ignore input that is distracting, and learn skills in the proper order.
- **Arranging and planning your learning:** The following strategies help the learner maximize the learning experience: take the time to understand how a language is learned; create optimal learning conditions, i.e., regulate noise, lighting and temperature; obtain the appropriate books, etc.; and set reasonable long-term and short-term goals.
- **Evaluate your learning:** The following strategies help learners assess their learning achievements: keep track of errors that prevent further progress and keep track of progress, e.g., reading faster now than the previous month.

Cognitive Strategies
Cognitive strategies are vital to second language acquisition; their most salient feature is the manipulation of the second language. The following are the most basic strategies: "Practicing", "Receiving and Sending Messages", "Analyzing and Reasoning", and "Creating Structure for Input and Output," which can be remembered by the acronym, "PRAC."

- **Practicing:** The following strategies promote the learner's grasp of the language: practice constant repetition, make attempts to imitate a native speaker's accent, concentrate on sounds, and practice in a realistic setting.
- **Receiving and sending messages:** These strategies help the learner quickly locate salient points and then interpret the meaning: skim through information to determine "need to know" vs. "nice to know," use available resources (print and non-print) to interpret messages.
- **Analyzing and reasoning:** Use general rules to understand the meaning and then work into specifics, and break down unfamiliar expressions into parts.
- **Creating structure for input and output:** Choose a format for taking meaningful notes, practice summarizing long passages, and use highlighters as a way to focus on main ideas or important specific details.

DEVELOP ENGLISH LEARNERS' ACADEMIC LANGUAGE
(e.g., frontloading vocabulary)

See 6.4

PROVIDE CLEAR MODELS OF EXPECTED PERFORMANCE OUTCOMES
Using rubrics to explain what is expected is an excellent way to clarify any misconceptions students may have about the assignment. Another excellent method is to show papers or projects from previous classes.

TRANSFORM TEXT FROM ONE GENRE TO ANOTHER GENRE
Examples are: Students can be asked to take a text and create a skit out of it. Skits could be changed into a short story.

PROVIDE OPPORTUNITIES FOR ENGLISH LEARNERS TO ENGAGE IN ANALYSIS AND INTERPRETATION OF TEXT, BOTH ORAL AND WRITTEN
Students can analyze and interpret texts with graphic organizers, journals, note-taking, and summaries. For beginners, teachers can provide graphics with sample entries filled in and as the students become more familiar with them, provide fewer and fewer clues.

Oral discourse may also be analyzed. Ask students how they felt about a dialogue. How would people in their culture respond during a similar situation? What was the main idea the speaker was making? Why do you believe or disbelieve this speaker?

PROVIDE ENGLISH LEARNERS WITH OPPORTUNITIES TO LEARN AND USE FORMS OF ENGLISH LANGUAGE NECESSARY TO EXPRESS CONTENT-SPECIFIC ACADEMIC LANGUAGE FUNCTIONS
(e.g., analyzing, comparing, persuading, citing evidence, making hypotheses)

See 6.4

PROVIDE AUTHENTIC OPPORTUNITIES FOR ENGLISH LEARNERS TO USE THE ENGLISH LANGUAGE FOR CONTENT-RELATED COMMUNICATIVE PURPOSES WITH BOTH NATIVE AND NONNATIVE SPEAKERS OF ENGLISH

See 6.4

In addition to research projects, students will enjoy working on skits, role plays, drama, and singing. Games such as Pictionary and charades can be adapted to content for encouraging vocabulary learning.

ASSESS ATTAINMENT OF LESSON CONTENT USING MULTIPLE MODALITIES
(e.g., verbal, nonverbal)

For mini-assessments of lessons, the teacher can ask the students to give a "thumbs up" or "thumbs down" to questions about content. Teachers can use observation to determine if students understand and are progressing or if they did not and need help. These techniques are useful with beginners.

For more advanced learners, verbal assessment may be more appropriate. Students can be evaluated on rubrics, written work, answering structured and unstructured questions, free recall, completing graphic illustrations of text, and word associations. Formal assessments include end of chapter tests and teacher-made tests.

PROVIDE COMPREHENSIBLE AND MEANINGFUL CORRECTIVE AND POSITIVE FEEDBACK TO ENGLISH LEARNERS
Feedback is valuable only if the student understands it. Teachers can illustrate the correct response, "go over the test" providing the correct answers and illustrating the most common errors, and even using mime or translators if necessary.

Skill 7.3   Selects materials and implements strategies that support English language learners' achievement of reading standards (WIDA ELD, 2011 Massachusetts Curriculum Framework for English Language Arts and Literacy).

See 5.3 for background on WIDA and the Massachusetts curriculum frameworks.

The Massachusetts standards draw on both literary and informational reading as essential parts of all students' literacy development. Reading texts of varying types should be part of an integrated program that helps students develop reading, writing, speaking, and listening skills. Further, instructional strategies should attempt to build on ELL students' existing literacy skills. Students with strong reading skills in their home language are often able to transfer reading strategies (e.g., decoding, the use of context clues for meaning, etc.) to English.

Reading instruction should include strategies for research and analysis of potential sources of information, particularly when using online research. Direct instruction progressing to greater independence is particularly important for ELL students as they increasingly read for content-area knowledge. Use of scaffolding techniques is an essential part of this progression.

Massachusetts standards emphasize a 'staircase' of reading complexity as students build towards college and career readiness. As students work with increasingly sophisticated texts, they are expected to draw increasingly complex conclusions, make deeper and more extensive connections between ideas, recognize evidence, and become able to respond to ambiguous meanings.

WIDA defines six levels of language proficiency: Entering, Emerging, Developing, Expanding, Bridging, and Reaching. At the final level, Reaching, language development is sufficient for students to read grade level texts in different content areas independently. In designing instruction for earlier levels, WIDA defines three types of support that ESOL teachers should consider.

- Sensory supports - Includes things like illustrations, photos, realia, and videos
- Graphic supports - Includes charts, graphs, timelines
- Interactive supports - Includes partner or group work, work with a mentor, and even support in L1

WIDA emphasizes as well that English Language Development should occur across the content areas. ESOL teachers should use the WIDA supports and levels as guides for instruction and support of ELL students. Instructional strategies using these supports in reading may include timelines to help clarify the plot of a novel, graphic organizers to help with annotation of texts, or literature circles to help students build understanding together.

Additional information on instruction can be found in 7.2

Skill 7.4   Applies understanding of characteristics of various types of formal and informal reading assessments and their advantages and limitations for use with English language learners

Formal reading assessments are used for state and district accountability purposes. They usually include multiple-choice questions. Some utilize the **cloze or maze** formats, where a word or words are omitted and a choice of three or four words are given to fill-in the missing content.

Examples are:

- **Test of Reading Comprehension:** 30-minute standardized test that can be administered by teacher or reading specialists individually or to a group of students from ages 7-17. The test has 8 sub-tests and evaluates general vocabulary, syntactic similarities, paragraph reading, and sentence sequencing. The end result is a Reading Comprehension Quotient. The TORC-3 gives information about a student's strengths and weaknesses in each of the comprehension components it tests.

- **Woodcock-Johnson III Diagnostic Reading Battery:** An individually administered measure used to diagnose a student student's strengths and weaknesses for needed areas of instruction. Used with students in K-16.9.

- **Gates-MacGinitie Reading Tests (GMRT):** Norm-referenced, group-administered instrument that has been scientifically researched and is effective in screening K-12 students and adults. Test identifies instructional needs and generates a **lexile score.** A lexile score is a calculation of the level of comprehension a student will have with a text. The GMRT estimates that a student will understand 75% of the lexile score, and using software, generates a list of texts based on this score.

- **Degrees of Reading Power (DRP):** A standardized test that uses maze (or modified cloze). Students are given passages with missing words and are required to supply missing word from a multiple-choice selection. Tests for Grades 1-12 are available. DRP scores can be matched with books of appropriate reading levels.

Informal reading assessments include:

- **Informal Reading Inventories (IRIs):** Graded reading passages and comprehension questions
    - may include both narrative and expository passages
    - may include narrative and expository retelling checklists
    - may incorporate prior knowledge questions for each passage
    - purposes:
        - used to gauge oral reading comprehension
        - assess silent reading comprehension
        - passages read aloud by a test administrator to test listening comprehension

- **Regular student observations:** Used to observe and evaluate student comprehension performance

- **Teacher-made and textbook assessments**

(Adapted from Medina & Pilonieta in Schumm, 2006)

Skill 7.5   Analyzes and apply formal and informal assessment data; recognizes bias and differentiates between normed reading assessments for native speakers of English and normed assessments for English language learners

As a teacher of English Language Learners, it is important to advocate for the use of appropriate assessment tools for students. Commonly used norm-referenced tests can be problematic when used with ELL students because of the bias inherent within them.

Norm-referenced tests seek to determine whether a test-taker performed better or worse than an 'average' student. The performance of the hypothetical 'average' student is determined by analyzing the performance on the test of a sampling of students of the same age and grade. In the development of the norm-referenced tests and the process of norming the tests themselves, test creators select their norm group from amongst the target population for the test. Because they are generally not from the intended population for the test, ELL students (and even sub-groups of American students) taking a norm-referenced test in the United States will often be at a disadvantage.

For example, even an ELL student with strong English reading skills may have great difficulty answering a series of reading comprehension questions related to a passage dealing with the US government. The student may be, for example, unfamiliar with references to Congress or election campaigns that other students would take for granted. The unfamiliar terminology and context could make it impossible for the ELL student to answer questions correctly that would otherwise be at her/his reading level.

Tests like the Peabody Picture Vocabulary test and the Woodcock-Muñoz Language Survey are examples of norm-referenced assessment tools. The Peabody test assesses a student's receptive vocabulary and potential scholastic aptitude but is not intended for students whose first language is not English. Because the images used in the test are representations of 'mainstream' culture, any student not from the dominant/majority cultural group may perform below his/her level because of cultural background - not ability.

Similarly, the Woodcock-Muñoz Language Survey is designed to be a measure of overall proficiency in reading, writing, speaking, and listening. However, it is normed for American students from Hispanic backgrounds. Therefore, it would be a useful assessment for some ELL students but not for others.

The most essential thing to remember about norm-referenced tests is their validity. As noted by Kim and Zabelina (2015), "[i]f the cultural or linguistic backgrounds of the individuals being tested are not adequately represented in the norming group, the validity and reliability of the test are questionable (Padilla and Borsato, 2008)."

Validity and reliability take on great importance if the purpose of testing is to determine placement in special programs, evaluation for potential learning disabilities, or planning for interventions. ESOL teachers play an invaluable role not only in testing, but in ensuring that appropriate tools are used. Translation of a norm-referenced test does not remove potential bias.

Skill 7.6   Develops and utilizes guidelines for selecting and administering various types of reading assessments; interprets and uses assessment information, including differentiation between normal variation in performance and performance that may indicate possible reading or learning disabilities

The Massachusetts Department of Education (MA DOE) tests students in the English language each year to comply with the mandates of the Every Student Succeeds Act (ESSA). Students are tested in the four language skill areas: speaking, listening, reading, and writing. Detailed information of guidance and classification of Limited English Proficiency (LEP) students is available at http://www.doe.mass.edu/mcas/access/.

DISABILITIES

Students with disabilities are guaranteed an education under Public Law 94-142 of 1975. A key feature of the law is the requirement of an individualized education program (IEP) for any student receiving special funds for special education. However, the classification of many ELLs or the "dumping" of ELLs in special education classes has been of concern to many educators. Those testing ELLs for placement in different classes must be certain that the tests used are both reliable and valid. Reliability can be established using multiple assessment measures, objective tests, multiple raters, and clearly specified scoring criteria (Valdez-Pierce, 2003). For a test to be valid, it must first be reliable (Goh, 2004).

Learning disabilities refer to physical, emotional, cognitive, or social components, which severely limit what is considered "normal" functioning behavior. Children who fall into this category can be one or more of the following: emotionally challenged, hearing-, vision-, or speech-impaired or learning disabled.

See Skill 3.6 for more information on students with possible learning disabilities.
See Skill 7.4 and 7.5 for more information about reading assessments.

Skill 7.7   Understands the impact on English language reading literacy of the similarities and differences between first language(s) and the English language (e.g. directionality, orthographic depth, morphology, sentence structure, discourse structure, etc.)

Teachers can use the similarities and differences of the different languages to teach learning strategies. For example, the adjective comes before the noun in English but in Spanish it comes after the noun. A text written in English is expected to have a main idea and several supporting details to explain or support it. Other languages are more descriptive and depend on the beauty of the language to convey the writer's meaning. By using the concept of cognates, both true and false, teachers can improve vocabulary development.

See 2.6

Additionally, recent research has shown that, for English language learners, phonological awareness in the native language (L1) predicts successful literacy acquisition in both L1 and a second language (L2). In other words, phonological awareness skills developed in L1 transfer to L2 and facilitate L2 literacy development. Phonological awareness skills are known to develop in a predictable pattern, which is the same from one language to another (i.e., from larger to smaller units of sound - from word to syllable to onset-rime to phoneme). Phonological awareness skills developed in one language can transfer to another language.

In a sense, people learn to read only once. If they can read in their native language, they will apply the same cognitive processes of decoding text to make meaning. Learning to read in a new language involves the same skills but with (potentially) a new alphabet, new sounds, and new vocabulary. It is important for ELLs to increase their vocabulary and knowledge of the structure of English, their second language. By building on what the ELL already knows about literacy, language, and experiences in his or her native language, teachers will be able to improve the reading level of the ELL in English. For this reason, it is ideal to evaluate the ELL in his or her first, native, or heritage language to initiate the best reading instruction in English.

For these transitional readers, explanations in the L1 will be beneficial because they will be able to compare and contrast new information with information about their L1.

Sometimes ELLs entering the U.S. school system have not had schooling in their L1 or the opportunity to learn to read in the L1. In this case, it may be necessary to begin reading instruction in English. These students will not have the benefit of academic instruction in reading and will need to begin reading instruction like that of beginning native speakers. However, teachers should bear in mind that their native language may or may not contain linguistic features that are similar to the English language. Dulay, Burt, & Krashen (1982 in Quiocho & Ulanoff, 2009) state that a knowledge of how young native speakers construct the rules and structure of English will benefit teachers more in understanding ELLs' difficulties with the language than contrastive linguistics.

Teaching initial literacy should focus on concepts about print (Clay, 1983 in Quiocho & Ulanoff, 2009), phonemic awareness, and phonics (Chall, 1983 in Quiocho & Ulanoff, 2009). Zainuddin et al (2007) claims that ELLs who come from different backgrounds and varying literacy experiences may benefit from instruction that emphasizes skill building at the word and sentence levels as well as comprehension of different types of reading materials. Texts, such as predictable stories, poems, public signs, advertisement clips, and songs, are all helpful in exploring the purpose and nature of reading.

COMPETENCY 8.0   WRITING INSTRUCTION AND ASSESSMENT FOR
                  ENGLISH LANGUAGE LEARNERS

Skill 8.1   **Demonstrates knowledge of approaches, practices, and strategies
             used to promote English language learners' writing development and
             writing skills (e.g., Language Experience Approach, dialogue
             journals); selects purposeful writing activities appropriate for a
             range of ages, reading abilities, and English proficiency levels**

Writing in a new language involves a great deal of risk-taking as errors in spelling, word
choice, and syntax are inevitable. While some ELL students may not be concerned
about this, others may feel reluctance, embarrassment, or frustration as they build
writing skills in English. It is therefore important to use methods that encourage students
to see learning to write as a developmental process towards self-expression.

Correcting every error in a writing sample can discourage participation and cause
students to shut down to learning. Keeping track of errors that students repeat allows
the teacher to reteach specific skills or address specific needs, either with a group of
students who all need to master that skill, or individually for a student who has not yet
mastered a skill with others in the class.

Using the Language Experience Approach to introduce children into the art of writing.
Involves the following steps:

- Provide an experience
- Talk about the experience
- Record the dictation
- Read the text

Sometimes, children are reluctant to 'write' their own stories later because their writing
is not a "perfect" model as the teacher's was. However, this may be overcome if the
teacher alternates with the children when writing the stories.

There are many ways to get students to practice writing without grading the writing:
learning logs, journals, and quick-writes. Teachers can devise prompts that allow the
ELLs to reflect on their learning and class discussions or explore new ideas. They may
rewrite complex ideas in their own words and compare, evaluate, critique, or interpret.
At the end of the period, students may quickly write what they learned during the class.
ELLs can write dialogues either in pairs or individually. They can try using vocabulary
words from their text in comprehensible paragraphs. Another idea is to write from the
perspective of another person, place or thing (Adapted from Zwiers, 2007).

Some English language learners may be fairly sophisticated in their manipulation of
language. However, their language may value other aspects of writing that are very
different from the U.S. idea of a sentence (s-v-o) or a paragraph (the topic sentence and
its supporting details). In essays, the idea of developing sentences of varying lengths

and structures, and connecting them through the skillful use of connectors must be taught through skillful modeling and examples. Supplying ample resources, such as dictionaries and lists of vocabulary conventions or connectors, will be invaluable to ELLs in upper levels.

Also, students who are learning to write need to read as much as possible of the genre that they are going to be writing about. As writing takes place in multiple genres (narrative prose, poetry, mathematical proofs, historical accounts, case studies, essays, emails, and letters), students should be exposed to each particular type of writing—its organization, the thinking behind the form, the grammar, and the correct terms used in each genre—so that they are able to replicate the appropriate phrases and syntax in their writing. As nonmainstream students will not have had as much exposure to the models as native speakers, it is necessary to point out the conventions of each genre as it is studied in the classroom.

To improve children's writing, the following activities may be used:

- **Frontloading vocabulary and language functions:** Frontloading vocabulary and language function is simply pre-teaching the vocabulary and language functions that might be unfamiliar to the students during a content lesson or reading session. The goal is to increase reading comprehension.
- **Interactive journals:** Any type of journal that requires the student to write about classroom content or comment on their feelings. Journals are a low-stakes method of keeping the teacher and the student engaged in a personal dialogue.
- **Shared reading:** In this type of reading exercise, students are given their own copy of a text to follow along in while the teacher reads to them. Unrau (2008) points out some of the benefits of shared reading:
  - demonstrates the natural rhythm and beauty of the language
  - builds bridges between texts and students' lives
  - provides practice in strategies that make a text comprehensible
  - models fluent reading
  - helps students build knowledge of texts and their world
- **Learning logs:** Records of what students have learned or what they are struggling to understand. Students can be asked to summarize what they have learned from a text. Teachers give daily feedback of what is expected in a summary. Teachers and students can use learning logs to negotiate a text's meaning.
- **Process writing:** Unrau (2008) lists 5 stages of process writing:
  - Pre-writing: Planning by brainstorming, researching, note taking, listing, clustering, organizing
  - Drafting: Selecting a format, writing drafts, deciding on an audience
  - Revising: Review or reflect on earlier drafts by rethinking, adding, dropping, rearranging, rewriting
  - Proofreading: Prepare for publication by polishing, correcting spelling, punctuation, and grammatical problems

- o Publishing: Share with an audience by reading, displaying, anthologizing, submitting for publication
- **Graphic organizers:** Unrau (2008) enumerates graphic organizers as:
  - o Clusters are also known as mind-mapping, semantic mapping, mindscaping, and webbing. A simpler and less-structured form than the formal outline.
  - o Characteristics outliner: similar to a cluster but more structured. Students draw an ellipse or circle in the center and then place arrows or lines between the term and its characteristics.
  - o Process organizer or Flowchart: Used to organize each step in a process
  - o Cause-Effect Organizer: Causes are connected to their effect by an arrow or line
  - o Problem-Solution-Evaluation Organizer: Appropriately labeled boxes are filled in with the corresponding information and connected by lines or arrows
  - o Compare/Contrast Organizer: A simple Venn diagram or three columns can be used to show the similarities and differences. The overlapping circles (or center column) are used to illustrate items that are the same in each concept.
- **Prereading activities:** Those activities which prepare the student for reading (Schumm, 2006):
  - o Activating or building background knowledge
  - o Making predictions
  - o Word maps
  - o Previewing
  - o Picture Walk (previewing the story using the illustrations)
  - o Going beyond the printed page (e.g. using globes, films, maps, simulation games, role playing, and field experiences)
  - o Setting the Mood

When planning meaningful and purposeful literacy activities teachers of very young children may set up activities for:

- Using literacy materials in dramatic play centers
- Making posters about favorite books
- Labeling classroom items
- Writing morning messages
- Recording questions and information on charts
- Writing notes to parents
- Reading and writing letters to pen pals
- Reading and writing charts and maps

For older ELLs, similar non-threatening activities may be used to provide needed practice. O'Malley and Pierce (1996) recommend scaffolding techniques to reduce the language demands on ELLs by:

- **Exhibits or projects:** ELLs can be involved in presenting projects or demonstrations that illustrate the concepts or procedures being tested.
- **Visual displays:** ELLs can use graphic organizers (e.g. diagrams or semantic maps) to illustrate their understanding of vocabulary and concepts.
- **Organized lists:** ELLs can present lists of concepts or terms and demonstrate understanding by organizing or sequencing them.
- **Tables or graphs:** ELLs can complete or construct and label tables and graphs to demonstrate their understanding of how data is organized and interpreted
- **Short answers:** ELLs can give short answers or explanations that focus on the content area concepts.

ELLs need to be taught listening, speaking, reading, and writing skills in an integrated fashion which attempt to mimic real-life communicative incidents. The reading of a newspaper article may lead to an oral discussion or an oral discussion may lead to research on a topic and writing about it. Since much of the same vocabulary is being used in each of these communicative incidents, each act reinforces the other and students are able to engage in meaningful learning.

Skill 8.2 Demonstrates knowledge of the writing process and its applications in developing English language learners' writing proficiency

The writing process needs to be taught since many students come from backgrounds where writing a text or paper is very different from the U.S. conventions. They may be unfamiliar with the concept of planning a paper, doing research, organizing the material, developing a thesis statement, deciding on methods of development, and drafting, revising, and editing. To help ELLs, ESOL teachers can devise scoring rubrics that are appropriate to process writing and take into consideration both the process and the product.

Reid (1987) explains the **writing process** as steps to be followed:

Composing process
Prewriting
- Choosing a subject
- Identify your audience
- Decide on the purpose of the paper
Generating material
- Narrow the topic
- Collect ideas from personal experience, observation, interviews and/or research
- Generate details about the topic through brainstorming, clustering, outlining, listing, treeing, flow-charting
- Select the most pertinent ideas and facts for the paper
Organizing the material
- Write the main idea of the essay in thesis statement

- o Statement of opinion and/or
- o Statement of intent
- Develop paragraphs of support for thesis statement using:
  - o Topic sentences
  - o Supporting sentences which include:
    - Facts
    - Examples
    - Physical description
    - Personal experience
- Decide on methods of development to present your ideas
  - o Process
  - o Extended definition
  - o Comparison/contrast
  - o Classification
  - o Cause/effect

Drafting
- Begin writing
- Don't worry about errors
- Reread what you have written
  - o Reflect on what you have said
  - o Reconsider your ideas
  - o Evaluate your support

Once the paper is written, the students should begin the **revision process**. If this is presented as an integral part of the writing process, students will accept it more readily.

Revision process
Focus on the audience: make the essay memorable and interesting
Focus on the Purpose: make the main idea clear and strong
Editing:
- **Coherence:**
  - o all information should directly relate to the thesis statement
  - o the information in each paragraph should relate to the topic sentence
  - o use transitions between paragraphs
  - o use paragraph hooks (repetition of words that unites paragraphs)
- **Organization**
  - o The sequence of ideas must be clear
  - o The thesis statement should be narrow enough to support the author's ideas
- **Development**
  - o Clear, credible details
  - o Use of most important information
  - o Eliminate useless details or less important information
  - o Define terms where necessary

- Simplify information where possible
- **Mechanics:**
  - Use clear, correct, and precise vocabulary
  - Strive for varied and correct sentenced structure
  - Use some short, emphatic sentences
  - Revise grammar, especially verb tenses and subject/verb agreement
  - Spell check all work
  - Use correct punctuation

Teaching the writing process is a lengthy, cumulative effort across the curriculum and amplified over the years. The youngest children learn basic story structure, middle-graders develop paragraph writing skills, and high school students learn the intricacies of the academic essay. Many times, teachers will need to give mini-lessons in the writing process as it becomes necessary in the development of a particular child's writing efforts.

Skill 8.3   **Demonstrates knowledge of formal elements of written English and explicit, systematic strategies for developing students' knowledge and use of different text structures (e.g., narrative, expository, persuasive) and conventions of written Standard English (e.g., mechanics, syntax, grammar, spelling)**

As ELLs develop their language skills, the **four main functions of writing** should be introduced. The types of writing may be introduced formally in class, and followed up by appropriate exercises for practice. One good way to introduce the different types of exposition is through literature.

- **Narrative:** Used to tell fictional or nonfictional stories or accounts. May relate one incident or several.
- **Descriptive:** Provides information about a person, place, or thing. Descriptive writing may be fictional (as in a story) or nonfictional (as in newspaper stories or in describing a vacation spot).
- **Expository:** Explains and clarifies ideas. Frequently found in textbooks or user manuals.
- **Persuasive:** Used to convince the reader of something.

As ELLs develop formal written English, they will need instruction in the conventions of written Standard English. This instruction is best understood as a long-term process in which the writer is engaged throughout the school years.

Mechanics
Mechanics includes spelling, punctuation, capitalization, and grammar. Teaching of mechanics is one of the goals of Language Arts instruction, and as such, is taught systematically over the course of the school years.

Syntax (See Skills in Competency 1.0)

Syntax is best taught in context. As ELLs develop their reading skills, they are exposed to the syntax of English. They are introduced to the grammar of English, how words are put together to form sentences, the mechanics of English, word forms, and the different kinds of sentences (simple, compound, and compound-complex).

Grammar

One way to instruct ELLs is to use their own papers for mini-lessons on relevant points. Grammar begins to have more meaning as students become more fluent in the language. Direct instruction in grammar can be achieved through formal lessons for the entire class and through mini-lessons. In mini-lessons, the teacher may wish to focus on past tense verbs. Students can then look for examples of these forms in their journals or papers and correct them for practice.

Spelling

ELLs will need instruction to progress through the five stages of spelling:

- **Emergent spelling:** Students experiment with spelling/Teacher models adult writing/Encourage ELLs to talk about their writing/Encourage ELLs to notice environmental words and letters in names
- **Letter-name spelling:** Instruction in how to form letters/Encourage listening to pronunciation of words/Post a word wall/ teach consonants, consonant digraphs, and short vowels
- **Within-word spelling:** Teach long vowel spelling rules, vowel digraphs and r-controlled vowels/develop a visual sense of whether a word looks right or not/focus on silent letters in one-syllable words/ have students sort words according to patterns/use interactive writing
- **Syllables and affixes spelling:** Teach rules of syllabication and rules for inflectional endings/teach schwa sounds and spelling patterns/teach homophones, contractions, compound words, and possessives
- **Derivational relations:** Teach root words and derivational affixes/ make word clusters using root words/sort words into roots or language of origin

(Adapted from Tompkins: Language Arts: Patterns of Practice)

| Skill 8.4 | **Selects materials and implements strategies that support English language learners' achievement of writing standards (WIDA ELD, 2011 Massachusetts Curriculum Framework for English Language Arts and Literacy).** |

See 5.3 for background on WIDA and the Massachusetts curriculum frameworks.

Both WIDA and the Massachusetts standards emphasize students' ability to express ideas, defend claims, relate personal experiences, and demonstrate knowledge in increasingly complex ways. As writers, they must learn to tailor their work for different audiences and purposes while incorporating evidence from diverse sources to support a point of view. In the content areas, they must be able to communicate ideas in different disciplines using relevant vocabulary and terminology. As students progress in their writing skills, they must be able to produce clear written work in situations requiring a 'one draft' deadline, while also developing the habits and skills to revise, edit, and improve written work.

As in writing, WIDA defines six levels of language proficiency: Entering, Emerging, Developing, Expanding, Bridging, and Reaching. At the final level, Reaching, ELL students have developed sufficient skills to communicate ideas and information using different text types in different content areas independently. To support students at earlier levels of language development, WIDA defines three types of support that ESOL teachers should consider.

- Sensory supports - Includes things like illustrations, photos, realia, and videos
- Graphic supports - Includes charts, graphs, timelines
- Interactive supports - Includes partner or group work, work with a mentor, and even support in L1

Instructional strategies to support ELL students using these types of supports might include the use of graphic organizers, peer editing and review, or conferencing to help students refine their writing.

Additional information on instruction can be found in 8.1 and 8.2

Skill 8.5   Demonstrates knowledge of characteristics, selection, and administration of various types of formal and informal writing assessments and interpretation and use of assessment information, including differentiation between normal variation in writing development and performance that may indicate possible disabilities

Assessment is the gathering of information to make decisions. In education, assessments typically focus on student performance, progress, and behavior.

PURPOSES OF ASSESSMENT
In the education of students with exceptionalities, assessment is used to make decisions about the following:

- Screening and initial identification of children who may need services
- Diagnosis of specific learning disabilities
- Selection and evaluation of teaching strategies and programs
- Determination of the child's present level of performance in academics
- Classification and program placement
- Development of goals, objectives, and evaluation for the IEP
- Eligibility for a program
- Continuation of a program
- Effectiveness of instructional programs and strategies
- Effectiveness of behavioral interventions

- Accommodations needed for mandated or classroom testing

TYPES OF ASSESSMENT

Assessment types can be categorized in many ways, most commonly in terms of what is being assessed, how the assessment is constructed, or how it is to be used. It is important to understand these differences to be able to correctly interpret assessment results.

Formal vs. Informal

This variable focuses on how the assessment is constructed or scored. **Formal assessments** are assessments such as standardized tests or textbook quizzes; objective tests that include primarily questions for which there is only one correct, easily identifiable answer. These can be commercial or teacher made assessments, given to either groups or individuals. **Informal assessments** have less objective measures, and may include anecdotes or observations that may or may not be quantified, interviews, informal questioning during a task, etc. An example might be watching a student sort objects to see what attribute is most important to the student, or questioning a student to see what he or she found confusing about a task.

Standardized Tests

Formal tests are those that are administered to either groups or individuals in a specifically prescribed manner, with strict rules to keep procedures, scoring, and interpretation of results uniform in all cases. Such tests allow comparisons to be made across populations, ages, or grades, or over time, for a student. Intelligence tests and most diagnostic tests are standardized tests.

Norm-Referenced vs. Criterion Referenced

This distinction is based on the standard to which the student's performance is being compared. *Norm-referenced* tests establish a ranking and compare the student's performance to an established norm, usually for age or grade peers. What the student knows is of less importance than how similar the student's performance is to a specific group. *Norm-referenced* tests are, by definition, standardized. Examples include intelligence tests and many achievement tests. Norm referenced tests are often used in determining eligibility for special needs services.

Criterion Referenced tests measure a student's knowledge of specific content, usually related to classroom instruction. The student's performance is compared to a set of criteria or a pre-established standard of information the student is expected to know. On these tests, what the student knows is more important than how he or she compares to other students. Examples include math quizzes at the end of a chapter, or some state mandated tests of specific content. Criterion referenced tests are used to determine whether a student has mastered required skills.

Group vs. Individual Assessments

This variable simply refers to the manner of presentation, whether given to a group of students or on a one to one basis. Group assessments can be formal or informal, standardized or not, criterion or norm referenced. Individual assessments can be found in all these types as well.

Authentic Assessments

Authentic assessments are designed to be as close to real life as possible so they are relevant and meaningful to the student's life. They can be formal or informal, depending upon how they are constructed. An example of an authentic test item would be calculating a 20 percent sales discount on a popular clothing item after the student has studied math percentages.

Rating Scales and Checklists

Rating scales and checklists are self-appraisal instruments completed by the student or observation-based instruments completed by teacher or parents. The focus is frequently on behavior or affective areas such as interest, motivation, attention, or depression. These tests can be formal or informal and some can be standardized and norm-referenced. Examples of norm referenced tests of this type would be ADHD rating scales or the Behavior Assessment System for Children.

Screening, Diagnosis, and Placement

Intelligence tests have historically been considered good predictors of school performance. These tests are standardized and norm-referenced. Examples are the *Wechsler Intelligence Scale for Children-Fourth Edition (WISC-IV)*, Stanford-*Binet IV*, and *Kaufman Assessment Battery for Children-Second Edition (KACB-II)*. Some intelligence tests are designed for use with groups and are used for screening and identification purposes. The individual tests are used for classification and program placement. Since intelligence is a quality that is difficult to define precisely, results of intelligence tests should not be used to discriminate or define the person's potential. In many cases a significant discrepancy between scores helps to identify if an ELL has specific learning disabilities and/or language gaps. This information can also help show how a disability impacts performance in different areas of the curriculum.

There are many standardized achievement and educational skills tests, including state mandated testing, that are also used by school systems to help determine eligibility and placement.

MAKING INSTRUCTIONAL DECISIONS BASED ON ASSESSMENT RESULTS

Assessment is a key to providing differentiated and appropriate instruction to all students, and this is the area in which teachers will most often use assessment. Teachers should use a variety of assessment techniques to determine the existing knowledge, skills, and needs of each student. Depending on the age of the student and the subject matter under consideration, diagnosis of readiness may be accomplished through pretest, checklists, teacher observation, or student self-report. Diagnosis serves two related purposes—to identify those students who are not ready for the new instruction and to identify for each student what prerequisite knowledge is lacking.

Student assessment is an integral part of the teaching-learning process. Identifying student, teacher, or program weaknesses is only significant if the information so obtained is used to remedy those concerns. Lesson materials and lesson delivery must be evaluated to determine relevant prerequisite skills and abilities. The teacher must be able to determine whether a student's difficulties lie with the new information, with a lack of significant prior knowledge, or with a core learning disability that must be addressed with specialized lesson plans or accommodations. The goal of any diagnostic or assessment endeavor is improved learning. Thus, instruction is adapted to the needs of the learner based on assessment information.

USING ASSESSMENT INFORMATION TO MODIFY PLANS AND ADAPT INSTRUCTION

Assessment skills should be an integral part of teacher training. Teachers are able to use pre- and post-assessments of content areas to monitor student learning, analyze assessment data in terms of individualized support for students and instructional practice for teachers, and design lesson plans that have measurable outcomes and definitive learning standards. Assessment information should be used to provide performance-based criteria and academic expectations for all students in evaluating whether students have learned the expected skills and content of the subject area.

For example, in an Algebra I class, teachers can use assessment to see whether students have the prior knowledge to engage in the proposed lesson. If the teacher provides students with a pre-assessment on algebraic expression and ascertains whether the lesson plan should be modified to include a pre-algebraic expression lesson unit to refresh student understanding of the content area, then the teacher can create, if needed, quantifiable data to support the need of additional resources to support student learning. Once the teacher has taught the unit on algebraic expression, a post-assessment test can be used to test student learning, and a mastery examination can be used to test how well students understand and can apply the knowledge to the next unit of math content learning.

A teacher working with students with learning disabilities will use assessment information in additional ways. For example, if assessments show a student has extreme difficulty organizing information in the visual field, a teacher may modify a worksheet in math to present only one problem positioned in a large, squared off field with lots of white space around it, or even set up problems to be presented one problem at a time on 4x6 inch cards, etc.

By making inferences on teaching methods and gathering clues for student performance, teachers can use assessment data to inform and have an impact on instructional practices. By analyzing the various types of assessments, teachers can gather more definitive information on projected student academic performance. Instructional strategies for teachers would provide learning targets for student behavior, cognitive thinking skills, and processing skills that can be employed to diversify student learning opportunities.

APPROPRIATE WRITING ASSESSMENTS FOR ELLS WOULD BE:

Formal Assessments

- The National Assessment of Educational Progress (NAEP) (primary trait scoring)
- Test of English as a Foreign Language (TOEFL) Writing Test (holistic scoring)
- International English Language Test System (IELTS) (analytic scoring)
- Test of English for Educational Purposes (TEEP) (analytic scoring)
- Michigan Writing Assessment (analytic scoring)
- Essays with preestablished rubrics specific to the type of assignment
- Portfolios which include several pieces of writing

Informal Classroom Assessments

For teachers concerned with assessing writing in the regular classroom, Weigle (2002) offers the following criteria:

- Evaluate out-of-class writing as well as in-class writing.
- Evaluate more than one writing sample.
- Build authenticity and interactiveness into timed writing tasks.
- Use scoring instruments (e.g. rubrics) specific to the assignment and to the instructional focus of the class. Provide useful feedback to the students.

Pros of Writing Portfolio Assessment

Assessment is:

- **Integrative:** Combines curriculum and assessment which means evaluation is developmental, continuous, comprehensive, and fairer, representing program goals and reflecting writing progress over time, and genre
- **Valid:** Closely related to material taught and what students can do
- **Meaningful:** Students see portfolios as a record of work and progress
- **Motivating:** Presents a range of challenging writing experiences in different genres; students can see similarities and differences between assignments
- **Process-oriented:** Focuses on multi-drafting, feedback, collaboration, revision, etc.
- **Coherent:** Assignments build on each other rather than being isolated assignments
- **Flexible:** Teachers can adopt different selection criteria, evaluation methods and response practices over time, emphasizing different features of writing
- **Reflexive:** Students can evaluate their improvement and consider their weaknesses, which encourages greater responsibility and independence in writing
- **Formative:** Grading may be delayed until end of course allowing teacher to provide constructive feedback without the need for early, potentially discouraging, evaluation

Cons of Writing Portfolio Assessment

- **Logistic:** May produce considerable work for teachers
- **Design:** Grading criteria needs to be understood by all teachers
- **Reliability:** Need to ensure standardized grading by all raters across genres, portfolios and courses
- **Product variation:** Problem in fairly assigning a single grade to a collection varied in genre, complexity and quality, especially if assigned by a variety of teachers in different departments
- **Task variation:** Some tasks may be more interesting than others and therefore, elicit better writing
- **Authenticity:** Some students may get considerable outside help or plagiarize since portfolios are compiled without close teacher supervision.

(Adapted from Hyland, 2002)

Skill 8.6	Analyzes and applies formal and informal assessment data; recognizes bias and differentiates between normed reading assessments for native speakers of English and normed assessments for English language learners

As noted in 7.5, norm-referenced tests may not provide valid or reliable results when used with ELL students. Writing tests have their own potential pitfalls when used with English language learners because many elements of writing are influenced by culture.

American education usually emphasizes an essay structure that values a strong, clear argument supported by evidence. The author works hard to convince his/her audience that their point of view is correct. In other cultures, however, this style is not valued and may even be perceived as arrogant, especially the idea of a student presenting him/herself as an authority on a topic.

A norm-referenced writing assessment could, in such a case, be an unreliable measure of a student's writing ability. The ELL student may simply not have mastered the writing type or genre being assessed but still be able to express complex ideas in other formats. Again, if the results of this type of norm-referenced assessment are being used to screen for things like program eligibility or learning disabilities, the test would not be an appropriate measure. It could be an important indicator, however, of areas for growth or for instructional planning.

See also 7.5.

Skill 8.7	Understands the impact on English language writing literacy of the similarities and differences between first language(s) and the English language (e.g. directionality, orthographic depth, morphology, sentence structure, discourse structure, etc.)

See 7.7

COMPETENCY 9.0   UNDERSTANDS INSTRUCTION AND ASSESSMENT METHODS THAT SUPPORT THE LANGUAGE DEVELOPMENT AND CONTENT AREA KNOWLEDGE OF ENGLISH LANGUAGE LEARNERS

Skill 9.1   Utilizes effective research-based instructional approaches and methods to support English language learners' academic language proficiency

Literary Texts

Literary genres are collections of works with a similar theme or style. Some literary genres are grouped under large umbrella terms like biography and nonfiction, whereas others, like folktales, are further classified as fables, tall tales, fairy tales, and myths. Additionally, under fiction, there are other literary genres: historical fiction, mystery, realistic fiction, fantasy, science fiction, etc. Students should be made aware of these different genres and the different formats and styles that make them distinct.

Learning about the features of new text types provides students with additional tools for understanding complex texts. For example, learning that an essay typically starts with the author's main point, then continues on to incorporate his/her evidence or arguments, and then ends with a conclusion, will help all students (particularly ELL students) to identify main ideas, look for key points, or even to construct a contrary opinion. The concept of genre and its purpose becomes more complicated as children advance to a higher grade level.

Informational Texts and Purposes for Reading

According to Shanahan (2008), people make decisions based on information that comes from multiple viewpoints in multiple formats (e.g., letters, essays, reports, advertisements, lectures) through various media (e.g., newspapers, television, websites, books, magazines). This is evident in content-area subjects as well. For example, historians supply evidence from multiple sources (e.g., film, newspapers, letters, interviews, fictional accounts) to prove their point of view regarding a historical event. The views regarding a specific event might change based on the era in which historians were doing the writing and who the historians were. Historians not only read multiple genres when collecting information but also write them (e.g., scholarly books, journals, articles, lectures). This is also true for other disciplines, such as science and mathematics. Students must also learn to gather information or present their own ideas in different genres and formats.

These multiple genres within a single topic make reading even more challenging for ESL learners. This struggle is magnified when these genres communicate contradictory purposes and messages depending on the author and the context. These genres and their purposes for writing change across disciplines; therefore, teachers need to make students aware of these differences so they can become critical readers. Shanahan (2008) suggests what teachers could do to help students to understand complex texts of different genres:

- Preteach potentially troublesome vocabulary.
- Provide information to build background knowledge. Use an anchor text or experience before reading a more difficult text.
- Teach students to use strategies that will help them to better interpret texts. This includes teaching the key features of different text types.
- Teach students about various genres and structures used in texts and how texts within those genres signal important information.
- Teach students information about the discipline in which they are reading as well as how experts in that discipline approach and use information in texts to build upon existing knowledge.
- Set up cooperating group structures that allow students who are weaker readers to be supported in their reading by better readers.
- Find easier texts or annotate existing texts to make them easier if the difficult texts are so challenging that students become unmotivated, even with all the support they receive.

Graphic Organizers and Mind Maps: Graphic organizers and mind maps can help students evaluate and comprehend more complex informational texts by helping English language learners visualize information or raw data. These can be used by the teacher for simplification of complex materials, data, and complicated relationships in content areas. Students use them to analyze data, organize information, and clarify concepts. Examples are: pie charts, flow charts, bar diagrams, Venn diagrams, family trees, spider maps, organizational charts, and strip maps. Still other graphic organizers are webbing, concept mapping, passwords and language ladders, and brainstorming.

- With webbing, students learn to associate words or phrases within a topic or concept.
- By using concept maps, students learn the relationships between the different elements of a topic and how to organize them from the most general to the most specific. This is different from webbing, where relationships between words or phrases are shown, but not ranked.

Passwords and Language Ladders: Words of the Day and Language Ladders are motivating ways to teach chunks of language to ELLs. The Word of the Day is language that can range from content-specific language to words/phrases needed for daily student life. After the words or phrases are explained, they are posted on the board, and must be used before leaving the room or participating in some activity. Language ladders are associated words, such as different ways to say hello or good-bye.

Brainstorming: Brainstorming consists of students contributing ideas related to a concept or problem-centered topic. The teacher initially accepts all ideas without comment. Students then categorize, prioritize, and select proposed ideas for further investigation.

Vocabulary Study: See 3.3 for details on vocabulary study.

Skill 9.2   **Applies knowledge of sheltered teaching strategies and selects materials to support the ability of English language learners' to communicate for social and instructional purposes as described in the WIDA ELD Standards**

WIDA identifies three primary types of strategies that teachers may employ to support ELL students. These are sensory (e.g., word walls, math manipulatives, audio books), graphic (e.g., Venn diagrams, graphic organizers, tables or word webs), and interactive (partner or group work, cooperative learning strategies, mentors).

In designing learning opportunities, the ESOL teacher must be responsive to the needs of learners. Flexibility in the use of materials and in instructional practices will ensure that students can maximize learning and progress in language acquisition. Employing these methods will allow students to build social language skills while also developing communicative skills for academic purposes.

Skill 9.3   **Applies strategies for teaching subject matter in English and for developing English language learners' cognitive-academic language proficiency (e.g., providing comprehensible input, providing explicit instruction in academic language and vocabulary, integrating content and language objectives, supporting students' use of English to discuss and consider subject matter content)**

It is important to implement powerful instructional strategies that actively engage students from linguistically and culturally diverse backgrounds instead of allowing them to be passive participants or observers. Krashen (1981, 1982) states that students must be instructed at a level slightly higher than their competence level, i.e. $i + 1$. He believes that for a student to learn, the input must be comprehensible.

Chamot and O'Malley (1994) stated that teachers need to be aware of their students' approaches to learning and how to expand the students' repertoire of learning strategies.

Arreaga-Mayer (1998) puts forward constructs for effective instruction to linguistically and culturally diverse students:

1. **Challenge**
   - Implicit (cognitive challenge, use of higher-order questions)
   - Explicit (high but reasonable expectations)

2. **Involvement**
   - Active involvement of all students

3. **Success**
   - Reasonable activities that students can complete successfully.

4. Scaffolding/cognitive strategies
- Visual organizers, adequate background information, and support provided by teachers to students by thinking aloud, building on and clarifying their input

5. Mediation/feedback
- Strategies provided to students
- Frequency and comprehensibility stressed

6. Collaborative/cooperative learning
- Opportunities for students to work together, solve problems, and complete projects

7. Techniques for second-language acquisition/sheltered English
- Extended discourse
- Consistent language
- Incorporation of students' language

8. Respect for cultural diversity
- Respect and knowledge of cultural diversity

Additionally, **peer-mediated instruction** is effective in promoting higher levels of language and academic learning and social interaction. Research has shown that cooperative, peer-mediated instruction contributes more to content mastery than do whole-class instruction, workbook activities, and question-answer sessions. This method gives ELLs opportunities to actively practice a concept, the amount of discourse produced, the degree of negotiation of meaning, and the amount of comprehensible linguistic input. The essential components of peer-mediated learning strategies are: (a) cooperative incentives, (b) group rewards, (c) individual accountability, and (d) task structures.

In this method, students of varied academic abilities and language proficiency levels work together in pairs and small groups toward a common goal. In these groups, the success of one student depends on the help of the others. In peer-mediated instruction the learning task assigned to groups varies, but the format of learning always includes interaction and interdependence among the students.

Similarly, **peer tutoring** is a method developed to improve the acquisition and retention of basic academic skills. In this method, students are either paired randomly or matched by ability or language proficiency to partners each week. Student's roles are switched during the daily tutoring session, allowing each child to be both the tutor/teacher and the tutee/student. Students are trained in the procedures necessary to act as tutors and tutees. The four basic components of this method are:

- Weekly competing teams (heterogeneous grouping)

- Highly structured teaching procedure (content material, teams, pairing, error correction, system of rewards)
- Daily, contingent, individual tutee point earning and public postings of individual and team scores
- Direct practice of functional academic and language skills to mastery

Academic tasks tend to increase in their cognitive demands as students progress in their schooling, but the context becomes increasingly reduced. ELLs who have not developed CALP need additional teacher support to achieve success. Contextual support in the form of realia, demonstrations, pictures, graphs, etc. provide the ELL with scaffolding and reduce the language difficulty level of the task. Both content and ESOL teachers should incorporate teaching academic skills in their lessons. The following are essential elements to include in teaching academic English:

1. Integrate listening, speaking, reading, and writing skills in all lessons for all proficiencies;
2. Teach the components and processes of reading and writing;
3. Focus on vocabulary development;
4. Build and activate prior knowledge;
5. Teach language through content and themes;
6. Use native language strategically;
7. Pair technology with instruction; and
8. Motivate ELLs with choice.

Many program models have been developed to meet the needs of language minority students involving the integration of language and content instruction. In this approach, the second or foreign language is used as the medium of instruction for mathematics, science, social studies, and other academic subjects; it is the vehicle used for teaching and acquiring subject-specific knowledge. The focus of the second language classroom should be on something meaningful, such as academic content, and modification of the target language facilitates language acquisition and makes academic content accessible to second-language learners.

Integrated language-and-content instruction offers a means by which English as a Second Language (ESL) students can continue their academic or cognitive development while they are also acquiring academic language proficiency. In **theme-based programs**, a language curriculum is developed around selected topics drawn from one content area (e.g., marketing) or from across the curriculum (e.g., pollution and the environment). The theme could be a week or two long and focuses on language taught in a meaningful way. The goal is to assist learners in developing general academic language skills through interesting and relevant content. There are a variety of strategies to teach the integrated approach to language teaching of which the four most important are (Crandall, 1994):

 1. **Cooperative learning:** In this method, students of different linguistic and educational backgrounds and different skill levels work together on a common

task for a common goal to complete a task pertaining to the content being taught in the classroom. The focus is also on an implicit or explicit language feature that the students acquire through negotiation of meaning.

2. **Task-based or experiential learning:** Appropriate contexts are provided for developing thinking and study skills as well as language and academic concepts for students at different levels of language proficiency. Students learn by carrying out specific tasks or projects that they complete with a focus on the content, but learning language and academic skills as well.

3. **Whole language approach:** The philosophy of whole language is based on the concept that students need to experience language as an integrated whole. It focuses on the need for an integrated approach to language instruction within a context that is meaningful to students (Goodman, 1986). The approach is consistent with integrated language and content instruction, as both emphasize meaningful engagement and authentic language use, and both link oral and written language development (Blanton, 1992). Whole language strategies that have been implemented in content-centered language classes include dialogue journals, reading response journals, learning logs, process-based writing, and language experience stories (Crandall, 1992).

4. **Graphic organizers:** These frameworks provide a "means for organizing and presenting information so that it can be understood, remembered, and applied" (Crandall, 1992). Graphs, realia, tables, maps, flow charts, timelines, and Venn diagrams are used to help students place information in a comprehensible context. These props enable students to organize information obtained from written or oral texts, develop reading strategies, increase retention, activate schema as a prereading or prelistening activity, and organize ideas during the prewriting stage (Crandall, 1992).

An approach to teach vocabulary and to build prior knowledge about the content for readers is the **language experience approach**. Pressley (2008) states that good readers make use of background knowledge to make inferences that are necessary for understanding a text. This process helps readers create new knowledge from the text (*top-down processing*). In this view, the language experience approach supports children's concept development and vocabulary growth while offering many opportunities for meaningful reading and writing activities. It also helps in the development of shared experiences that expand children's knowledge of the world around them. In this approach, students' attention is focused on an experience in their daily life such as taking a class walk to collect leaves, blowing bubbles, making popcorn, apple picking, or experimenting with magnets. Students are involved in planning, experiencing, responding to, and recording the experience. The teacher initiates a discussion eliciting narrative from the students while providing appropriate vocabulary. In the end, the students compose oral individual or group stories which the teacher writes down and reads with students.

Skill 9.4 **Applies knowledge of sheltered teaching strategies and selects materials to support the content-area achievement of English Language Learners' as described in the Massachusetts curriculum frameworks (comprehensible input).**

See also 9.3.

Though ELL students, particularly in the early stages of English language development, face challenges in learning content, research-based theories and strategies can maximize content-area learning. The following language learning theories support specific instructional strategies. Many of these theories overlap in theory and in practice.

Theory: Language learners will learn authentic language and gain a truer picture of the complexities and richness of English when used as a real means of interacting and sharing among people

Strategy: Integrated Language Teaching
The two main types of integrated language teaching are Content-Based Instruction and Task-Based Instruction. Both of these approaches require students to use language authentically to obtain information and to communicate information. Content-based instruction requires students to practice all the language skills in a highly integrated, communicative way while learning content (Oxford, 2001). The three main models of content-based instruction are:

- Theme-based models: Language skills are integrated in the study of themes or broad topics (e.g., cities, recycling, homelessness)
- Adjunct model: Language and content courses are taught separately but closely coordinated
- Sheltered model: English is simplified to ELL's level of proficiency while teaching content. (Oxford, 2001)

Task-based learning is another way of achieving Integrated Language Teaching. Students are guided through tasks (Prabhu, 1987) formulated so that they are as realistic as possible. Three main trends in tasks are:

- Communicativeness: Learning is achieved through activities promoting real conversation between learners.
- Tasks: Learners who use language in a meaningful way to carry out tasks will learn language.
- Meaningfulness: Learners need to find meaning in the task for the learning tasks to be most effective.

Theory: When learners are instructed through content-based instruction such as mathematics, science, social studies etc., they tend to achieve a much higher proficiency level in the target language, than if they were only instructed in the target language through ESL methods.

Strategy: The Cognitive Academic Language Learning Approach (CALLA) integrates the following tenets:

- The L2 learners' actual grade level in the main subject areas of mathematics, science, and social studies etc., should be the deciding factor for content.
- The L2 learners should be exposed to and gradually acquire the specific language used when studying in the subject areas, such as: add this column of numbers; determine "x" in this algebraic problem; identify the properties of this cell, etc.
- The L2 learners should be encouraged to use higher level cognitive processes such as application, analysis and synthesis.

The CALLA teacher needs to first introduce basic literacy skills. If possible, these should be introduced in the native or heritage language of the child. For older students, the Language Experience Approach has proven effective. Another technique to use with older students is to have them read such everyday items as signs, menus, ads, and recipes because there is an immediate association with these materials and the need to learn to read (Chamot & O'Malley, 1994).

Some examples of methods to help ELL students begin developing basic English literacy before transitioning to more academic English include:

- Creating illustrated autobiographies: ("All about Me" or "The Story of My Life") can help ease ELLs into the academic challenges of a new school and culture. Students use as much English as they can and draw pictures to illustrate other points. This is an integrative activity because ELLs are not singled out, but are part of the group.
- Dialogue journals: Can be used with students of all ages. Provide all students with blank journals and allow them to draw or write in the language of their choice. The instructor should respond to the journals periodically. Journals are an excellent way to develop a personal relationship with the students while at the same time introducing literacy to the class.
- Themes: Such as "Where We Were Born" or "Family Origins" make good starting points to bring in home cultures and activate prior knowledge of all students. (Adapted from Peregoy and Boyle, 2008)

Theory: Students can learn content while developing their English language skills

Strategy: Sheltered Content Teaching
In sheltered content teaching, students from diverse linguistic backgrounds are grouped together allowing content instruction through English adapted to the proficiency level of the students. Emphasis is on content, though English language learning is also expected. Specifically Designed Academic Instruction in English (S.D.A.I.E.) is one example of this type of instruction. Sheltered content teaching—which is based upon the theories of Krashen (comprehensible input and affective environment) and Cummins

(Basic Interpersonal Communication Skills—BICS and Cognitive Academic Language Proficiency--CALP) are indispensable components of Sheltered Content Teaching.

Some of the features of Sheltered Content Teaching would be:

- Comprehensible input
- Assessing prior knowledge
- Scaffolding
- Hands-on activities
- Visual clues (realia, word lists, pictures, models, gestures, body language)
- Cooperative learning
- Reduced language demands (teachers monitor their syntax, rate of speech, and language structures)
- Cultural affirmation and multicultural appreciation
- Graphic organizers
- Active learning with higher order thinking skills
- Teacher as a facilitator of learning

Depending on student population sizes and staffing levels, schools often employ different models of programs to support ELL students' content-area learning. Some programs focus on 'push-in' with specialist teachers working with ELL students in content-area classes while others are 'pull-out', working English learners in special classes. Still others combine push-in and pull-out. They generally share as goals the intent to teach English language learners to communicate in social settings, engage in academic tasks, and use English in socially and culturally appropriate ways. Some of these models are:

Content-based instruction: Instruction in English that attempts to develop language skills and prepare ELLs to study grade-level content material in English. Emphasis on language, but with gradual introduction to content areas, vocabulary, and basic concepts.

Structured English immersion: The goal is English proficiency. ELLs are pulled out for structured instruction in English so that subject matter is comprehensible. Used with sizeable groups of ELLs who speak the same language and are in the same grade level or with a diverse population of language minority students. There is little or no first/home language support. Teachers use sheltered instructional techniques and often have strong receptive skills in the students' native or heritage language.

Submersion with primary language support: The goal is English proficiency. Bilingual teachers or aides support the minority students in each grade level who are ELLs. In small groups, the ELLs are supported by reviewing the content areas in their primary language. The teachers may use the L1 to support English content classes.

Skill 9.5 Selects and adapts formal and informal methods of assessing students' language development and content-area knowledge and skills

The first step in personalizing instruction is for ESOL teachers to assess English Language Learners' proficiency in literacy and oracy. In addition, teachers might also consider a learner's:

- age and grade level
- level of home language proficiency
- social-emotional well being
- comfort levels with group work and independent work
- proficiency and comfort level with the five core skills (reading, writing, listening, viewing and speaking)

After analyzing assessment data, teachers can make action plans for individuals and groups of students. Aspects of instruction that can be personalized include:

- Teaching tools and resources (including technology and media)
- Production tasks
- Revising communicative, academic literacy and content-based goals

An important part of any personalized action plan for students, particularly students who are not meeting language literacy or content-area goals, is for the ESOL teacher to communicate with families and with the students themselves about learning or performance gaps and about the strategies teachers are going to use to support ELLs development.

The WIDA English Language Development Standards cover some research-based essential actions strategies for effective instruction with ELLs. (https://www.wida.us/standards/eld.aspx#essentialactions)

A few are adapted below:

- Create and utilize language proficiency profiles for each student
- Design language teaching and learning with attention to the sociocultural context
- Create meaningful, language-rich, and safe environments for English Language Learners that provide them with differentiated language practice and use. This means providing ample time for students to practice who need more and appropriate challenges for students who need less. That way all students are working to their potential and no students 'finish' before others.
- Use instructional supports and scaffolds
- Communicate and plan with other teachers in order get to know students' strengths and challenges outside of your classroom. This can help in planning personalized learning opportunities inside it.

Finally, when students are encouraged to be metacognitive learners, their ability to take responsibility for and personalize their own learning increases. This results in students becoming more active learners and has a positive effect on English language and content-area learning.

Skill 9.6 **Analyzes and applies formal and informal assessment data; recognizes bias and possible differences between content-area performance for native speakers of English and for English language learners**

In analyzing both formal and informal assessment data, ESOL teachers should carefully consider whether the content-area performance task provides native speakers and ELLs equal opportunities to succeed. The construct of a content-area performance task should not necessarily involve a high level of English language proficiency. If it does, it might make it difficult for ELLs to perform well, even if they have considerable knowledge and skills in the content-area. This puts ELLs at a disadvantage. Linguistic demands need to be clear and fair, if testing content-area knowledge and skills.

Other possible assessment areas for consideration include the ways in which students are asked to demonstrate knowledge and skills. Providing ELLs (and all students) with multiple opportunities and ways to demonstrate their knowledge and skills is more likely to produce better performance outcomes. Carefully consider the weighting of test items. If some items are weighted heavily because they require longer written responses, this could put ELLs at a disadvantage, as these written tasks will require more English language skills so they can express content-area knowledge.

Finally, the language used in the assessment should be accessible for both assessment directions and items/questions to give native speakers and English language learners equal opportunities to express what they know.

See competencies 7 and 8 for more on assessments

Skill 9.7 **Applies knowledge of characteristics of and guidelines for using various formal and informal procedures and instruments for assessing students' cognitive-academic language proficiency and content area concepts and skills and interpretation and use of assessment information, including differentiation between normal variation in performance and performance that may indicate possible learning disabilities**

The 1993 Massachusetts Education Reform Law, state law M. G. L. Chapter 69, section 1I, mandates that all students in the tested grades who are educated with Massachusetts public funds participate in the Massachusetts Comprehensive Assessment System (MCAS), the Massachusetts test which assesses students' academic performance based on the Massachusetts Curriculum Frameworks. This includes ELL students in elementary and secondary school with one exception.

Students enrolled in a US school after a specified date (see http://www.doemass.org/mcas/accessibility/) who did not appear in a SIMS report, are not required to participate in ELA testing. They must still write the Mathematics and Science and Technology test results are used for diagnostic purposes and are not included in accountability reporting or summary results.

The MCAS tests each public school student in Massachusetts in English Language Arts and mathematics each year in grades 3-8 and once in high school (Grade 10). Students must also take a science and engineering/technology test once in elementary, middle, and high school (http://www.doe.mass.edu/mcas/tdd/).

In addition, ELL students are required to participate in ACCESS for ELLs tests, which replaced MEPA tests. ACCESS for ELLs tests are given annually and measure English language listening, reading, writing and speaking proficiency based on the WIDA ELD standards and performance indicators. (See Skill 5.3 for details on speaking standards). The assessment also measures the progress students are making in learning English.

The general test-taking time allotted for the ACCESS for ELLs in Massachusetts is:

- Listening (up to 40 minutes),
- Reading (up to 50 minutes),
- Writing (up to 65 minutes, depending on the student's English proficiency), and
- Speaking (up to 30 minutes)

Language Classification Recommendations
School teams, using ACCESS for ELL data, make determinations as to a student's reclassification (removing a student's EL classification). If a student achieves a Level 5.5 or greater in both reading and writing and a Level 6 (Reaching) in speaking and listening, s/he should no longer be classified as EL and can reasonably be considered to have achieved English language proficiency comparable to their English proficient peers without specialized language supports. See (http://www.doe.mass.edu/ell/Guidance.pdf) for details.

English language learners with academic difficulties (e.g., learning disabilities, speech-language impairments, etc.) may qualify to take ACCESS for ELLs with accommodations. English language learners with significant cognitive disabilities may quality to take the Alternate ACCESS for ELLs assessment. (https://www.wida.us/assessment/alternateaccess.aspx#participation-criteria)

DISTINCTION BETWEEN ELL AND STUDENTS WITH DISABILITIES
One way to serve the student with disabilities and the ELL student is to accurately assess their disability or limitation. Differentiating between ELLs with learning disabilities from those who are simply struggling with learning a second language can be problematic. Many of the problems associated with second language learning are also identified as learning difficulties: for example, should processing difficulties, behavioral differences, reading difficulties, and expressive difficulties (Lock & Layton, 2002) be

associated with the difficulties of second language learning or with learning difficulties? While some learning difficulties can be partially identified by observation over a time or by the lack of academic improvement (Gersten & Baker, 2003), they are also often typical of ELLs struggling with the complexities of language and a new school environment.

Therefore, it is of critical importance to assess the concerned student using a variety of testing procedures. Chalfant & Psch (1981) recommend using a Teacher Assistance Team (TAT) consisting of regular classroom teachers who meet with the referring teacher to discuss problems, brainstorm possible solutions, and develop an action plan. After the plan has been implemented, the TAT and the referring teacher have a follow-up meeting to evaluate the results and to develop other recommendations if necessary. The TAT ultimately decides whether the student should be referred for a special education evaluation.

Suggestions concerning the testing procedure are:

- Tests that are nondiscriminatory based on race or culture
- Tests conducted in both the student's primary language (not translated, but designed to assess speakers of the language) and English
- Identify student using observations from school, home, and community
- Alternative assessments combined with formal assessments
- Criterion-referenced assessments
- Curriculum-based assessments
- Portfolio of student's work
- Informal assessments: rubrics, dynamic assessment (test-teach-test), learning logs, self-evaluations
- Comparison of student's cultural teaching style (e.g., teacher centered) with the school's teaching style (e.g., student centered)

Further Reading on ELLs with Disabilities
A major obstacle in working with ELLs with disabilities is the lack of guidelines dealing specifically with the two limitations. While both learning disabilities and teaching English to language group minorities or immigrants have been studied extensively, little research has been done on how to best integrate the two disciplines (Gersten & Baker, 2003; Ortiz, 1997 in Gurel 2004). The following suggestions for further reading are offered to those who wish for more enlightenment.

- Aron, L.Y. & Loprest, P.J. (2007) Meeting the Needs of Children with Disabilities. Urban Institute Press.
- Echevarria, J. & Graves, A. (1998) Sheltered content Instruction: Teaching English-Language Learners with Diverse Abilities. Allyn and Bacon. .
- Wynne, S. 2011. Praxis 0353. Special Education: Knowledge-Based Core Principles. Teacher Certification Exam. Boston: XAMonline.

- Zehr, Mary Ann (2008) "Bilingual Students with Disabilities Get Special Help." *Education Week*. Nov. 7, 2001.
- http://www.eric.ed.gov/
- http://www.edweek.org/ew/articles/2001/11/07/10clark.h21.html?print=1
- http://learningdisabilities.about.com

Changes in Requirements for IEPs

Individualized Education Plans (IEPS) continue to have multiple sections. One section, *present levels of educational performance (PLEP),* now addresses *academic achievement and functional performance.* Annual IEP goals must now address the same areas.

IEP goals should be aligned to state standards, therefore, short term objectives are not required on every IEP. Students with IEPs must not only participate in regular education programs to the full extent possible, they must also show progress in those programs. Therefore, goals must be written to reflect academic progress.

For students who must participate in alternate assessment, there must be alignment to *alternate achievement standards.*

Significant change has been made in the definition of the IEP team. It now states that *not less than 1 teacher* from each of the areas of special education and regular education be present.

IDEA 2004 recognized that the amount of required paperwork placed upon teachers of students with disabilities should be reduced if possible. For this reason, some states will participate in a newly developed pilot program that uses multi-year IEPs. Individual student inclusion in this program will require consent by both the school and the parent.

IDENTIFICATION

Identification of a student's learning problem begins when comparisons are made between a given student's academic and behavioral characteristics and those of the peer population. For example, when a student exhibits a significant difference between her/his academic performance and that of other students, teachers can identify potential issues.

All children and youth exhibit behaviors that deviate from normative expectations at times. But overall, it is the intensity of the behavior, the degree to which it is shown, and the frequency and length of time that it persists or has occurred that is significant. Behavior rating scales, checklists, inventories, and sociograms are used to determine whether a particular behavior is occurring and to what extent.

Students with disabilities are usually identifiable by a combination of academic and social behaviors that deviate significantly from those of their classmates. The longer it takes to identify these students, the further they fall behind their age-mates in school.

INTERVENTION

Once a student is identified as being at-risk academically or socially, remedial interventions are attempted within the regular classroom. Federal legislation requires that sincere efforts be made to help the child learn in the regular classroom.

In some states, school-based teams of educators are formed to solve learning and behavior problems in the regular classroom. These informal problem-solving teams have a variety of names that include concepts of support (school support teams, student support teams), assistance (teacher assistance teams, school assistance teams, or building assistance teams), and appraisal (school appraisal teams) (Pugach & Johnson 1989b).

Regardless of what the teams are called, their purpose is similar. Chalfant, Psch, and Moultrie (1979) state that **teacher assistance teams (TAT)** are created to make professional suggestions about curricular alternatives and instructional modifications. These teams may be composed of a variety of participants, including regular education teachers, ESOL teachers, building administrators, guidance counselors, special education teachers, and the student's parent(s). The make-up of teams varies based on the type of referral, the needs of the student, availability of educational personnel, and state requirements.

Instructional modifications are used to accommodate the student in the regular classroom. Effective instruction is geared toward individual needs and recognizes differences in how students learn. Modifications are tailored to individual student needs. Some strategies for modifying regular classroom instruction shown in the table below are effective with at-risk students with disabilities and students without learning or behavior problems.

REFERRAL

Referral is the process through which a teacher, a parent, or some other person formally requests an evaluation of a student to determine eligibility for special education services. The decision to refer a student may be influenced by the following:

- Student characteristics, such as the abilities, behaviors, or skills (or lack thereof) that students exhibit;
- Individual differences among teachers, in their beliefs, expectations, or skill in dealing with specific kinds of problems;
- Expectations for assistance with a student who is exhibiting academic or behavioral learning problems;
- Availability of specific kinds of strategies and materials;
- Parents' request for referral or opposition to referral; and
- Institutional factors that may facilitate or constrain teachers in making referral decisions. Fewer students are referred when school districts have complex procedures for referral, psychological assessments are backlogged for months, special education classes are at capacity, or principals and other administrators do not fully recognize the importance of special services.

Everyone must clearly understand referral procedures, and they must be coordinated among all school personnel. All educators should be able to identify characteristics typically exhibited by special needs students. Also, the restrictiveness of special service settings must be known and the appropriateness of each clearly understood. The more restrictive special education programs tend to group students with similar disabilities for instruction. Last, the specialized services afforded through equipment, materials, teaching approaches, and specific teacher-student relations should be clearly understood.

EVALUATION

If instructional modifications in the regular classroom have not proven successful, a student may be referred for multidisciplinary evaluation. The evaluation is comprehensive and includes:

- Norm- and criterion-referenced tests (e.g., IQ and diagnostic tests)
- Curriculum-based assessment
- Systematic teacher observation (e.g., behavior frequency checklist)
- Samples of student work
- Parent interviews

The purpose of the evaluation is twofold: to determine eligibility for special education services and to identify a student's strengths and weaknesses to plan an individual education program.

The wording in federal law is very explicit about the manner that evaluations must be conducted, and about the existence of due process procedures that protect against discrimination. Provisions in the law include the following:

- The testing of children in their native or primary language unless it is clearly not feasible to do so
- The use of evaluation procedures selected and administered to prevent cultural or ethnic discrimination.
- The use of assessment tools validated for the purpose for which they are being used (e.g., achievement levels, IQ scores, adaptive skills)
- Assessment by a multidisciplinary team using several pieces of information to formulate a placement decision

Furthermore, parental involvement must occur in the development of the child's educational program. According to the law, parents must:

- Be notified before initial evaluation or any change in placement by a written notice in their primary language describing the proposed school action, the reasons for it, and the available educational opportunities; and
- Give consent, in writing, before the child is initially evaluated.

Parents may then:

- Request an independent educational evaluation if they feel the school's evaluation is inappropriate;
- Request an evaluation at public expense if a due process hearing decision is that the public agency's evaluation was inappropriate;
- Participate on the committee that considers the evaluation, placement, and programming of the student.

All students referred for evaluation for special education should have on file the results of a current vision and hearing screening. This will determine the adequacy of sensory acuity and ensure that learning problems are not due to a vision and/or hearing problem.

ELIGIBILITY

Eligibility is based on criteria defined in federal law or state regulations, which vary from state to state. Evaluation methods correspond with eligibility criteria for the special education classifications. For example, a multidisciplinary evaluation for a student being evaluated for intellectual disabilities would include the individual's intellectual functioning, adaptive behavior, and achievement levels. Other tests are based on developmental characteristics exhibited (e.g., social, language, and motor).

A student evaluated for learning disabilities is given reading, math, and spelling achievement tests, an intelligence test to confirm average or above average cognitive capabilities, and tests of written and oral language ability. Tests need to show a discrepancy between potential and performance. Classroom observations and samples of student work (such as impaired reading ability or impaired writing ability) also provide indicators of possible learning disabilities.

Eligibility for services in behavior disorders requires documented evidence of social deficiencies or learning deficits that are not because of intellectual, sensory, or physical conditions. Therefore, any student undergoing multidisciplinary evaluation for this categorical service is usually given an intelligence test, diagnostic achievement tests, and social and/or adaptive inventories. Results of behavior frequency lists, direct observations, and anecdotal records collected over an extended period often accompany test results.

Additional information frequently used when making decisions about a child's eligibility for special education include the following:

- Developmental history
- Past academic performance
- Medical history or records
- Neurological reports
- Classroom observations
- Speech and language evaluations

- Personality assessment
- Discipline reports
- Home visits
- Parent interviews
- Samples of student work

If considered eligible for special education services, the child's disability should be documented in a written report stating specific reasons for the decision.

Domain III   **INTEGRATION OF KNOWLEDGE AND UNDERSTANDING**

COMPETENCY 10.0   **ANALYSIS AND INTEGRATION**

In this section of the exam, you will need to integrate your knowledge and understanding of second language instruction and **issues related to content-area learning in a second language. See the practice test for sample questions.**

REFERENCES

Alderson, J. 1992. Guidelines for the evaluation of language education. In: Ellis, R. 1997. The empirical evaluation of language teaching materials. ELT Journal Vol. 51, No. 1 Jan.

Allen, V.G. (1994) Selecting materials for the instruction of ESL children. In: Zainuddin (2007).

Au, K. H. 1993. Literacy instruction in multicultural settings. Orlando, FL.: Harcourt Brace.

------ 2002. Multicultural factors and effective instruction of students of diverse backgrounds. In A. Farstrup and S. J. Samuels (eds.) *What research says about reading Instruction*. Newark, DE: International Reading Assn. Coral Gables: U of Miami. 392-413.

Banks, J. A. 1988. Multicultural Leader. Vol. 1, No. 2. Educational Materials & Services Center. Spring.

Baker, K. 1998. Structured English Immersion: Breakthrough in Teaching Limited-English-Proficient Students. Phi Delta Kappan, Nov. pp199-204.

Barton, L. 1997. Quick Flip Questions for Critical Thinking. Dana Point, CA: Edupress.

Bebe, V.N & Mackey, W.F. 1990. *Bilingual schooling and the Miami experience*. Coral Gables, FL University of Miami. Institute of Interamerican Studies. Graduate School of International Studies.

Bennett, C. 1995. Comprehensive multicultural education: Theory and practice (3rd ed.). Massachusetts: Allen & Bacon.

Berko Gleason, J. 1993. *The Development of Language* (3rd ed.) New York: Macmillan.

Bialystok, E. (ed.). 1991. *Language Processing in Bilingual Children*. Cambridge: CUP.

Blakey, E. & Spence, S. 1990. Developing Metacognition (ED327218). ERIC Clearinghouse on Information Resources. Syracuse, NY.

Brisk, M. E. 1998. Bilingual Education: From compensatory to quality schooling. Mahwah, N. J. Lawrence Erlbaum.

Burstall, C., Jamieson, M., Cohen, S. and Hargreaves, M. 1974. *Primary French I the balance*. Slough: NFER.

California Department of Education. Testing & Accountability. CELDT Questions and Answers. http://www.cde.ca.gov/ta/tg/el/celdtfaq.asp Rev. 11/03/09.

Candlin, C. 1987. In Batstone, R. 1994. *Grammar*. Oxford: OUP.

Chalfant, J.C. & Pysh, M.V. 1981. Teacher assistance teams—A model for within building problem solving. Counterpoint. Nov. p 16-21.

Chalfant, J.C., Pysh, M.V. & Moultrie, R. 1979. Teacher Assistance Teams: A Model for Within-Building Problem Solving. Learning Disability Quarterly. v2, n3 Summer, p. 85-96. Council for Learning Disabilities.

Chamot, A.U. and O'Malley, J. M. 1994. *The Calla Handbook*. Reading, MA: Addison-Wesley.

Collier, V.P. 1989. "How long? A synthesis of research on academic achievement in second language." *TESOL Quarterly*, 23. 509-531.

-----. 1992. A synthesis of studies examining long-term language minority student data on academic achievement. *Bilingual Research Journal*, 16 (1-2). 187-212.

-----. 1995. "Acquiring a second language for school." Directions in Language & Education. Washington, DC: NCBE. 1(4), 1-10.
Conflict Research Consortium. Online Training Program on Intractable Conflict (OTPIC) Conflict Management and Constructive Confrontation: A Guide to the Theory and Practice. University of Colorado Revised July 20, 1999. http://conflict.colorado.edu
Crawford, J. 1998. Ten Common Fallacies About Bilingual Education. ERIC Clearinghouse on Language & Linguistics . Washington, D.C. Nov. ERIC Id ED424792.

Criteria for Evaluating Instructional Materials: Kindergarten Through Grade Eight. Reading/Language Arts Framework for California Public Schools. California Department of Education. 2007.

Cruz, J. 2005. Second Language Acquisition Programs: An Assessment of the Bilingual Education Debate. McNair Scholars Journal: Vol. 9, Iss. 1, Art. 6. http://scholarworks.gvsu.edu/mcnair/vol/iss1/6

Cummins, J. 1981. Bilingualism and Minority Language Children. Toronto: Institute for Studies in Education.

Cummins, J. 1984. Bilingualism and special education: Issues in assessment and pedagogy. San Diego: College-Hill.

Cummins, J. 1998. Rossell and Baker: Their case for the effectiveness of bilingual education. The Journal of Pedagogy Pluralism & Practice. Issue 3, Vol. 1: Fall.

Cummins, J. & Genzuk, M. 1991. Analysis of final report longitudinal study of structured English immersion strategy, early-exit and late-exit transitional bilingual education programs for language-minority students. California Association for Bilingual Education Newsletter, 13.

Curry, D. 1989. Illustrated American Idioms. Washington, DC. English Language Program Division. Bureau of Educational and Cultural Affairs. USIA.

Díaz-Rico, L.T. and Weed, K.Z. 1995. Language, and Academic Development Handbook: A Complete K-12 Reference Guide. Needham Heights, MA: Allyn and Bacon.

Diaz-Rico, L.T. 2008. Strategies for Teaching English Learners. 2nd ed. Boston: Pearson.

Dulay, H. and Burt, M. 1974. "You can't learn without goofing" in J. Richards' (ed.) Error Analysis, Perspectives on Second Language Acquisition. New York: Longman.

Ellis, R. 1985. Understanding Second Language Acquisition. Oxford: OUP.

------ 1994. The Study of Second Language Acquisition. Oxford: OUP.

Entwhistle, N.J. and Entwhistle, D. 1970. The relationships between personality, study methods and academic performance. British Journal of Educational Psychology. Vol 40(2). doi.apa.org. 132-143.

Fillmore, L.W. 2001. Scott, Foresman ESL:Accelerating English Language Learning. In: Zainuddin (2007).

Friend, M. and Bursuck, W. D. 2005. *Models of Coteaching: Including Students with Special Needs: A Practical Guide for Classroom Teachers*. (3rd ed.) Boston, MA: Allyn and Bacon.

Garcia, E. 1994. *Understanding and Meeting the Challenge of Student Cultural Diversity*. Boston: Houghton Mifflin.

Garinger, D. 2002. Textbook Evaluation. TESL Web Journal Vol. 1, No. 3.

Genesee, F. 1987. *Learning through Two Languages: Studies of Immersion and Bilingual Education*. Cambridge, MA: Newbury House.

------ (ed.) 1994. *Educating Second Language Children: The Whole Child, the Whole Curriculum, the Whole Community*. Cambridge: CUP.

Grellet, F. 1981. *Developing Reading Skills*. Cambridge: CUP.

Gersten, R. & Baker, S. 2000. What we know about effective instructional practices for English-Language Learners. Exceptional Children, 66(4) June, p. 454-470.

Gersten, R. & Baker, S. 2003. English-Language Learners with Learning Disabilities. In H. L. Swanson, K. R. Harris & S. Graham (eds.) Handbook of Learning Disabilities. (pp. 94-109). NY: Guilford.

Grasha, A. F. 1996. Your teaching style. Pittsburgh, PA: International Alliance of Teacher Scholars.

Gregorc, A.1982. An adult's guide to style. Maynard, MA: Gabriel Systems.

Gurel, Sarah M. (2004) Teaching English Language Learners with Learning Disabilities: A Compiled Convergence of Strategies. College of William and Mary. School of Education, Curriculum and Instruction.

Harris, M. and McCann, P. 1994. *Assessment*. Oxford: Heinemann.
Jerald, C.D. 2006. School Culture: "The Hidden Curriculum". The Center for Comprehensive School Reform and Improvement. Issue Brief. December.
www.centerforcsri.org

Heywood, D. 2006. Using Whole Discourse Tasks for Language Teaching. www.jalt-publications.org/tlt/chaprep/ Jan.

Hruska-Reichmann, S. & Grasha, A.F. 1982. The Grasha-Reichmann Student Learning Scales: Research findings and applications. In. J. Keefe (Ed.). Student learning styles and brain behavior. Reston, VA: NASSP.

Hyland, K. 2002. Teaching and Researching Writing. Harlow, England: Pearson.
Keirsey, D. 1998. Please understand me II. Del Mar, CA: Prometheus Nemesis.

KH Kim, D Zabelina. Cultural Bias in Assessment: Can Creativity Assessment Help? The International Journal of Critical Pedagogy, 2015

Kolb, D. A. 1976. The learning style Inventory technical manual. Boston: McBer.

Kramsch, C. 1998. *Language and Culture*. Oxford: OUP.

Krashen, S. 1981. *Second Language Acquisition and Second Language Learning*. Oxford: Pergamon Press.

------1982. *Principles and Practice in Second Language Acquisition*. Oxford: Pergamon Press.

Lambert, W. and Klineberg, O. 1967. Children's views of foreign peoples: A crossnational study. New York: Appleton. (Review in Shumann, J., Affective factors and the problem of age in second language acquisition, *Language Learning* 25/2. 1975. 209-235).

Lambert, W. E. 1990. Issues in Foreign Language and Second Language Education. In: Proceedings of the Research Symposium on Limited English Proficient Students' Issues. (1st, Washington, DC. September 10-12. ED 341 269. FI 020 030.

Language Development in Children. Child Development Institute (https://childdevelopmentinfo.com/child-development/language_development/#.WGdUApJ-hr1)

Larsen, D. and Smalley, W. 1972. *Becoming Bilingual, a Guide to Language Learning.* New Canadian: CT. Practical Anthropology.

Larsen-Freeman, D. 1997. Chaos/complexity science and second language acquisition. *Applied Linguistics,*18 (2). 141-165.

Leshinsky, J.G. 1995. Authentic listening and discussion for advanced students. Englewood Cliffs, NJ: Prentice-Hall Regents.

Lock, R.H. & Layton, C. A. 2002. Isolating Intrinsic Processing Disorders from Second Language Acquisition. Bilingual Research Journal. v 26n2 p. 383-94. Summer

Long, M. 1990. The lease a second language acquisition theory needs to explain. *TESOL Quarterly.* 24(4). 649-666.

Ludke, Karen M,Ferreira, Fernanda Overy, Katie. Singing can facilitate foreign language learning. *Memory & Cognition,* 2013; DOI: (10.3758/s13421-013-0342-5)

The Map of Standards for ELS. 2002. 3rd ed. West Education.

McArthur, T. ed. 1992. *The Oxford Companion to the English Language.* Oxford: OUP. 571-573.

McCarthy, B. 1983. The 4-MAT system: Teaching to learning styles with right-left mode techniques. Oak Brook, IL: Excel.

McClelland, D., Atkinson, J., Clark, R. & Lowell, E. 1953. *The Achievement Motive.* New York: Appleton, Century, Crofts.

McDonough, J. and Shaw, S. 1993. *Materials and Methods in ELT: A Teacher's Guide.* Blackwell.

McKay, S. L. 1987. Teaching Grammar: form, function, and technique. New York: Prentice Hall.

McLaughlin, B. 1990.The development of bilingualism: Myth and reality. In A. Barona & E. Garcia (eds.) *Children at Risk: Poverty, Minority Status and other Issues in Educational Equity* . Washington, D.C.: National Association of School Psychologists. 65-76.

Mitchell, V. 1990. Curriculum and instruction to reduce racial conflict. (ED322274). ERIC Clearinghouse on Urban Education. NY, NY.

Murphy, J. M. 1998. The eight disciplines. Grand Rapids, MI: Venture Management.

Naiman, N., Frolich, M., Stern, H., and Todesco, A. 1978. *The Good Language Learner*. Toronto: The Modern Language Centre, Ontario Institute for Studies in Education.

National Center for Research on Cultural Diversity and Second Language Learning. 1999. Two-Way Bilingual Education Programs in Practice: A National and Local Perspective. Center for Applied Linguistics, Online Resources: Digest. July.

National Center on Education and the Economy. 2001. California Performance Standards.

Nieto, S. 1992. "We Have Stories to Tell: A Case Study of Puerto Ricans in Children's Books." In Harris, V.J. (Ed.), Teaching Multicultural Literature in Grades K-8. Norwood, MA: Christopher-Gordon Publishers.

Nunan, D. 1989. *Designing Tasks for the Communicative Classroom*. Cambridge, CUP.

O'Malley, J. M. and Pierce, L. V. 1996. *Authentic Assessment for English Language Learners*. Longman.

Ovando, C.J., Coombs, M.C., and Collier, V.P. eds. 2006. *Bilingual and ESL Classrooms: Teaching in Multicultural Contexts* (4th ed.) Boston: McGraw-Hill.

Oxford, R. 2001. Integrated skills in the ESL/EFL classroom. Center for Applied Linguistics. Online Digests. Sept. EDO-FL-01-05.

Padilla, Amado M., Borsato N. Issues in Culturally Appropriate Psychoeducational Assessment. Research Gate. January 2008. (https://www.researchgate.net/publication/242580525_Issues_in_Culturally_Appropriate _Psychoeducational_Assessment)

Penfield, W. and Roberts, L. 1959. *Speech and Brain Mechanisms*. New York: Atheneum Press. (reviewed in Ellis, R. 1985).

Peregoy, S.F. and Boyle, O.F. 2008 *Reading, Writing, and Learning in ESL. 5th ed.* Boston: Pearson.

Prabhu, N. S. 1987. *Second Language Pedagogy: A Perspective*. London: Oxford, OUP.

Pugach, M.C. & Johnson, L.J. 1989. The Challenge of Implementing Collaboration between General and Special Education. Exceptional Children. V56.

Pugach, M.C. & Johnson, L.J. 1989. Prereferral Interventions: Progress, Problems, and Challenges. Exceptional Children. V56.

Quiocho, A. and Ulanoff, S.H. 2009. Differentiated Literacy Instruction for English Language Learners. Boston: Allyn & Bacon.

Reading/Language Arts Framework for California Public Schools. Kindergarten through Grade Twelve. 1999. Sacramento: CA DOE.

Reid, J. The learning style preferences of ESL students. *TESOL Quarterly,* 21(1): 86-103.

Rennie, J. 1993. ESL and Bilingual Program Models. Eric Digest.
http://www.cal.org/resources/Digest/rennie01.html

Richards, Platt, and Weber. 1985. quoted by Ellis, R. The evaluation of communicative tasks in Tomlinson, B (ed.) *Materials Development in Language Teaching*. Cambridge: CUP. 1998.

Rinvolucri, M. 1984. Grammar Games: Cognitive, affective and movement activities for EFL students. Cambridge, CUP.

Rinvolucri, M. and Davis, P. 1995. More Grammar Games: Cognitive, affective and movement activities for EFL students. Cambridge, CUP.

Rochman, H. 1993. Against Borders: Promoting Books for a Multicultural World. Chicago, IL: American Library Association.

Rosansky, E. 1975. The critical period for the acquisition of language: some cognitive developmental considerations. In: Working Papers on Bilingualism 6: 92-102.

Rosenberg, L. Global Demographic Trends. F&D: Finance and Development Sept. 2006, Vol. 43, No. 3.

Rosenblatt, L. 2005. Making meaning with texts: selected essays. Portsmouth, NH: Heinemann.

Samway, K.D. & McKeon, D. 1999. Myths and realities: Best practices for language minority students. Portsmouth, NH: Heinemann.

Schiffrin, D., Tannen, D., and Hamilton, H., eds. 2003. The Handbook of Discourse Analysis. Wiley, John & Sons.

Schimel, J. et al 2000. Running from the Shadow: Psychological Distancing From Others to Characteristics People Fear in Themselves. Journal of Personality and Social Psychology. Vol. 78, No. 3 446-462

Schmidt, R. W. 1990. The role of consciousness in second language acquisition. *Applied Linguistics*, 11(2). 129-158.

Schumm, J.S., ed. 2006. *Reading Assessment and Instruction for All Learners*. New York: The Guilford Press.

Sinclair, J. and Coulthard, M. 1975. Towards an Analysis of Discourse. Oxford: OUP. 93-94.

Slavin, R.E. and Cheung. 2003. *Effective Reading Programs for English Language Learners: A Best-Evidence Synthesis*. U.S. Dept. of Education. Institute of Education Sciences.

Snow, C. and Hoefnagel-Hohle, M. 1978. Age Differences in Second Language Learning. In *Second Language Acquisition,* Hatch ed. Rowley, MA.: Newbury House.

Sonbuchner, G. M. 1991. How to take advantage of your learning styles. Syracuse, NY: New Readers Press. .

Suid, M. & Lincoln, W. 1989. Recipes for Writing: Motivation, Skills, and Activities. Menlo Park, CA Addison-Wesley.

Taylor, O.L. 1990. Cross-Cultural Communication An Essential Dimension of Effective Education. Rev. ed. Chevy Chase, MD. Mid-Atlantic Equity Center.

Teachers of English to Speakers of Other Languages. 1997. *ESL Standards for Pre-K— 12 Students*. Alexandria, VA.: TESOL.

Teaching Tolerance. n.d. *Anti-Gay Discrimination In Schools*. Southern Poverty Law Center, (http://www.tolerance.org)

Tharp, R. 1989. Psychocultural variables and constants: Effects on teaching and learning in schools. American Psychologist, 44(2). 349-359.

Thomas, W. P., and Collier, V. P. 1995. Language minority student achievement and program effectiveness. Manuscript in preparation. (in Collier, V.P. 1995).

Tollefsen, J. 1991. *Planning Language, Planning Inequality.* New York, Longman.

Tompkins, G. 2009. *Language Arts: patterns of practice*. 7th ed. Upper Saddle River, N.J.: Pearson.

Traugott, E. C. and Pratt, M. L. 1980. *Linguistics for Students of Literature*. San Diego: Harcourt Brace Jovanovich.

Trim, J.M. 1981. Council of Europe Educational Objectives. Adapted from the report of a working party of the British National Congress on Languages in Education.

Two-Way Immersion Education: the Basics. 2005. Center for Applied Linguistics. http://www.alliance.brown.edu/pubs/twi and http://www.cal.org/twi

United Nations Cyberschoolbus. 1996. Understanding Discrimination. cyberschoolbus@un.org

Unrau, N. 2008. *Content Area Reading and Writing*. 2nd ed. Upper Saddle River, N.J.: Pearson.

Ur, P. 1996. *A Course in Language Teaching*. Cambridge: CUP.

Valsiner, J. 2003. Culture and its Transfer: Ways of Creating General Knowledge Through the Study of Cultural Particulars. In W. J. Lonner, D. L. Dinnel, S. A. Hayes, & D. N. Sattler (Eds.), Online Readings in Psychology and Culture (Unit 2, Chapter 12), (http://www.wwu.edu/~culture), Center for Cross-Cultural Research, Western Washington University, Bellingham, Washington.

Vohs, J. 2009. Parents Place Pointers. Massachusetts Parent Information & Resource Center (PIRC). Northhampton, MA.

Vygotsky, L.S. 1986. *Thought and language*. Cambridge, MA: MIT Press.

Vygotsky, L.S. 2006. *Mind in society*. Cambridge, MA: Harvard University Press.

Watson, S. (2011) Learning Disability Checklist. www.About.com

Weir, C. 1993. *Understanding and Developing Language Tests*. Hemel Hempstead: Prentice Hall International.

Willing, K. 1988. "Learning strategies as information management: Some definitions for a theory of learning strategies". *Prospect* 3/2: 139-55.

Yokota, J. 1993." Issues in Selecting Multicultural Children's Literature." Language Arts, 70, 156-167.

Zainuddin, H., et al. 2007. *Fundamentals of Teaching English to Speakers of Other Languages in K-12 Mainstream Classrooms.* 2nd ed. Dubuque: Kendall/Hunt.

Zebroski, J. T. 1994. Thinking through theory: Vygotskian perspectives on the teaching of writing. Portsmouth, NH: Boynton/Cook.

Zwiers, J. 2007. *Building Academic Language. Essential Practices for Content Classrooms, Grades 5-12.* San Francisco: Jossey-Bass.

SAMPLE TEST

1. In addition to learning and practicing with phonemes, English Language Learners must also be able to recognize and learn which additional aspects of phonology?
    (Competency 1.0)

    A. prefixes and suffixes
    B. pitch and stress
    C. phrases and clauses
    D. direct and indirect objects

2. The sentence: "The bus was late and he was late, but John still managed to catch it." is an example of a _____ .
    (Competency 1.0)

    A. simple sentence
    B. compound sentence
    C. complex sentence
    D. compound-complex sentence

3. Which one of the following is not a factor in people changing their register?
    (Competency 1.0)

    A. The relationship between the speakers
    B. The formality of the situation
    C. The attitude towards the listeners and subject
    D. The culture of the speakers

4. Which of the following characteristics of textbook language makes it difficult for ELLs to understand?
    (Competency 1.0)

    A. Genre
    B. Passive voice
    C. Pronoun reference
    D. All of the above

5. Which one of the following is not included in the study of "semantics"?
    (Competency 1.0)

    A. Culture
    B. The definition of individual words and meanings
    C. The intonation of the speaker
    D. Meaning which is "stored" or "inherent", as well as "contextual"

6. If you are studying "pragmatics", then you are studying:
    (Competency 1.0)

    A. the definition of individual words and meanings
    B. how context impacts the interpretation of language
    C. meaning which is "stored" or "inherent", as well as "contextual"
    D. all of the above

7. The theorist most associated with the study of communicative competence is:
(Competency 1.0)

A. Krashen
B. Fishman
C. Hymes
D. Pinker

8. The term diglossia means _____
(Competency 1.0)

A. use of language restricted to a limited close circle of speakers
B. speaking
C. use of separate dialects or use of separate language
D. a method of speaking when speakers do not share similar experiences or background

9. If you are studying "syntax", then you are studying:
(Competency 1.0)

A. intonation and accent when conveying a message
B. the rules for correct sentence structure
C. the definition of individual words and meanings
D. the subject-verb-object order of the English sentence

10. The ESOL teacher asks Sierra where her notebook is. Sierra answers, "He is in my bag." Which of the following explanations best helps you understand why the student used 'he' in her answer instead of, 'it'?
(Competency 1.0)

A. Sierra does not know what the word 'notebook means'.
B. Sierra's native language is one that marks objects as well as people by gender.
C. Sierra doesn't understand the difference between inanimate and animate objects in general.
D. Sierra is overgeneralizing rules for pronoun use.

11. Generally, why must phonographemic differences such as 'bare' and 'bear' be taught explicitly?
(Competency 1.0)

A. Sound-letter relationships in English are not always consistent.
B. Recognizing the difference in usage between homophones is difficult.
C. A and B
D. None of the above

12. Ralph Waldo Emerson's quote, "The English language is the sea which receives tributaries from every region under heaven," can be applied to which of the following phenomenon? *(Competency 1.0)*

   A. political rhetoric and sports metaphors contributing new words to the dominant culture, which changes the English language.

   B. technology and science contributing new words to the dominant culture(s), which changes the English language.

   C. immigrant cultures contributing new words to the dominant culture(s), which changes the English language.

   D. All of the above

13. If you are studying "morphemic analysis", then you are studying: *(Competency 1.0)*

   A. the smallest unit within a language system to which meaning is attached

   B. the root word and the suffix and/or prefix

   C. the way in which speech sounds form patterns

   D. answers A and B only

14. Learning about English morphemic analysis may provide students with: *(Competency 1.0)*

   A. an understanding of English grammar

   B. the tools necessary to understand English idioms

   C. the tools necessary to understand unfamiliar words

   D. all of the above

15. All of the following are examples of BICS except: *(Competency 1.0)*

   A. Call me.

   B. Text me after the game.

   C. Analyze and explain the causes of the Civil War.

   D. Please give me a fruit salad and a glass of milk.

16. When referring to a wealthy person as a "fat cat", the speaker is using a/an: *(Competency 1.0)*

   A. cognate

   B. derivational morpheme

   C. phrase

   D. idiom

17. Interlanguage is best described as: *(Competency 2.0)*

   A. a language characterized by overgeneralization

   B. bilingualism

   C. a language learning strategy

   D. a strategy characterized by poor grammar

18. Practicing, receiving and sending messages, analyzing and reasoning and creating structures for input and output are examples of:
(Competency 2.0)

A. cognitive strategies
B. metacognitive strategies
C. socioaffective strategies
D. social strategies

19. "The teacher 'writted' on the whiteboard" is an example of:
(Competency 2.0)

A. simplification
B. fossilization
C. inter-language
D. overgeneralization

20. An example of simplification by an English language learner is:
(Competency 2.0)

A. Adding 'ed' to irregular verbs to use the past tense
B. Stating 'I have a house beautiful in Miami' for 'I have a beautiful house in Miami'
C. Hispanics pronouncing words like 'student' as 'estudent'
D. Asking someone if 'You like?' instead of 'Do you like this one?

21. Young children are often considered better language learners than older children or adults. However, older children or adults may be able to progress more rapidly in developing literacy skills because:
(Competency 2.0)

A. they have more contextual knowledge to help them understand texts
B. their vocabulary concepts in L2 are less developed
C. they have more language learning experience
D. letter-sound relationships are the same between L1 and L2

22. Which of the following theorists is associated with social interaction as an important facilitator of language learning?
(Competency 2.0)

A. Krashen
B. Piaget
C. Vygotsky
D. Hymes

23. An intermediate/developing ELL, Miguel, was speaking in front of the class and telling them about his aunt, who had a big influence on him and his desire to learn. He introduced his aunt by saying, "Maria is a profesora." This is an example of:
(Competency 2.0)

A. dialect
B. inter-language
C. code-switching
D. formulaic speech

24. Chomsky's Language Acquisition Device (LAD) includes all of the following hypotheses except: *(Competency 2.0)*

    A. language learners form hypotheses based on the language they receive
    B. enter the world as a blank slate
    C. test out hypotheses in speech and texts
    D. construct language

25. Krashen's Natural Order hypothesis holds that: *(Competency 2.0)*

    A. Language instruction should follow a specific order.
    B. Learners follow a predictable pattern as they learn language.
    C. There are two basic ways of acquiring language.
    D. Classrooms must be orderly, safe environments for language acquisition to take place.

26. The Natural Approach theory is based on the idea that: *(Competency 2.0)*

    A. language is learned by imitating and practicing natural sounds
    B. language learning and skills grow naturally when learners are in an empathetic, supportive environment
    C. language is learned through natural principles taught through direct instruction
    D. language is learned subconsciously when interacting for natural, meaningful purposes

27. The Schema Theory of Carrell & Eisterhold suggests that for learning to take place, teachers must: *(Competency 2.0)*

    A. integrate content areas with ESOL techniques
    B. emphasize all four language skills
    C. present comprehensible input in a meaningful context
    D. relate new materials to previous knowledge

28. Which of the following statements is true of the Ramirez Report? *(Competency 3.0)*

    A. Investigators believe that students' perceptions of a program are essential to the evaluation of a program's effectiveness.
    B. Students in immersion and early-exit programs did not make as much progress in English language and literacy as those students in late-exit programs with consistent levels of primary language instruction.
    C. Teachers should reduce their English language demands when students are challenged cognitively, and vice versa.
    D. There is a higher level of more serious demand than by those being educated for higher levels of competence in foreign language and second languages than usually occurs in school-based programs.

29. When the teacher is correcting a student's language, the teacher should:
(*Competency 3.0*)

    A. carefully correct all mistakes
    B. consider the context of the error
    C. confirm the error by repeating it
    D. repeat the student's message but correct it

30. Which of the following methods is likely to be most effective in helping a student at the 'entering' level of English proficiency build vocabulary:
(*Competency 3.0*)

    A. TPR
    B. Word walls
    C. Pictionary
    D. charades

31. Abby is an enthusiastic child who always volunteers to go first in activities and presentations. She is sometimes too enthusiastic and jumps to conclusions before determining exactly what is being asked. Often, when asked why she made a choice or how she came to learn something, she can't answer the question. She doesn't know how she knows. Which of McCarthy's four learning styles most accurately describes her?
(*Competency 4.0*)

    A. Analytic learner
    B. Innovative learner
    C. Common Sense learner
    D. Dynamic learner

32. An affective factor that can impact language acquisition is:
(*Competency 4.0*)

    A. previous educational experience
    B. anxiety
    C. relationship between L1 and L2
    D. home environment

33. There are many socio-cultural factors that can affect language acquisition. Which of the following could negatively impact an ELL student's progress in learning English? The affective domain affects how students acquire a second language because:
(*Competency 4.0*)

    A. Learning English brings academic success but causes a 'break' from the family's home culture.
    B. An adolescent student is very reluctant to make mistakes in front of her/his peers.
    C. There are clear cultural differences between the student's new environment and where s/he is from.
    D. Facilitative anxiety determines our reaction to competition and is positive.

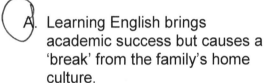

34. Which of the following activities is one of the easiest and/or most effective ways to learn new vocabulary?
(Competency 5.0)

A. Matching a vocabulary word with its definition
B. Labeling classroom objects
C. Singing
D. Listening to a tape and recording pertinent information in a graphic organizer

35. Advantages of informal assessment techniques include all the following except:
(Competency 5.0, 8.0)

A. recognizing opportunities for reteaching
B. giving feedback to students to improve learning
C. recognizing learning disabilities
D. adjusting or planning instructional opportunities

36. The ACCESS for ELLs 2.0 are a series of assessments for English language learners based on the WIDA English Language Development Standards. They are designed to assess:
(Competency 5.0)

A. only ELLS with learning or physical disabilities
B. students' proficiency in reading, writing, listening and speaking English
C. only ELLs in their first year at a new school
D. students' ability to think quickly in a timed testing situation

37. All of the following are characteristics of informal assessments except:
(Competency 5.0, 7.0, and 8.0)

A. are like frequent snapshots of learning
B. must be documented
C. can take many forms and be worked into common school routines
D. may take the form of observation of student performance

38. Formal assessments can be used to identify all of the following except:
(Competency 5.0)

A. a student's performance to grade level standards
B. a student's English language proficiency
C. a student's placement in special education classes
D. a student's performance in content-area knowledge

39. According to Ellis, two-way exchange of information shows more benefits in developing communication skills because:
(Competency 5.0)

A. open-ended tasks have no correct response
B. students enjoy chatting in class with peers
C. students can anticipate outcomes better
D. it requires more negotiation of meaning

40. When evaluating oral language, which one of the following is NOT an advantage of rubric-based scoring?
(Competency 5.0)

A. Allows students to compare their performance
B. Allows separate scoring of different criteria
C. Can be used to give descriptive feedback to students
D. Is performance-based

41. Which one of the following is not an effective activity used in developing speaking proficiency, especially with beginning and intermediate ELLs?
(Competency 5.0)

A. Choral reading
B. Individual reading (to the whole class)
C. Structured interviews
D. Role plays

42. Choose the best answer. TPR activities can contribute significantly to students listening comprehension proficiency because:
(Competency 5.0)

A. students are learning to follow simple commands, which they must do in the real world.
B. students are bonding with their classmates which helps create a positive learning environment.
C. students are actively involved in the listening process without being pressured to speak
D. students are getting some physical exercise; physically active students are more likely to learn

43. Which of the following would be the most effective activity to use with Entering or Beginning-level ELLs?
(Competency 5.0)

A. asking comprehension questions after completing a listening activity
B. frontloading vocabulary
C. identify a picture that matches specific passages or parts of passages that ESOL teacher is playing for the students
D. quiz

44. Which one of the scaffolding methods would be most effective in helping ELLs develop listening skills?
(Competency 5.0)

A. Frontloading or pre-teaching vocabulary
B. Asking ELLs to compare/contrast a listening activity with a text passage
C. Allowing students to listen several times
D. Creating a word wall

45. Cooperative learning tasks, races and team drawings are examples of:
(Competency 5.0)

A. metacognitive tasks
B. Chomsky's Language Acquisition Device (LAD)
C. two-way exchanges of information
D. linguistic modifications

46. Which of the following is not a step in the Language Experience Approach?
(Competency 5.0)

A. Students draw a picture to represent something personal about an experience
B. Students dictate their story to the teacher
C. The teacher reads the story revising where necessary
D. The story is read in later days as a follow-up activity

47. All of the following can help more advanced ELLs improve listening and speaking proficiency except:
(Competency 5.0)

A. memorization of long vocabulary lists that students will encounter in various texts and be expected to use when analyzing the texts
B. requiring students to integrate information and evidence from diverse media sources
C. emphasizing the authentic use of language (e.g. presentations or debates rather than memorization of language patterns)
D. integrating speaking, listening, reading and writing

48. In a "top down" strategy of literacy development, which one of the following undesirable strategies might not help a reader with comprehension?
(Competency 6)

A. Make guesses about what is going to happen
B. Look up and record each unfamiliar word
C. Anticipate the contents of the text
D. Infer meaning from sentences and paragraphs

49. Activities that help students develop phonological awareness, fluency in word recognition and the ability to sound out words are all key components of instructional strategies designed to:
(Competency 6)

    A. build cognitive and metacognitive skills
    B. build semantic and pragmatic skills
    C. build critical thinking skills
    D. build literacy skills

50. In the cooperative learning task "jigsaw", students:
(Competency 6)

    A. use open-ended questions
    B. pool meaning
    C. write headlines
    D. interview other students

51. ESOL instruction frequently requires the teacher to change his/her instruction methods. One of the most difficult may be:
(Competency 6.0)

    A. wait time
    B. establishment of group work
    C. show and tell based on different cultures
    D. extensive reading time

52. Which one of the following is not an effective instructional literacy practice for elementary ESOL teachers?
(Competency 6.0)

    A. Providing direct explicit instruction of reading/writing skills based on ongoing student assessment
    B. Devoting less than 50% of the day's instructional time to reading/writing
    C. Assessing student work based on common rubrics
    D. Promoting conversation through purposeful and guided discussions about a book, piece of writing, or topic

53. Activities which focus on increasing fluency in academic reading include all of the following strategies except:
(Competency 6.0)

    A. modeled reading
    B. repeated reading of a familiar text
    C. checking for understanding by asking if there are any questions
    D. coached reading of appropriate materials

54. To build reading fluency, a skill that helps students build reading comprehension skills, among other things, ESOL teachers can use all of the following strategies except:
(Competency 6.0)

A. choose texts carefully that students can read with some fluency

B. read aloud daily to students to model reading fluency

C. consistently quiz students after reading fluency activities to ensure success

D. have students re-read texts that they have heard before to build fluency

55. Successful ESOL teaching encourages tasks that:
(Competency 6.0)

A. alternate reading and listening passages accompanied by quizzes

B. give learners flexibility in problem solving

C. encourage learners to focus on accurate language use

D. are cognitively and linguistically demanding

56. Which researcher is most associated with problem solving activities for language learning?
(Competency 6.0)

A. Russell and Baker

B. Prabhu

C. Penfield and Roberts

D. Vygotsky

57. Common activities of the "post-reading phase" include:
(Competency 6.0)

A. building background knowledge

B. summarizing and organizing information

C. asking questions

D. annotating text

58. Cummin's interdependence hypothesis states that:
(Competency 6.0)

A. children are active learners who co-construct their worlds.

B. language is controlled by external influences and social interactions

C. the degree of knowledge and processes evident in the first language determines the ease of transfer to the new language

D. children are more prone to use their Language Acquisition Device (LAD), while adults are better able to use their inductive reasoning because of more fully developed cognitive faculties.

59. Asking students to make inferences increases learning in which domain?
(Competency 6.0)

A. Psychomotor

B. Cognitive

C. Affective

D. Naturalistic

60. When teaching initial literacy, teachers should focus on all of the following literacy skills except:
(Competency 7.0)

A. effect of culture on language learning
B. phonemic awareness
C. phonics
D. comprehension of different types of reading materials

61. Why is an ELL student's ability to read and then successfully paraphrase a text a good indicator of literacy development?
(Competency 7.0)

A. It demonstrates that the student can recognize main ideas.
B. It demonstrates that the student is overcoming anxiety about language learning.
C. This is an important element of BICS.
D. The student is using appropriate register for an academic setting.

62. Of the following questions, which one would be most effective in helping ELLs learn to infer meaning?
(Competency 7.0)

A. How can we synthesize what you just said?
B. What conclusions can you draw?
C. What is the relationship between...?
D. What evidence can you find...?

63. Which one of the following skills would probably have the most positive effect on developing literacy skills in ELLs?
(Competency 7.0)

A. Oral storytelling traditions
B. Watching documentaries on TV
C. Visiting art museums
D. Attending concerts

64. Which of the following are advantages to the instructor's of use of students' home language(s) in the English language classroom or in English language instruction?
(Competency 7.0)

A. It can reduce anxiety and fear
B. It can permit explanation of differences and similarities of home and new languages
C. It can reduce time-consuming explanations of abstract concepts
D. All of the above.

65. By acquiring knowledge of as few as _____ words, the ELL can understand _____ percent of the words used in conversation and comprehension of an academic text.
(Competency 7.0)

A. 1000; 74
B. 1500; 80
C. 2000; 95
D. 2500; 60

66. In helping students develop reading strategies for use in analyzing the plot of a novel, which one of the following suggestions is most likely to help build comprehension?
(Competency 7.0)

A. Morphemic analysis focusing on prefixes, roots, and suffixes
B. Annotations with arrows showing the relationship between events
C. The study of cognates
D. A word wall of commonly used words

67. Incorporating prior knowledge into second language learning does not:
(Competency 7.0)

A. provide opportunities for beginning English language readers to learn and remember more ⟶ *restraining*
B. inhibit the English language reading skills of beginning ELLs
C. help new English language readers to evaluate and understand new ideas
D. improve the reading comprehension skills of English language learners

68. Which one of the following questions would be least effective in promoting critical-thinking skills when looking at a butterfly collection?
(Competency 7.0)

A. Looking at this collection, what parts do the different butterflies have in common?
B. What evidence do you find to support the idea that butterflies are able to fly long distances?
C. How would you classify a butterfly compared to other animals that you know about?
D. What colors are the butterflies?

69. Which of the following is a metacognitive strategy?
(Competency 7.0)

A. Practicing new language
B. Summarizing long passages
C. Skimming for necessary information
D. Evaluating learning

70. To analyze oral discourse, which of the following is not an analytical question?
(Competency 7.0)

A. How did you feel about the dialogue?
B. How would you restate what the speaker said?
C. How would people from your country act in a similar situation?
D. Do you agree or disagree with what is said in the dialogue?

71. A science teacher is reluctant to incorporate partner work into a project. As an ESL teacher, what would be the most persuasive argument you could give to encourage your colleague to try partners for a project about an experiment?
(Competency 7.0, 8.0)

A. Partner work will allow native speakers of English to help ELL students.
B. Partner work can bridge the gap between native speakers and ELL students to create a more open classroom culture.
C. Partner work encourages authentic use of language and allows both students to use prior knowledge in demonstrating learning.
D. All of the above.

72. Which one of the following is not a way to establish reliability when placing students with disabilities?
(Competency 7.0)

A. Using multiple raters
B. Including multiple assessment measures
C. Establishing clearly specified scoring criteria
D. Using the Woodcock-Johnson III Diagnostic Reading Battery

73. Norm-referenced assessments may not provide accurate results when used with ELL students because:
(Competency 7.0)

A. The test is not in the student's home/first language.
B. The student will not understand the test.
C. The tests are too difficult for ELL students.
D. The norm group may not be reflective of the ELL student.

74. WIDA defines three types of support for ELL students. Which of the following is NOT one of them?
(Competency 7.0)

A. Sensory supports such as illustrations
B. Graphic supports such as timelines
C. Institutional supports such as bilingual assistants
D. Interactive supports such as partner work

75. Encouraging non-graded writing practice can really help English language learners develop writing fluency. Which of the following is not a task that encourages students to practice non-graded writing?
(Competency 8.0)

A. Writing a dialog in pairs
B. Rewriting a passage or summary in the ELL's own words
C. Writing from the perspective of another
D. Writing a summary or journal entry to hand in

76. The purpose of frontloading vocabulary is:
(Competency 8.0)

A. vocabulary development
B. increase reading comprehension
C. explaining content
D. increasing spelling proficiency

77. Reid (1987) divides the writing process into two broad divisions. They are:
(Competency 8.0)

A. composing; pre-writing
B. pre-writing; drafting
C. brainstorming; drafting
D. composition; revision

78. Which one of the following writing activities is not appropriate for different proficiency levels?
(Competency 8.0)

A. Reading and writing letters to friends, businesses or penpals
B. Writing directions for solving a problem
C. Writing long form book reports
D. Writing and organizing lists

79. Which one of the following is not an appropriate activity for engaging ELLs in real-life communicative activities?
(Competency 8.0)

A. Oral discussion based on a news story
B. Researching an assigned topic and reporting back to peers
C. Reporting on a new video game
D. Discussing a movie with a friend

80. Emerging ELLs need instruction in conventions of written Standard English such as:
(Competency 8.0)

A. syntax
B. discourse
C. vocabulary
D. types of written texts

81. Which one of the following is not a valid purpose of assessment?
(Competency 8.0)

A. Determining a student's potential
B. Determination of a student's present academic performance level
C. Eligibility for a program
D. Diagnosis of special learner disabilities

82. Tests which evaluate an individual as compared to others are:
(Competency 8.0)

A. standardized
B. authentic
C. norm referenced
D. criterion referenced

83. A student support team is looking over the assessment results from the ACCESS for ELLs 2.0 assessments, the MCAS ELA assessment and some formal and informal in-class assessments. For a few students, they notice a gap between the scores on the standardized tests and the scores on informal classroom assessments in science and social studies. Which of the following cannot be inferred by this gap?
(Competency 8.0)

A. Some students may work very hard to understand and express their understanding in the subjects they love, but may be challenged with lower cognitive skills than the team initially thought

B. Some students may be so nervous taking formal assessments and standardized tests that it impacts their performance.

C. Some teachers may be scoring informal assessments too high because they know what the student wanted to express.

D. Some students may have higher cognitive levels and content-area knowledge than the team initially thought but may be challenged by lack of English proficiency/fluency.

84. Which one of the following goals will not be discovered through assessment?
(Competency 8.0)

A. If student is ready for new information

B. Strategies for improving programs

C. If student is lacking prerequisite skills

D. Program weaknesses

85. Which of the following writing assessments uses holistic scoring?
(Competency 8.0)

A. International English Language Test System (IELTS)

B. National Assessment of Educational Progress (NAEP)

C. Test of English as a Foreign Language (TOEFL)

D. Michigan Writing Assessment

86. Which one of the following is a disadvantage of portfolio assessment?
(Competency 8.0)

A. They are integrative

B. They produce variable samples

C. They are motivating

D. They are formative

87. Sheltered content teaching allows teachers to do all of the following except:
(Competency 9.0)

A. use realia, word lists, gestures, etc.

B. reduce language demands

C. facilitate learning

D. instruct in heritage language

88. Vocabulary development is an essential component of learning for ELL students. To support this, teachers should focus on:
(Competency 6.0, 9.0)

A. Finding opportunities for students to use words in realistic situations
B. Have students do memorization drills
C. Emphasize correct pronunciation
D. Writing down definitions

89. Arreaga-Mayer (1998) suggests all of the following constructs for successful ELLs except:
(Competency 9.0)

A. collaborative/cooperative learning
B. input slightly above competence level
C. involvement
D. mediation/feedback

90. Which one of the following is not one of the three basic strategies that WIDA recommends to support ELL students building content-area knowledge, skills and vocabulary?
(Competency 9.0)

A. sensory strategies (e.g., word walls, math manipulatives)
B. graphic strategies (e.g., venn diagrams, word webs)
C. interactive strategies (e.g. mentors, group work)
D. homework strategies (e.g. vocabulary study, reading comprehension questions and answers

91. All of the following are part of an integrated approach to language teaching except:
(Competency 9.0)

A. Language Experience Approaches
B. Cooperative learning activities
C. Task-based or experiential learning tasks
D. Note-taking and planning with graphic organizers

92. Which of the following is a model of content-based instruction, part of the Integrated Language Teaching strategy:
(Competency 9.0)

A. theme based models (language is integrated in the study of themes or broad topics)
B. peer tutoring model (cooperative peer mediated instruction of language and content)
C. adjunct model (language and content taught separately but closely coordinated)
D. sheltered model (English is simplified to ELL's level of proficiency while teaching content)

93. According to Chomsky's Universal Grammar (UG) and Language Acquisition Device (LAD) theories, younger learners have less difficulty learning language because:
(Competency 9.0)

A. language is controlled by external factors
B. after puberty, the critical period shuts down
C. their LAD is still active
D. language abilities increase with age

94. All of the following are true about the Massachusetts Comprehensive Assessment System (MCAS) except:
(Competency 9.0)

A. Each public school student in the state is tested in grades 3-8 and once in high school in English.
B. The Massachusetts Curriculum Frameworks forms the basis of the test battery.
C. Each public school student in the state is tested in grades 3-8 and once in high school in mathematics.
D. Each public school student in the state is tested in grades 3-8 and once in high school in history and social studies.

95. To distinguish between ELLs and ELLs with disabilities, which one of the following testing procedures is not recommended?
(Competency 9.0)

A. Intelligence quotient (IQ) test
B. Criterion-referenced assessments
C. Curriculum-referenced assessments
D. Observations from school, home, and community

96. Culture plays an important role in our lives and can affect classroom teaching and learning in several ways. Which of the following is not a way that culture can affect ELL students in the classroom:
(Competency 9.0)

A. concepts and practices around roles and interpersonal relationships
B. concepts and practices around food and religion
C. concepts and practices around time and physical space
D. All of the above

97. Teacher Assistance Teams (TATS) should be composed of all of the following except the:
(Competency 9.0)

A. school administrators
B. guidance counselors
C. media specialists
D. parent(s)

98. When considering referrals for specialized services, all of the following are considered except: *(Competency 9.0)*

    A. student characteristics
    B. parents' request for/against referral
    C. multidisciplinary evaluation
    D. institutional factors

99. To protect students from inequities in the referral process, federal law explicitly provides for: *(Competency 9.0)*

    A. non-discriminatory evaluation procedures
    B. an independent education evaluation
    C. a multidisciplinary team using several pieces of information to formulate a referral
    D. testing of the child in L1 unless clearly not feasible to do so

100. Information for placing students with learning or behavioral disabilities will usually include all of the following except: *(Competency 9.0)*

    A. past academic performance
    B. neurological reports
    C. notes from auxiliary/substitute teachers
    D. speech and language evaluations

ANSWER KEY

1.	B	43.	C	85.	C
2.	B	44.	C	86.	B
3.	D	45.	C	87.	D
4.	D	46.	C	88.	A
5.	A	47.	A	89.	B
6.	B	48.	B	90.	D
7.	B	49.	D	91.	A
8.	C	50.	B	92.	B
9.	B	51.	A	93.	C
10.	B	52.	B	94.	D
11.	C	53.	C	95.	A
12.	D	54.	C	96.	D
13.	D	55.	B	97.	C
14.	C	56.	B	98.	C
15.	C	57.	B	99.	B
16.	D	58.	C	100.	C
17.	C	59.	B		
18.	A	60.	A		
19.	D	61.	A		
20.	D	62.	D		
21.	A	63.	A		
22.	C	64.	D		
23.	C	65.	C		
24.	B	66.	B		
25.	B	67.	B		
26.	D	68.	D		
27.	D	69.	D		
28.	B	70.	B		
29.	D	71.	C		
30.	A	72.	D		
31.	D	73.	D		
32.	B	74.	C		
33.	A	75.	D		
34.	C	76.	B		
35.	C	77.	D		
36.	B	78.	C		
37.	B	79.	B		
38.	C	80.	A		
39.	D	81.	A		
40.	A	82.	C		
41.	B	83.	D		
42.	C	84.	B		

RATIONALES

1. **In addition to learning and practicing with phonemes, English Language Learners must be able to recognize and learn which additional aspects of phonology?**
   (Competency 1.0)

   A. prefixes and suffixes
   B. pitch and stress
   C. phrases and clauses
   D. direct and indirect objects

The correct answer is B. pitch and stress.
Pitch and stress (at the word and sentence level) affects the meaning being communicated. Until ELLs learn to recognize and interpret these aspects of phonology, they may be confused about the meaning of specific words and sentences they are listening to or reading.

2. **The sentence: "The bus was late and he was late, but John still managed to catch it." is an example of a _____.**
   (Competency 1.0)

   A. simple sentence
   B. compound sentence
   C. complex sentence
   D. compound-complex sentence

The correct answer is B. compound sentence
Answer A may be eliminated since the sentence contains three independent clauses. Since there are no independent clauses, Answer C and D may be eliminated. Thus, Answer B is the correct choice.

3. **Which one of the following is not a factor in people changing their register?**
   (Competency 1.0)

   A. The relationship between the speakers
   B. The formality of the situation
   C. The attitude towards the listeners and subject
   D. The culture of the speakers

The correct answer is D. The culture of the speakers
People change their register depending on the relationship between the speakers, the formality of the situation, and the attitudes towards the listeners and the subject. Answer D—culture of the speakers—is not a reason for people to change their register.

4. **Which of the following characteristics of textbook language makes it difficult for ELLs to understand?**
   (Competency 1.0)

   A. Genre
   B. Passive voice
   C. Pronoun reference
   D. All of the above

The correct answer is D. All of the above
Answer A: each genre has a distinct organizational pattern and writing style. Answer B: The passive voice is common in textbooks, especially science textbooks. Answer C: To whom or what a pronoun refers can be obscure and cause problems for ELLs, too. Thus, D is the correct choice. Textbook language is difficult for most ELLs for many reasons.

5. **Which one of the following is not included in the study of "semantics"?**
   (Competency 1.0)

   A. Culture
   B. The definition of individual words and meanings
   C. The intonation of the speaker
   D. Meaning which is "stored" or "inherent", as well as "contextual"

The correct answer is A. Culture
Since semantics refers to the definition of individual words and meanings, the intonation of the speaker, and meaning which is "stored" or "inherent", as well as "contextual", option A is the best response.

6. **If you are studying "pragmatics", then you are studying:**
   (Competency 1.0)

   A. the definition of individual words and meanings
   B. how context impacts the interpretation of language
   C. meaning which is "stored" or "inherent", as well as "contextual"
   D. all of the above

The correct answer is B. how context impacts the interpretation of language
The definition of individual words and meanings refers to semantics. Meaning which is "stored" or "inherent", as well as "contextual" refers to the lexicon of a language. The best option is B as pragmatics refers to studies of how context impacts the interpretation of language.

7. **The theorist most associated with the study of communicative competence is:**
   (Competency 1.0)

   A. Krashen
   B. Fishman
   C. Hymes
   D. Pinker

The correct answer is B. Hymes
A Krashen formulated The Monitor Model, and the Natural Approach, among other theories. B. Fishman was famous for his work on diglossia, Pinker wrote about language instinct. Hymes wrote about communicative competence and his model of discourse analysis that explained the relationship between society, culture and language and can be more easily remembered with the acronym SPEAKING.

8. **The term diglossia means _____.**
   (Competency 1.0)

   A. use of language restricted to a limited close circle of speakers
   B. speaking
   C. use of separate dialects or use of separate language
   D. a method of speaking when speakers do not share similar experiences or background

The correct answer is C. use of separate dialects or use of separate language
Answer A refers to Bernstein's restricted code and D to his elaborated code. Answer B is an acronym Hymes devised to explain the abilities of a native speaker. Answer C is a definition of diglossia and the correct choice.

9. **If you are studying "syntax", then you are studying:**
   (Competency 1.0)

   A. intonation and accent when conveying a message
   B. the rules for correct sentence structure
   C. the definition of individual words and meanings
   D. the subject-verb-object order of the English sentence

The correct answer is B. the rules for correct sentence structure
The intonation and accent used when conveying a message refer to pitch and stress. The definition of individual words and meanings is semantics. The subject-verb-object order of the English sentence refers to is the correct order for most English sentences, but the rules for correct sentence structure refers to syntax, so B is the best option.

10. The ESOL teachers asks Sierra where her notebook is. Sierra answers, "He is in my bag." Which of the following explanations best helps you understand why the student used 'he' in her answer instead of 'it'?

    A. Sierra does not know what the word 'notebook means'.
    B. Sierra's native language is one that marks objects as well as people by gender.
    C. Sierra doesn't understand the difference between inanimate and animate objects in general.
    D. Sierra is overgeneralizing rules for pronoun use.

The correct answer is B. Sierra's native language is one that marks objects as well as people by gender.

Many languages, including Spanish, French and Italian mark inanimate objects for gender. This type of mistake is very common with English language learners whose native languages do this. Although it is possible that Sierra overgeneralized, this is more common with rules that learners try to apply across the board, like rules around tense use. Sierra probably wouldn't think that all of the inanimate objects were gendered as male, so her mistake is more likely a result of her native language.

11. Generally, why must phonographemic differences such 'bare' and 'bear' be taught explicitly?
    (Competency 1.0)

    A. Sound-letter relationships in English are not always consistent.
    B. Recognizing the difference in usage between homophones is difficult.
    C. A and B
    D. None of the above

The correct answer is C. A and B

Some languages have consistent sound-letter relationships (e.g., Spanish and Turkish), but English does not. ELL students may not recognize the distinction between 'bear' and 'bare' and use the 'wrong' word with the 'right' spelling. Because the two words in this example sound exactly alike, it would be difficult to distinguish when to use the appropriate word without explicit practice and instruction.

12. Ralph Waldo Emerson's quote, "The English language is the sea which receives tributaries from every region under heaven," can be applied to which of the following phenomenon?
(Competency 1.0)

    A. political rhetoric and sports metaphors contributing new words to the dominant culture, which changes the English language.
    B. technology and science contributing new words to the dominant culture(s), which changes the English language.
    C. immigrant cultures contributing new words to the dominant culture(s), which changes the English language.
    D. All of the above

The correct answer is D. All of the above.
There are so many influences on the English language including war, politics, sports, new cultures, technology and science, text messaging/internet language, work related jargon and even geography. This is what makes English such a dynamic, living language.

13. If you are studying "morphemic analysis", then you are studying:
(Competency 1.0)

    A. the smallest unit within a language system to which meaning is attached
    B. the root word and the suffix and/or prefix
    C. the way in which speech sounds form patterns
    D. answers A and B only

The correct answer is D. answers A and B only
The study of the way in which speech sounds form patterns is called phonology. The smallest unit within a language system to which meaning is attached is a morpheme. The root word and the suffix and/or prefix are components of morphemes and basic to the analysis of a word. Therefore, both A and B are necessary for the study of morphemic analysis so the correct answer is D.

14. Learning about English morphemic analysis may provide students with: *(Competency 1.0)*

   A. an understanding of English grammar
   B. the tools necessary to understand English idioms
   C. the tools necessary to understand unfamiliar words
   D. all of the above

The correct answer is C. The tools necessary to understand unfamiliar words
Morphemes are the smallest units of a language that have meaning. Though some morphemes (e.g., and) can provide grammatical information in a sentence, they do not provide an understanding of grammar. Similarly, they do not give insights into idioms. Morphemic analysis can, however, help in breaking down a word and understanding it. For example, 'disrespectful' contains the morphemes 'dis' and 'ful'. Knowing their meaning can help in understanding the whole word.

15. All of the following are examples of BICS except: *(Competency 1.0)*

   A. Call me.
   B. Text me after the game.
   C. Analyze and explain the causes of the Civil War.
   D. Please give me a fruit salad and a glass of milk.

The correct answer is C. Analyze and explain the causes of the Civil War.
BICS (basic interpersonal communication skills) refers to the ability to communicate with peers, teachers, friends, people in stores, etc. in routine social situations. C is an example of Cognitive Academic Language Proficiency (CALP); CALP includes the language skills necessary to fully participate in academic discourse.

16. When referring to a wealthy person as a "fat cat", the speaker is using a/an: *(Competency 1.0)*

   A. cognate
   B. derivational morpheme
   C. phrase
   D. idiom

The correct answer is D. idiom
Idioms are new meanings assigned to words that already have a meaning in a language. The expression 'fat cat' literally means a cat that is fat. However, it has become an idiomatic way to say someone is a wealthy person.

17. Interlanguage is best described as:
    (Competency 2.0)

    A. a language characterized by overgeneralization
    B. bilingualism
    C. a language learning strategy
    D. a strategy characterized by poor grammar

The correct answer is C. a language learning strategy
Interlanguage occurs when the second language learner lacks proficiency in L2 and tries to compensate for his or her lack of fluency in the new language. Three components are overgeneralization, simplification, and L1 interference or language transfer. Therefore, answer A is only one component of interlanguage making option C the correct answer.

18. Practicing, receiving and sending messages, analyzing and reasoning and creating structures for input and output are examples of:
    (Competency 2.0)

    A. cognitive strategies
    B. metacognitive strategies
    C. socioaffective strategies
    D. social strategies

The correct answer is A. cognitive strategies
Cognitive strategies are strategies that related to how learners internalize language rules and learn vocabulary in a second language. The cognitive strategies listed above are often remembered using the acronym, PRAC. Metacognitive strategies refer to students thinking about their own learning, socioaffective strategies relate more to emotions and social strategies are more related to working with others.

19. "The teacher 'writted' on the whiteboard" is an example of:
    (Competency 2.0)

    A. simplification
    B. fossilization
    C. inter-language
    D. overgeneralization

The correct answer is D. overgeneralization
In this case, the ELL has tried to apply the rule of /ed/ endings to an irregular verb to form the past tense verb, i.e., s/he has used 'overgeneralization' to create an incorrect verb form. The correct answer is D.

20. An example of simplification by an English language learner is:
    (Competency 2.0)

    A. Adding 'ed' to irregular verbs as a way to use the past tense
    B. Stating 'I have a house beautiful in Miami' for 'I have a beautiful house in Miami'
    C. Hispanics pronouncing words like 'student' as 'estudent'
    D. Asking someone if 'You like?' instead of 'Do you like this one?

The correct answer is D. Asking someone if 'You like?' instead of 'Do you like this one?'
Simplification is a common learner error involving simplifying the language where the correct structures have not been internalized. In this case, the correct question form has not been acquired through the ELLs meaning is clear.

21. Young children are often considered better language learners than older children or adults. However, older children or adults may be able to progress more rapidly in developing literacy skills because:
    (Competency 2.0)

    A. they have more contextual knowledge to help them understand texts
    B. their vocabulary concepts in L2 are less developed
    C. they have more language learning experience
    D. letter-sound relationships are the same between L1 and L2

The correct answer is A. they have more contextual knowledge to help them understand texts
Answers B and C would depend on the individuals involved in the learning situation. For answer D, it is possible that letter-sound relationships are the same between languages. If this is true, it could make learning to read easier for an already literate ELL student. However, many languages do not have the same relationships, and many do not even use the same alphabet as English, so this answer would not hold true. The correct answer is A. Older learners can apply their worldly experience and schema developed in L1 to understanding L2 texts as well as other language learning situations.

22. Which of the following theorists is associated with social interaction as an important facilitator of language learning?
    (Competency 2.0)

    A. Krashen
    B. Piaget
    C. Vygotsky
    D. Hymes

The correct answer is C. Vygotsky
Answer A: Krashen formulated The Monitor Model. Answer B: Bernstein researched restricted and elaborated codes. Answer D: Hymes theorized on communicative competence. Answer C: Vygotsky theorized on the importance of social interaction in the language learning process.

23. An intermediate/developing ELL, Miguel, was speaking in front of the class and telling them about his aunt, who had a big influence on him and his desire to learn. He introduced his aunt by saying, "Maria is a profesora." This is an example of:
    (Competency 2.0)

    A. dialect
    B. inter-language
    C. code-switching
    D. formulaic speech

The correct answer is C. code-switching
Dialect is any form or variety of a spoken language peculiar to a region, community, social group, etc. Inter-language is the language spoken by ELLs that is between their L1 and L2. Formulaic speech refers to speech that is ritualistic in nature and perhaps used for social politeness rather than information.

Sociolinguistics is a very broad term used to understand the relationship between language and people including the phenomenon of people switching languages during a conversation. One person may switch languages when a word is not known in the other language. Option C is the correct option.

24. Chomsky's Language Acquisition Device (LAD) includes all of the following hypotheses except:
(Competency 2.0)

A. language learners form hypotheses based on the language they receive
B. enter the world as a blank slate
C. test out hypotheses in speech and texts
D. construct language

The correct answer is B. enter the world as a blank slate
The essence of Chomsky's theory is that children do not enter the world as a blank slate, but rather have a LAD which permits the construction of their language regardless of which language it may be. The LAD is innate. Therefore, Option B is the correct choice as it does not support Chomsky's theory.

25. Krashen's Natural Order hypothesis holds that:
(Competency 2.0)

A. Language instruction should follow a specific order.
B. Learners follow a predictable pattern as they learn language.
C. There are two basic ways of acquiring language.
D. Classrooms must be orderly, safe environments for language acquisition to take place.

The correct answer is B. Learners follow a predictable pattern as they learn language.
Krashen's Natural Order hypothesis holds that language learners acquire different aspects of language in a typical order. Some grammatical structures, for example, are learned early while others are acquired later in the language learning process. Though this has implications for instruction, it does not determine language instruction.

26. The Natural Approach theory is based on the idea that:
    (Competency 2.0)

    A. language is learned by imitating and practicing natural sounds
    B. language learning and skills grow naturally when learners are in an empathetic, supportive environment
    C. language is learned through natural principles taught through direct instruction
    D. language is learned subconsciously when interacting for natural, meaningful purposes

The correct answer is D. language is learned subconsciously when interacting for natural, meaningful purposes

The underlying assumption of The Natural Approach is that any learner of any age can receive comprehensible speech input and determine its pattern, without someone else having to spell it out for them and that speech emerges from motivated language use and not artificial practice.

27. The Schema Theory of Carrell & Eisterhold suggests that for learning to take place, teachers must:
    (Competency 2.0)

    A. integrate content areas with ESOL techniques
    B. emphasize all four language skills
    C. present comprehensible input in a meaningful context
    D. relate new materials to previous knowledge

The correct answer is D. relate new materials to previous knowledge

The schema theory of Carrell & Eisterhold suggests that schema must be related to previous knowledge or learning does not take place. When activated, schema are able to evaluate the new materials in light of previous knowledge. If the arguments are made convincing to the learner, he or she accepts them and integrates the new knowledge into his/her data bank. Otherwise, the new materials are unconvincing, and the new knowledge is rejected by the learner.

28. Which of the following statements is true of the Ramirez Report?
(Competency 3.0)

   A. Investigators believe that students' perceptions of a program are essential to the evaluation of a program's effectiveness.
   B. Students in immersion and early-exit programs did not make as much progress in English language and literacy as those students in late-exit programs with consistent levels of primary language instruction.
   C. Teachers should reduce their English language demands when students are challenged cognitively, and vice versa.
   D. There is a higher level of more serious demand than by those being educated for higher levels of competence in foreign language and second languages than usually occurs in school-based programs.

The correct answer is B. Students in immersion and early-exit programs did not make as much progress in English language and literacy as those students in late-exit programs with consistent levels of primary language instruction.
Answer A refers to the Amigos Program reported on by Cabazon, Lambert & Hall, 1992. Answer C refers to statements of Gersten and Baker, 2001. Answer D is a distinction discovered by Lambert, 1990. Answer B is the correct one since it was a conclusion of the U.S. Department of Education, 1991, and informally known as the Ramirez Report.

29. When the teacher is correcting a student's language, the teacher should:
(Competency 3.0)

   A. carefully correct all mistakes
   B. consider the context of the error
   C. confirm the error by repeating it
   D. repeat the student's message but correct it

The correct answer is D. repeat the student's message but correct it
To carefully correct all mistakes a student makes would raise the affective filter and probably cause the student to hesitate before speaking. Considering the context of the error gives the teacher insight into the student's learning, but it isn't a method of correction. To confirm the error by repeating it would suggest to the student that his or her utterance was correct and is not good practice. The best option is D which corrects the error, but in a way that shows the student the correct form without embarrassing him or her.

30. Which of the following methods is likely to be most effective in helping a student at the 'entering' level of English proficiency build vocabulary? *(Competency 3.0)*

   A. TPR
   B. Word walls
   C. Pictionary
   D. charades

The correct answer is A. TPR
Though all four of these techniques are potentially effective in building vocabulary, B, C, and D would likely be difficult for students at the entering level. Pictionary and charades would likely be intimidating and raise students' affective filter because of their lack of proficiency. Word walls might be useful if the student can decode words in English. TPR, on the other hand, allows students to follow simple instructions with teacher guidance to build vocabulary.

31. Abby is an enthusiastic child who always volunteers to go first in activities and presentations. She is sometimes too enthusiastic and jumps to conclusions before determining exactly what is being asked. Often, when asked why she made a specific choice or how she came to learn something, she can't answer the question. She doesn't know how she knows. Which of McCarthy's four learning styles most accurately describes her? *(Competency 4.0)*

   A. Analytic learner
   B. Innovative learner
   C. Common Sense learner
   D. Dynamic learner

The correct answer is D. Dynamic Learner
Analytic learners (Answer A) think through ideas and concepts carefully and Abby clearly does not do this. Innovative learners (Answer B) learn more by getting personally involved in their learning through social interaction. From the information given in the scenario, we cannot tell if this is true for Abby and we cannot tell if she is a common sense learner either. Dynamic learners like to learn intuitively; they like to take risks and they sometimes jump to conclusions. Therefore, Abby is a dynamic learner, Answer D.

32. An affective factor that can impact language acquisition is:
    (Competency 4.0)

    A. previous educational experience
    B. anxiety
    C. relationship between L1 and L2
    D. home environment

The correct answer is B. Anxiety.
Though previous educational experience and the relationship between L1 and L2 can play a role in a student's language acquisition, anxiety is an affective factor. ESOL teachers can minimize this factor by creating a classroom environment that feels 'safe' for language learners.

33. There are many socio-cultural factors that can affect language acquisition. Which of the following could negatively impact an ELL student's progress in learning English? The affective domain affects how students acquire a second language because:
    (Competency 4.0)

    A. Learning English brings academic success but causes a 'break' from the family's home culture.
    B. An adolescent student is very reluctant to make mistakes in front of her/his peers.
    C. There are clear cultural differences between the student's new environment and where s/he is from.
    D. Facilitative anxiety determines our reaction to competition and is positive.

The correct answer is A. Learning English brings academic success but causes a 'break' from the family's home culture.
Answers B and D describe affective factors that could impact a student's language learning. Answer C represents a socio-cultural factor that could have an effect on learning, but there is no reason to expect that the effect would necessarily be negative. Answer A is a clear socio-cultural factor that some students experience. Learning English can be viewed as a rejection of the culture in which a student was raised. When this occurs, it is most often in environments in which the student's home culture/language are looked down on and not respected.

34. Which of the following activities is one of the easiest and/or most effective ways to learn new vocabulary?
(Competency 5.0)

    A. Matching a vocabulary word with its definition
    B. Labeling classroom objects
    C. Singing
    D. Listening to a tape and recording pertinent information in a graphic organizer

The correct answer is C. Singing
Both Answers A and B are passive activities which do not require the learner to use the language. Answer D is an effective listening strategy, but the learner is trying to understand and remember the material, not learn vocabulary. Only Answer C facilitates the learning of language and/or vocabulary. In several studies, including one written about in Memory & Cognition, 2013; DOI, participants who learned through singing phrases performed much better than those who learned by speaking the same phrases; they were more likely to have better pronunciation of the words and sentences and better able to recall the phrases with greater accuracy for a longer amount of time.

35. Advantages of informal assessment techniques include all of the following except:
(Competency 5.0, 8.0)

    A. recognizing opportunities for reteaching
    B. giving feedback to students to improve learning
    C. recognizing learning disabilities
    D. adjusting or planning instructional opportunities

The correct answer is C. Recognizing learning disabilities
Informal or formative assessments are useful opportunities to give feedback to students on progress towards learning goals. They are also useful for teachers in planning instruction or determining if content needs to be retaught. Though informal assessments may indicate to a teacher the presence of a problem, to determine learning disabilities, more formal, diagnostic assessments are needed.

36. The ACCESS for ELLs 2.0 are a series of assessments for English language learners based on the WIDA English Language Development Standards. They are designed to assess:
(Competency 5.0)

A. only ELLS with learning or physical disabilities
B. students' proficiency in reading, writing, listening and speaking English
C. only ELLs in their first year at a new school
D. students' ability to think quickly in a timed testing situation

The correct answer is B. proficiency in reading, writing, listening and speaking English
Answer A may be discarded since in Massachusetts all ELLs, including those with disabilities are required to take the ACCESS for ELLs 2.0. Answer C may be discarded as ELLs are required to take the ACCESS for ELLs 2.0 until they reach a minimum level 5.5 or 6 in all standards. Answer D may be discarded as the ACCESS for ELLs 2.0 does not assess students based on the amount of time they take to complete the assessments. Only Answer B is correct. Proficiency in reading, writing, listening and speaking are the components evaluated by the ACCESS for ELLs 2.0.

37. All of the following are characteristics of informal assessments except:
(Competency 5.0, 7.0, and 8.0)

A. are like frequent snapshots of learning
B. must be documented
C. can take many forms and be worked into common school routines
D. may take the form of observation of student performance

The correct answer is B. must be documented
Informal or formative assessments take many forms and include conferences with students, observations, checks for understanding, exit tickets, and polls. These assessments frequent and form the 'picture' teachers form of students as they progress throughout the year. Though teachers may document the results of these informal assessments, they do not all need to be recorded.

38. Formal assessments can be used to identify all of the following except:
(Competency 5.0)

   A. a student's performance to grade level standards
   B. a student's English language proficiency
   C. a student's placement in special education classes
   D. a student's performance in content-area knowledge

The correct answer is C. a student's placement in special education classes
In Massachusetts, formal assessments, including the ACCESS for ELLs 2.0 and the MCAS are used to measure students' proficiency and performance in areas listed in Answers A, B, and D. Only Answer C is inaccurate as many factors, as well as different types of reports and records, lead up to placement in special education classes, not just formal assessments.

39. According to Ellis, two-way exchange of information shows more benefits in developing communication skills because:
(Competency 5.0)

   A. open-ended tasks have no correct response
   B. students enjoy chatting in class with peers
   C. students can anticipate outcomes better
   D. it requires more negotiation of meaning

The correct answer is D. it requires more negotiation of meaning
Only Answer D was a conclusion of Ellis' study.

40. When evaluating oral language, which one of the following is NOT an advantage of rubric-based scoring?
(Competency 5.0)

   A. Allows students to compare their performance
   B. Allows separate scoring of different criteria
   C. Can be used to give descriptive feedback to students
   D. Is performance-based

The correct answer is A. Allows students to compare their performance
Rubrics are an ideal way to assess student performance in a presentation or discussion. The rubric can allow the teacher to evaluate overall performance while separating out criteria such as oral fluency or vocabulary. A student may perform very well in one area and not as well in another. The rubric can then be used to give students feedback on areas of strength/weakness. Though students can theoretically compare rubrics, each one gives information that is much more individualized and is therefore not about comparison.

41. Which one of the following is not an effective activity used in developing speaking proficiency, especially with beginning and intermediate ELLs? *(Competency 5.0)*

   A. Choral reading
   B. Individual reading (to the whole class)
   C. Structured interviews
   D. Role plays

The correct answer is B. Individual reading (to the whole class).
Answers A, C, and D are all effective strategies for developing speaking skills. According to the findings of the National Literacy Panel on Language-Minority Children and Youth, ELL may be very self-consciousness about making mistakes in front of their peers and/or about having an 'accent'. If pressured to read aloud in front of the entire class, this can have a negative impact on their reading fluency. Answer A is the correct choice.

42. Choose the best answer. TPR activities can contribute significantly to students listening comprehension proficiency because: *(Competency 5.0)*

   A. students are learning to follow simple commands, which they will have to do in the real world.
   B. students are bonding with their classmates which helps create a positive learning environment.
   C. students are actively involved in the listening process without being pressured to speak
   D. students are getting some physical exercise; physically active students are more likely to learn

The correct answer is C. Students are actively involved in the listening process without being pressured to speak.
Studies show that incorporation other skills and activities into listening comprehension can help students retain and use the new language. In addition, many ELLs may understand but struggle to produce language by speaking or writing. TPR gives students the opportunity to show that they understand without the challenges of producing language. Although answers B and C may be true, they are not as closely correlated to improved listening comprehension proficiency.

43. **Which of the following would be the most effective activity to use with Entering or Beginning level ELLs?**
    (Competency 5.0)

    A. asking comprehension questions after completing a listening activity
    B. frontloading vocabulary
    C. identify a picture that matches specific passages or parts of passages that ESOL teacher is playing for the students
    D. quiz

The correct answer is C. Identify a picture that matches specific passages or parts of passages that ESOL teacher is playing for the students.
Answer A is ineffective because students will frequently "tune out" of listening activities because they don't understand and listening is hard work. Answer B may be effective for helping the ELL to understand what he/she is going to hear but may also confuse a beginning English language learner. Answer D is the least effective option because it may raise anxiety levels and block learning. Answer C is the best choice because students will be listening to the entire passage and actively engaging with it.

44. **Which one of the scaffolding methods would be most effective in helping ELLs develop listening skills?**
    (Competency 5.0)

    A. Frontloading or pre-teaching vocabulary
    B. Asking ELLs to compare/contrast a listening activity with a text passage
    C. Allowing students to listen several times
    D. Creating a word wall

The correct answer is C. Allowing students to listen several times
While all the answers are effective scaffolding techniques, until understanding is achieved, learning does not occur. The best option would be C, allowing ELL students to listen several times.

45. Cooperative learning tasks, races and team drawings are examples of: *(Competency 5.0)*

A. metacognitive tasks
B. Chomsky's Language Acquisition Device (LAD)
C. two-way exchanges of information
D. linguistic modifications

The correct answer is C. two-way exchanges of information.
Ellis concluded that two-way exchanges of information show more benefits for ELLs partly because they require more negotiation of meaning. When learning cooperatively, participating in TPR races, or team drawing, students are focusing on comprehension and on producing the language in some form - whether by drawing, physical movement or communicating with other students. Answer B. Chomsky's LAD refers to children not entering the world as a blank slate. Answer A refers to task where students think about how they learn and how they think.

46. Which of the following is not a step in the Language Experience Approach? *(Competency 5.0)*

A. Students draw a picture to represent something personal about an experience
B. Students dictate their story to the teacher
C. The teacher reads the story revising where necessary
D. The story is read in later days as a follow-up activity

The correct answer is C. The teacher reads the story revising where necessary
In the Language Experience Approach, the teacher writes the revised sentences on the storyboard making the necessary corrections.

47. All of the following can help more advanced ELLs improve listening and speaking proficiency except:
(Competency 5.0)

A. memorization of long vocabulary lists that students will encounter in various texts and be expected to use when analyzing the texts
B. requiring students to integrate information and evidence from diverse media sources
C. emphasizing the authentic use of language (e.g. presentations or debates rather than memorization of language patterns);
D. integrating speaking, listening, reading and writing

The correct answer is A. memorization of long vocabulary lists that students will encounter in various texts and be expected to use when analyzing the texts
Answers B, C, and D are examples of materials and strategies that support English language learners' achievement of listening and speaking WIDA ELD standards. Answer A, encouraging students to memorize long vocabulary lists is not effective. Although vocabulary building is an important aspect of listening and speaking English language development, ESOL teachers should try to carefully pre-teach only those words which are important to understand the text - long vocabulary lists will be too difficult to learn and retain.

48. In a "top down" strategy of literacy development, which one of the following strategies might not help a reader with comprehension?
(Competency 6)

A. Make guesses about what is going to happen
B. Look up and record each unfamiliar word
C. Anticipate the contents of the text
D. Infer meaning from sentences and paragraphs

The correct answer is B. Look up and record each unfamiliar word
Options A, C, and D are all advantages of a "top down" strategy and are desirable reading strategies. Only Option B might not help an English language learner build reading comprehension skills. Looking up and recording definitions of words can impede reading fluency, and decontextualize the text.

49. Activities that help students develop phonological awareness, fluency in word recognition and the ability to sound out words are all key components of instructional strategies designed to:
(Competency 6)

   A. build cognitive and metacognitive skills
   B. build semantic and pragmatic skills
   C. build critical thinking skills
   D. build literacy skills

The correct answer is D. build literacy skills
Answers A, B, and C are all skills that help students academically but they are not specifically focused on literacy development. The correct answer is D.

50. In the cooperative learning task "jigsaw", students:
(Competency 6)

   A. use open-ended questions
   B. pool meaning
   C. write headlines
   D. interview other students

The correct answer is B. pool meaning
Answer A is utilized in many cooperative learning activities including Information Gap Activities. Answer C, writing headlines, is a way to summarize information. Answer D, interviewing other students, is another Communicative Language Activity. A characteristic of "jigsaw" is that students pool their information in order to fully understand a text. Answer B is the correct choice.

51. ESOL instruction frequently requires the teacher to change his/her instruction methods. One of the most difficult may be:
(Competency 6.0)

   A. wait time
   B. establishment of group work
   C. show and tell based on different cultures
   D. extensive reading time

The correct answer is A. wait time
Answer B, C, and D can all be discounted since they are standard practice for language arts teachers. Answer A, the amount of time a teacher waits for an answer from students, can be very difficult to change. Teachers may be somewhat impatient ('Let's get on with it'), lack understanding ('If they knew the answer, they would respond'), and unaware of differences between the U.S. and other cultures. Answer A is the correct response.

52. Which one of the following is not an effective instructional literacy practice for elementary ESOL teachers?
(Competency 6.0)

    A. Providing direct explicit instruction of reading/writing skills based on ongoing student assessment
    B. Devoting less than 50% of the day's instructional time to reading/writing
    C. Assessing student work based on common rubrics
    D. Promoting conversation through purposeful and guided discussions about a book, piece of writing, or topic

The correct answer is B. Devoting less than 50% of the day's instructional time to reading/writing
Only Answer B is an ineffective strategy. Recommendations are that ESOL teachers devote at least 50% of instructional time to reading and writing a daily basis. Studies have shown that even when teachers have a 90-minute reading block scheduled, for example, often only 10 - 15 minutes of that time is devoted to students actually reading. Successful ESOL and ELA teachers work hard to ensure that their students spend half the day (or half of the instructional time) in reading and writing activities.

53. Activities which focus on increasing fluency in academic reading include all of the following strategies except:
(Competency 6.0)

    A. modeled reading
    B. repeated reading of a familiar text
    C. checking for understanding by asking if there are any questions
    D. coached reading of appropriate materials

The correct answer is C. checking for understanding by asking if there are any questions
Answers A, B, and D are appropriate for developing fluency. Answer C would probably not improve the reading of academic texts or literature. It is not an effective way to check for understanding for two reasons. One, students may not feel comfortable asking questions in front of the class, and two, waiting until the end of class to gauge understanding is not going to give the ESOL teacher timely feedback needed to adapt instruction, particularly if students don't remember their questions because they had to wait.

54. To build reading fluency, a skill that helps students build reading comprehension skills, among other things, ESOL teachers can use all of the following strategies except:
    (Competency 6.0)

    A. choose texts carefully that students can read with some fluency
    B. read aloud daily to students to model reading fluency
    C. consistently quiz students after reading fluency activities to ensure success
    D. have students re-read texts that they have heard before to build fluency

The correct answer is C. consistently quiz students after reading fluency activities to ensure success
Reading instruction should include explicit instruction in A, B, and D to develop fluency. Answer C is a will not develop fluency development and may even inhibit it as students become nervous about performing.

55. Successful ESOL teaching encourages tasks that:
    (Competency 6.0)

    A. alternate reading and listening passages accompanied by quizzes
    B. give learners flexibility in problem solving
    C. encourage learners to focus on accurate language use
    D. are cognitively and linguistically demanding

The correct answer is B. give learners flexibility in problem solving
Answers A, C, and D are ineffective ESOL practice and are not recommended. Effective ESOL instruction gives the ELL many opportunities to show what he/she knows and understands. Thus, the correct choice is B.

56. Which researcher is most associated with problem solving activities for language learning?
    (Competency 6.0)

    A. Russell and Baker
    B. Prabhu
    C. Penfield and Roberts
    D. Vygotsky

The correct answer is B. Prabhu
Option A. Russell and Baker were associated with evaluating bilingual education programs. Option C. Penfield and Roberts developed the critical period hypothesis. Option D. Vygotsky theorized on the importance of social interaction in the language learning process. The correct option is B. Prabhu who developed the idea of "gap" activities which include Reasoning and problem solving.

57. Common activities of the "post-reading phase" include:
(Competency 6.0)

A. building background knowledge
B. summarizing and organizing information
C. asking questions
D. annotating text

The correct answer is B. Summarizing and organizing information
Peregoy and Boyle described different reading phases. During the post-reading phase, a common strategy is to summarize and organize information gleaned from the text. This helps to build deeper understanding and to retain information. Annotation and questions are common during reading, and building background knowledge is a feature of the pre-reading phase.

58. Cummin's interdependence hypothesis states that:
(Competency 6.0)

A. children are active learners who co-construct their worlds.
B. language is controlled by external influences and social interactions
C. the degree of knowledge and processes evident in the first language determines the ease of transfer to the new language
D. children are more prone to use their Language Acquisition Device (LAD), while adults are better able to use their inductive reasoning because of more fully developed cognitive faculties.

The correct answer is C. the degree of knowledge and processes evident in the first language determines the ease of transfer to the new language.
According to Cummins, ELLs need to develop oral language in order to develop reading skills which in turn further develop oral language skills. This aligns with the central hypothesis of Answer C. Answer D refers to research by Romansky, Answer B refers to research by Piaget and Answer A refers to research by contemporary researchers and theorists.

59. Asking students to make inferences increases learning in which domain?
    (Competency 6.0)

    A. Psychomotor
    B. Cognitive
    C. Affective
    D. Naturalistic

The correct answer is B. Cognitive

Answer A deals with motor skills, communication and creating. Answer C concerns feelings, attitudes, and values. Answer D may be dismissed as this is one of the eight multiple intelligences of Gardner. Answer B is the domain where mental operations occur.

60. When teaching initial literacy, teachers should focus on all of the following literacy skills except:
    (Competency 7.0)

    A. effect of culture on language learning
    B. phonemic awareness
    C. phonics
    D. comprehension of different types of reading materials

The correct answer is A. effect of culture on language learning

Answers B, C, and D are all important literacy skills. Answer A is not a literacy skill, but culture, especially the characteristics of the heritage language, may affect transfer of language skills to L2. Answer A is the correct choice.

61. Why is an ELL student's ability to read and then successfully paraphrase a text a good indicator of literacy development?
    (Competency 7.0)

    A. It demonstrates that the student can recognize main ideas.
    B. It demonstrates that the student is overcoming anxiety about language learning.
    C. This is an important element of BICS.
    D. The student is using appropriate register for an academic setting.

The correct answer is A. It demonstrates that the student can recognize main ideas.

As students develop literacy skills, the ability to recognize central ideas from a text is an important skill. It has applicability to research, writing, and discussion/debate. Paraphrasing, or restating an idea in one's own words, requires recognition of what is important and synthesis to successfully convey meaning.

62. Of the following questions, which one would be most effective in helping ELLs learn to infer meaning?
    (Competency 7.0)

    A. How can we synthesize what you just said?
    B. What conclusions can you draw?
    C. What is the relationship between...?
    D. What evidence can you find...?

The correct answer is D. What evidence can you find...?
Answer A is a paraphrasing technique. Both Answers B and C refer to drawing conclusions. Only Answer D asks the student to support meaning which is inferred.

63. Which one of the following skills would probably have the most positive effect on developing literacy skills in ELLs?
    (Competency 7.0)

    A. Oral storytelling traditions
    B. Watching documentaries on TV
    C. Visiting art museums
    D. Attending concerts

The correct answer is A. Oral storytelling traditions
While all of the above could positively affect literacy development, the most probable would be Answer A. Oral storytelling encourages developing readers to follow a story line, look for the climax or main idea, and compare the written word to prior knowledge.

64. Which of the following are advantages to the instructor's of use of students' home language(s) in the English language classroom or in English language instruction?
    (Competency 7.0)

    A. It can reduce anxiety and fear
    B. It can permit explanation of differences and similarities of home and new languages
    C. It can reduce time-consuming explanations of abstract concepts
    D. All of the above.

The correct answer is D. All of the above.
There are quite a few benefits to using the home language to scaffold instruction. A caveat is that ESOL teachers need to be judicious in their use of the home language(s) because one danger of this method is that some students may become so dependent on instruction in their first language that they will hesitate to use their knowledge of the second language.

65. By acquiring knowledge of as few as _____ words, the ELL can understand _____ percent of the words used in conversation and comprehension of an academic text.
(Competency 7.0)

A. 1000; 74
B. 1500; 80
C. 2000; 95
D. 2500; 60

The correct answer is C. 2000; 95
The correct figures are 2000; 95—Answer C. ELLs need to acquire the 2000 most used words and work on academic content words at the same time to comprehend most academic texts.

66. In helping students develop reading strategies for use in analyzing the plot of a novel, which one of the following suggestions is most likely to help build comprehension?
(Competency 7.0)

A. Morphemic analysis focusing on prefixes, roots and suffixes
B. Annotations with arrows showing the relationship between events
C. The study of cognates
D. A word wall of commonly used words

The correct answer is B. Annotations with arrows showing the relationship between events
Though strategies A, B, and D can help students build vocabulary and, by extension, reading comprehension, only B (annotations showing the relationships between events) would have a direct impact on understanding the plot of a novel. Teachers may model this strategy for students as a way of keeping track of the plot development with novels and stories, especially as students begin to work with more complex texts.

67. Incorporating prior knowledge into second language learning does not: *(Competency 7.0)*

   A. provide opportunities for beginning English language readers to learn and remember more
   B. inhibit the English language reading skills of beginning ELLs
   C. help new English language readers to evaluate and understand new ideas
   D. improve the reading comprehension skills of English language learners

The correct answer is B. inhibit the English language reading skills of beginning ELLs
Activating schema and incorporating previous knowledge into second language learning will strengthen the learning process. It does not inhibit reading skills. It helps ELLs learn and remember, evaluate and understand and improve their reading comprehension skills.

68. Which one of the following questions would be least effective in promoting critical-thinking skills when looking at a butterfly collection? *(Competency 7.0)*

   A. Looking at this collection, what parts do the different butterflies have in common?
   B. What evidence do you find to support the idea that butterflies are able to fly long distances?
   C. How would you classify a butterfly compared to other animals that you know about?
   D. What colors are the butterflies?

The correct answer is D. What colors are the butterflies?
Questions that support critical-thinking skills are A, B, and C. Answer D asks about color and is the correct selection. A critical-thinking skill about the myriad of colors of butterflies could be, "Based on what you know, why do butterflies have so many different colors?"

69. Which of the following is a metacognitive strategy? *(Competency 7.0)*

   A. Practicing new language
   B. Summarizing long passages
   C. Skimming for necessary information
   D. Evaluating learning

The correct answer is D. Evaluating learning
Answers A, B, and C are cognitive strategies. Answer D is a metacognitive strategy.

70. To analyze oral discourse, which of the following is not an analytical question?
(Competency 7.0)

   A. How did you feel about the dialogue?
   B. How would you restate what the speaker said?
   C. How would people from your country act in a similar situation?
   D. Do you agree or disagree with what is said in the dialogue?

The correct answer is B. How would you restate what the speaker said?
Answers A, C, and D are all analytical questions. Answer B is a comprehension question and the correct selection.

71. A science teacher is reluctant to incorporate partner work into a project. As an ESL teacher, what would be the most persuasive argument you could give to encourage your colleague to try partners for a project about an experiment.

   A. Partner work will allow native speakers of English to help ELL students.
   B. Partner work can bridge the gap between native speakers and ELL students to create a more open classroom culture.
   C. Partner work encourages authentic use of language and allows both students to use prior knowledge in demonstrating learning.
   D. All of the above.

The correct answer is C. Partner work encourage authentic use of language and allows both students to use prior knowledge in demonstrating learning.
In a science project, there is no clear reason to expect that native speaker students would know more than ELL students. Creating a more open classroom culture (answer B) is a worthy goal, but it is not the most pedagogically persuasive argument to be made as partnerships are not necessarily going to lead to an open culture. Partner work will, however, encourage students to use language in authentic ways and allow both to use prior knowledge in the content area.

72. Which one of the following is not a way to establish reliability when placing students with disabilities?
    (Competency 7.0)

    A. Using multiple raters
    B. Including multiple assessment measures
    C. Establishing clearly specified scoring criteria
    D. Using the Woodcock-Johnson III Diagnostic Reading Battery

The correct answer is D. Using the Woodcock-Johnson III Diagnostic Reading Battery
The Woodcock-Johnson III Diagnostic Reading Battery is widely used in formal reading assessments. While unquestionably reliable, it in of itself does not establish reliability for placement of students with special needs.

73. Norm-referenced assessments may not provide accurate results when used with ELL students because:
    (Competency 7.0)

    A. The test is not in the student's home/first language.
    B. The student will not understand the test.
    C. The tests are too difficult for ELL students.
    D. The norm group may not be reflective of the ELL student.

The correct answer is D. The norm group may not be reflective of the ELL student.
Norm-referenced tests are designed to measure an individual student's performance compared to an 'average' student. Test designers determine an 'average' student's performance by using the test with students from the target audience for the test. Typical norm-referenced reading comprehension tests in the U.S. are intended for American native speakers of English. An ELL student with a high level of English proficiency may still have difficulty with the test if there are reading passages about specific cultural experiences (like Halloween) or activities (like camping) that are unfamiliar. Even if the test is in the student's home language (Answer A), if it has been translated from English, the unfamiliar references will remain. Students may not understand parts of the test (Answer B), but this does not necessarily make the test inaccurate if it is measuring something like comprehension.

74. **WIDA defines three types of support for ELL students. Which of the following is NOT one of them?**
    (Competency 7.0)

    A. Sensory supports such as illustrations
    B. Graphic supports such as timelines
    C. Institutional supports such as bilingual assistants
    D. Interactive supports such as partner work

The correct answer is C. Institutional supports such as bilingual assistants.
Though some models of instruction for ELL students include bilingual assistants that can provide language support (particularly in the content areas), WIDA defines three types of support that teachers can easily provide - sensory, graphic, and interactive.

75. **Encouraging non-graded writing practice can really help English language learners develop writing fluency. Which of the of the following is not a task that encourages students to practice non-graded writing?**
    (Competency 8.0)

    A. Writing a dialog in pairs
    B. Rewriting a passage or summary in the ELL's own words
    C. Writing from the perspective of another
    D. Writing a summary or journal entry to hand in

The correct answer is D. Writing a summary to hand in
Answers A, B, and C are ways students can practice writing without a teacher's evaluation. They encourage students in meaningful activities that they can do collaboratively and/or independently in response to comprehensible and meaningful input. They are also activities that can be written and reflected upon and learned from by the student themselves. Answer D, writing a summary to be handed in, suggests evaluation, however informal. Students will not so much be engaged in 'practicing' writing to develop writing fluency if they know they are going to hand in their work. They will be more concerned about how the ESOL teacher or content-area teacher is going to judge their summary and/or journal entry.

76. **The purpose of frontloading vocabulary is:**
    (Competency 8.0)

    A. vocabulary development
    B. increase reading comprehension
    C. explaining content
    D. increasing spelling proficiency

The correct answer is B. increase reading comprehension
All of the answers are interrelated and valuable instructional goals. Nevertheless, the main goal is B, increasing reading comprehension.

77. Reid (1987) divides the writing process into two broad divisions. They are:
(Competency 8.0)

   A. composing; pre-writing
   B. pre-writing; drafting
   C. brainstorming; drafting
   D. composition; revision

The correct answer is D. composition; revision
Only Answer D considers the revision process which is an integral part of the writing process, and thus, the correct choice.

78. Which one of the following writing activities is not appropriate for different proficiency levels?
(Competency 8.0)

   A. Reading and writing letters to friends, businesses or penpals
   B. Writing directions for solving a problem
   C. Writing long form book reports
   D. Writing and organizing lists

The correct answer is C. Writing long form book reports
ELLs should work on purposeful, authentic writing activities. Answer A, B, and D are authentic tasks. Answer C is not. It is an artificial construct for the purposes of schooling.

79. Which one of the following is not an appropriate activity for engaging ELLs in real-life communicative activities?
(Competency 8.0)

   A. Oral discussion based on a news story
   B. Researching an assigned topic and reporting back to peers
   C. Reporting on a new video game
   D. Discussing a movie with a friend

The correct answer is B. Researching an assigned topic and reporting back to peers
Answers A, C, and D are authentic because they are engaging the learner in an activity they are interested in and are authentic. Research on assigned topics is not authentic and frequently uninteresting to students. The correct answer is B.

80. Emerging ELLs need instruction in conventions of written Standard English such as:
(*Competency 8.0*)

   A. syntax
   B. discourse
   C. vocabulary
   D. types of written texts

The correct answer is A. syntax
Answers B, C, and D are not conventions. Answer B is a type of connected speech or writing, Answer C is necessary to write well, and Answer D refers to genres and other types of texts. Only Answer A—syntax—refers to a convention of written Standard English.

81. Which one of the following is not a valid purpose of assessment?
(*Competency 8.0*)

   A. Determining a student's potential
   B. Determination of a student's present academic performance level
   C. Eligibility for a program
   D. Diagnosis of special learner disabilities

The correct answer is A. Determining a student's potential
Answers B, C, and D are all valid purposes of assessment. Answer A is a factor that tests, specifically I.Q. tests, are unable to define.

82. Tests which evaluate an individual as compared to others are:
(*Competency 8.0*)

   A. standardized
   B. authentic
   C. norm referenced
   D. criterion referenced

The correct answer is C. norm referenced
Answer D may be discarded as criterion referenced tests evaluate an individual's knowledge of specific content. Answer A might be true, but standardized tests may be criterion referenced. Answer B concerns tests being relevant to a student's life, and not necessarily comparing the student to others. Only Answer C is specifically designed to compare one individual with others.

83. A student support team is looking over the assessment results from the ACCESS for ELLs 2.0 assessments, the MCAS ELA assessment and some formal and informal in-class assessments. For a few students, they notice a gap between the scores on the standardized tests and the scores on informal classroom assessments in science and social studies. Which of the following cannot be inferred by this gap?
   (Competency 8.0)

   A. Some students may work very hard to understand and express their understanding in the subjects they love, but may be challenged with lower cognitive skills than the team initially thought
   B. Some students may be so nervous taking formal assessments and standardized tests that it impacts their performance.
   C. Some teachers may be scoring informal assessments too high because they know what the student wanted to express.
   D. Some students may have higher cognitive levels and content-area knowledge than the team initially thought but may be challenged by lack of English proficiency/fluency.

The correct answer is D. Some students may have higher cognitive levels and content-area knowledge than the team initially thought but may be challenged by lack of English proficiency/fluency.
With some formal assessments and standardized tests that do not specifically test for English language proficiency, a low score would not necessarily mean that a student had cognitive challenges, learning disabilities or needed additional assistance and support in the content-area. However, the ACCESS for ELLs 2.0 and the MCAS curricular framework tests are designed to take English language proficiency into account. In this case Answer D would not be a logical inference.

84. Which one of the following goals will not be discovered through assessment?
   (Competency 8.0)

   A. If student is ready for new information
   B. Strategies for improving programs
   C. If student is lacking prerequisite skills
   D. Program weaknesses

The correct answer is B. Strategies for improving programs
Answers A, C, and D may all be discovered through assessment. Answer B, strategies for improving programs, are not revealed through assessment. These are the result of analysis of the information discovered through assessment, and the teacher's knowledge of alternative strategies for teaching his/her charges.

85. Which of the following writing assessments uses holistic scoring? *(Competency 8.0)*

   A. International English Language Test System (IELTS)
   B. National Assessment of Educational Progress (NAEP)
   C. Test of English as a Foreign Language (TOEFL)
   D. Michigan Writing Assessment

The correct answer is C. Test of English as a Foreign Language (TOEFL)
Answer A (IELTS) and D (Michigan Writing Assessment) use analytic scoring. Answer B (NAEP) uses trait scoring. Only C (TOEFL) uses holistic scoring.

86. Which one of the following is a disadvantage of portfolio assessment? *(Competency 8.0)*

   A. They are integrative
   B. They produce variable samples
   C. They are motivating
   D. They are formative

The correct answer is B. They produce variable samples
Answers A, C, and D are all advantages of portfolio assessment. The disadvantage is they are produce variable samples; some tasks may elicit better writing because they are more interesting. The correct answer is B.

87. Sheltered content teaching allows teachers to do all of the following except: *(Competency 9.0)*

   A. use realia, word lists, gestures, etc.
   B. reduce language demands
   C. facilitate learning
   D. instruct in heritage language

The correct answer is D. instruct in heritage language
Answers A, B, and C are all part of Shelter Content Teaching strategies. Answer D is not an element of this strategy and is the correct choice.

88. Vocabulary development is an essential component of learning for ELL students. To support this, teachers should focus on:
(Competency 6.0, 9.0)

A. Finding opportunities for students to use words in realistic situations
B. Have students do memorization drills
C. Emphasize correct pronunciation
D. Writing down definitions

The correct answer is A. Finding opportunities for students to use words in realistic situations
Though learning new vocabulary will at time require students to write down definitions and memorize new words, the most effective way for them to learn and become adept at using new vocabulary is by using words in realistic contexts (writing, discussion, conversations). Perfect pronunciation is not the goal.

89. Arreaga-Mayer (1998) suggests all of the following constructs for successful ELLs except:
(Competency 9.0)

A. collaborative/cooperative learning
B. input slightly above competence level
C. involvement
D. mediation/feedback

The correct answer is B. input slightly above competence level
Answers A, C, and D are constructs put forth by Arreaga-Mayer, except B which Krashen theorized. Krashen stated his formula as i+ 1.

90. Which one of the following is not one of the three basic strategies that WIDA recommends to support ELL students building content-area knowledge, skills and vocabulary?
    (Competency 9.0)

    A. sensory strategies (e.g., word walls, math manipulatives)
    B. graphic strategies (e.g., venn diagrams, word webs)
    C. interactive strategies (e.g. mentors, group work)
    D. homework strategies (e.g. vocabulary study, reading comprehension questions and answers)

The correct answer is D. homework strategies (e.g. vocabulary study, reading comprehension questions and answers)
Answers A, B, and C make up the three basic strategies that WIDA recommends to support English language learners in developing content-area knowledge skills and vocabulary. Answer D, homework strategies, may help students academically (although there is much research to support only a limited amount of homework), but not a specific component of WIDA's strategies.

91. All of the following are part of an integrated approach to language teaching except:
    (Competency 9.0)

    A. Language Experience Approaches
    B. Cooperative learning activities
    C. Task-based or experiential learning tasks
    D. Note-taking and planning with graphic organizers

The correct answer is A. Language Experience Approaches
Answers B, C, and D are components of integrated approaches to language teaching. Answer A: LEA, targets vocabulary and reading development by building on prior knowledge. It is a specific and discrete method with its own teaching and learning strategies.

92. **Which of the following is a model of content-based instruction, part of the Integrated Language Teaching strategy:**
(Competency 9.0)

A. theme based models (language is integrated in the study of themes or broad topics)
B. peer tutoring model (cooperative peer mediated instruction of language and content)
C. adjunct model (language and content taught separately but closely coordinated)
D. sheltered model (English is simplified to ELL's level of proficiency while teaching content)

The correct answer is B. peer mediated model
Answers, A, B and C are all models of content-based instruction. Answer B is a separate model based on peer mediated instruction, where students are either paired randomly or matched by ability or language proficiency to partners each week to compete for points in a highly-structured teaching environment.

93. **According to Chomsky's Universal Grammar (UG) and Language Acquisition Device (LAD) theories, younger learners have less difficulty learning language because:**
(Competency 9.0)

A. language is controlled by external factors
B. after puberty, the critical period shuts down
C. their LAD is still active
D. language abilities increase with age

The correct answer is C. their LAD is still active
Answer A is based on Piaget's theory of language as controlled by external information and social interaction. Answer B is based upon the work of Krashen and Felix who both proposed theories for the close of the L2 critical period at puberty. Answer D is based on the research of Newport & Supalla supporting Piaget's theory. Only Answer C is part of Chomsky's theory of L2 development.

94. All of the following are true about the Massachusetts Comprehensive Assessment System (MCAS) except:
(Competency 9.0)

A. Each public school student in the state is tested in grades 3-8 and once in high school in English.
B. The Massachusetts Curriculum Frameworks forms the basis of the test battery.
C. Each public school student in the state is tested in grades 3-8 and once in high school in mathematics.
D. Each public school student in the state is tested in grades 3-8 and once in high school in history and social studies.

The correct answer is D. Each public school student in the state is tested in grades 3-8 and once in high school in history and social studies.
Answers A, B, and C are true of the MCAS test battery. Students are required to take a science and engineering/technology test once in elementary, middle, and high school. Answer D is the correct choice as right now, in Massachusetts, the History and Social Science assessment is not required.

95. To distinguish between ELLs and ELLs with disabilities, which one of the following testing procedures is not recommended?
(Competency 9.0)

A. Intelligence quotient (IQ) test
B. Criterion-referenced assessments
C. Curriculum-referenced assessments
D. Observations from school, home, and community

The correct answer is A. Intelligence quotient (IQ) test
Answers B, C, and D are effective procedures for determining placement for ELLs with disabilities. IQ tests are not recommended as they are frequently culturally biased. If used, they should be used in careful conjunction with more representative test types. Answer A is the correct choice.

96. Culture plays an important role in our lives and can affect classroom teaching and learning in several ways. Which of the following is not a way that culture can affect ELL students in the classroom:
    (Competency 9.0)

    A. concepts and practices around roles and interpersonal relationships
    B. concepts and practices around food and religion
    C. concepts and practices around time and physical space
    D. All of the above

The correct answer is D. All of the above

Peregoy and Boyle (2008) illustrate some of the many ways that culture can affect students in their participation, learning, and adjustment to a different society and its schools.

Even views on food and religion can play a role in classroom learning in the form of topics discussed in school and/or possible restrictions or proscriptions associated with the handling, offering, or discarding food.

97. Teacher Assistance Teams (TATS) should be composed of all of the following except the:
    (Competency 9.0)

    A. school administrators
    B. guidance counselors
    C. media specialists
    D. parent(s)

The correct answer is C. media specialists

Answer A, B, and D may all be members of a TAT. Media specialists could be consulted for additional materials that would help in special education cases, but would not form part of the normal TAT. Answer C is the correct choice.

98. When considering referrals for specialized services, all of the following are considered except:
    (Competency 9.0)

    A. student characteristics
    B. parents' request for/against referral
    C. multidisciplinary evaluation
    D. institutional factors

The correct answer is C. multidisciplinary evaluation

Answer A, B and D are all considered when evaluation of a student is requested by a teacher, parent, or other person. Answer C occurs after the referral. It is the next step in the lengthy process of establishing special services.

99. To protect students from inequities in the referral process, federal law explicitly provides for:
(Competency 9.0)

   A. non-discriminatory evaluation procedures
   B. an independent education evaluation
   C. a multidisciplinary team using several pieces of information to formulate a referral
   D. testing of the child in L1 unless clearly not feasible to do so

The correct answer is B. an independent education evaluation
Answers A, C, and D are all mandated by federal law. Answer B is an alternative that may be permitted when the parents feel the school's evaluation was inappropriate, but it is not mandated.

100. Information for placing students with learning or behavioral disabilities will usually include all of the following except:
(Competency 9.0)

   A. past academic performance
   B. neurological reports
   C. notes from auxiliary/substitute teachers
   D. speech and language evaluations

The correct answer is C. notes from auxiliary/substitute teachers
Answers A, B, and D are all important elements of the documentation needed for referral. Answer C, notes from auxiliary/substitute teachers, should not be dismissed out-of-hand, but followed-up on as a more formal, written report which details the observations, before this document is included in the student's file. Therefore, Answer C is the correct option.

Open-Response

As noted in the About This Test section, the open-response portion of the test will require you to prepare a detailed analysis that integrates your understanding of the foundations of second-language instruction and the relationship between second-language learning and content learning. This section focuses on the application of knowledge and will be assessed based on:

- How well your response addresses the task;
- How well you apply knowledge in completing the task;
- The evidence you use to support your argument; and
- Your understanding of the subject matter.

Read directions carefully, plan your response, and keep in mind that the goal in this section is to use evidence in applying your knowledge.

Directions: Use the information provided below to complete your open responses.

Open-response 1:

A high school ESL specialist working with students in social studies regularly uses formative, informal assessment techniques to check for student understanding, monitor progress, and determine next steps in teaching. Recently the teacher asked students read a short passage from a text and then summarize essential ideas and information. Below is an excerpt from the passage students had to read.

NAFTA
NAFTA, the North American Free Trade Agreement, is an agreement between the United States, Canada, and Mexico that came into effect in 1994. Prior to NAFTA, the United States and Canada had already signed a free trade agreement that had eliminated many tariffs on imported goods. NAFTA expanded this relationship to include Mexico.

Unlike the European Union, NAFTA did not allow for the free movement of people between the three countries and instead focused on making it easier for countries to sell goods and services between the three countries. Removing tariffs (taxes on imported goods) was intended to remove protections for domestic industries. As an example, cars produced by an American company (such as General Motors) or a Japanese company (such as Toyota) in Mexico or Canada could now be imported into the United States without having to pay import taxes. With the lower wages paid in Mexico, the auto industry in Mexico grew considerably. Concerns were raised, however, about the loss of manufacturing jobs in the United States.

The teacher asked students to describe the main ideas of the passage above. Here is the response of one student at the **expanding level** of English language proficiency.

NAFTA is from 1994. Mexico, US and Canada joined to sell things like cars. They can't go live in there like in European. They don't pay tariffs anymore. Now lots of cars come from Mexico. They want to sell stuff.

Based on your knowledge of second language acquisition and content-area learning, write a response that:

- Identifies one of the student's areas of strength as a language learner (e.g., comprehension, organization of ideas, use of writing conventions, content-area vocabulary, etc.);
- Describes an area in which the student needs to improve to maximize content-area learning and English language development; and
- Describes an instructional strategy you would use to help the student improve.

Use specific evidence and examples from the information provided in your response.

Open-response 2:

A middle school ESL teacher working with students in a language arts classroom is helping students develop their writing proficiency. Each student is working on a memoir/personal narrative about an important experience in his/her life. Below is an excerpt of the work from a student at the developing level of language proficiency.

I from a small place. I have a brother old and one sister little than me. One day we go together to the store to buy some stuff. My sister tell me she forget the list. I was mad and my brother too. She yell at her about forget. We have to go home again for the list. My sister look. I look. My brother look too but not a list. Then my sister laugh and I said what? She keep laughing and I look at her. She find the list in her pocket.

Based on your knowledge of WIDA language levels, second language acquisition, and content-area knowledge, prepare a response that:

- Identifies one of the student's strengths and how this can be further supported;
- Identifies an area for growth in the student's language development; and
- Explains instructional strategies you (the ESL teacher) would use and strategies you would recommend to other the student's other teachers in the content-areas.

CPSIA information can be obtained
at www.ICGtesting.com
Printed in the USA
BVHW01s1427020418
512247BV00022B/733/P